THE
JACKSON
PHENOMENON

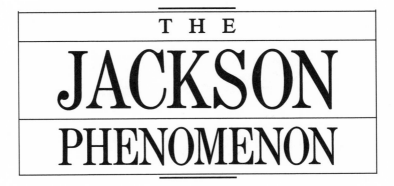

THE MAN,
THE POWER,
THE MESSAGE

Elizabeth O. Colton

DOUBLEDAY
New York London Toronto Sydney Auckland

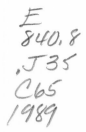

Published by Doubleday, a division of
Bantam Doubleday Dell Publishing Group, Inc.
666 Fifth Avenue, New York, New York 10103

Doubleday and the portrayal of an anchor
with a dolphin are trademarks of
Doubleday, a division of Bantam Doubleday Dell
Publishing Group, Inc.

Design by Richard Oriolo

Library of Congress Cataloging-in-Publication Data applied for

ISBN 0-385-26070-9

ACKNOWLEDGMENTS

I am especially grateful to a number of people who helped and encouraged me during the writing of this book: my agents Jonathon and Wendy Lazear; at Doubleday my editor Nan A. Talese and her associate Gail Buchicchio, and also Nancy Evans, Alberto Vitale, and Alex Gotfryd. I would like to thank Sabra Moore for her timely work in finding photographs, and my former colleagues—staff and journalists—on the Jackson campaign. I would also like to thank Susan Sgarlat, Kent Rush, Bill Borders, Beryl Abrams, Roger Cumming, Isabelle Fair, David Carey, Cely and Christopher Arndt, Judy Miller, Walter Washington, Joan Lucero, Doug Lea, Claudia Young, Constance Fowlkes, Sandra Hershberg, Roger Baroody, and Lee Elliott, and the many other friends whose support contributed immeasurably to this volume.

*This book is dedicated to
my parents Marie and Henry Colton
and
Almonia Thomas, Iona Rhodes, Helen Jackson*

CONTENTS

AUTHOR'S NOTE

The direct quotations in this book were taken either from notes that I made at the time of the campaign, from actual tape recordings, and from press reports; re-creations of incidents were in each case confirmed by more than two sources.

THE
JACKSON
PHENOMENON

1

GEARING
UP FOR '88

"Drama. That's what it's all about," Jesse Jackson remarked confidentially as he reached for the door handle preparing to spring from the back seat of the limousine.

"Your performance is always brilliant. It's really quite amazing to watch you in action," I said. I was sitting next to him after his appearance at the Bethel AME Church in downtown San Francisco. It was February 22, 1986. I was spending the day with Jesse Jackson to consider his proposition that I become his press secretary.

"It's all just drama," he repeated, almost as if to himself. But then he turned to emphasize his point as he emerged from the vehicle to greet the small waiting crowd.

A cluster of local photographers, reporters and well-wishers were gathered to see him before he entered St. Paul of the Shipwreck Church in the Hunters Point section of San Francisco.

Jackson turned on his magnetic personality, smiling broadly and lifting his arms in the afternoon sun. Minutes later, we were inside a bright, modern Roman Catholic church.

Jesse Jackson, the African-American who had defied the odds and run for the Democratic presidential nomination in 1984, had never ceased campaigning. He had never held an elected office, but he had a mission—to run for President of the United States of America.

That sunny day in San Francisco was in the winter of 1986, not even a presidential election year. A Republican President, Ronald Reagan, was in the middle of his second term. Most potential candidates for the 1988 race were quietly going about their interim business. But Jesse Jackson had not stopped campaigning since 1984. It had become his sole occupation, regardless of the year. The eternal candidate, he was building his political base every day.

At the altar a priest, fully garbed in white ecclesiastical robes, enthusiastically pointed toward the entrance of the church. His gesture was unnecessary. Everyone had already turned, and all eyes were fixed on the tall, dark and impressive figure who had just entered. Like a king, Jackson had his retinue in tow.

The priest shouted out the introduction above the music and clamor of the crowded church: "The Prince of Peace in our community." Such words seemed almost sacrilegious, and then the jubilant priest amended: "The drum major for Peace, the drum major for Justice—Jesse Jackson."

The Reverend Jesse Jackson needed no introduction. Dressed in a gray flannel three-piece suit with rep tie and blue pin-striped shirt, he strode down the aisle of the little church toward the sanctuary. The crowd inside St. Paul of the Shipwreck was cheering and shouting and crying as he made his way among them. All the time the gospel choir, unusual in a Catholic church, rocked along to its own singing.

The broad-shouldered, six-foot-three man held out his arms as if to embrace all the crowd. Jesse Jackson was a modern savior who had arrived in their midst. Mothers shoved babies at him, and he kissed them all, one by one.

From the pulpit, Jesse Jackson, a Baptist preacher, exhorted the Catholic congregation: "We've got to keep reminding America what it can be, not what it is." From the packed church came chants of "Yes, Jesse, yes."

On that day in February, Reaganism still held America in thrall despite some setbacks to the Republican administration. It was a month after the space shuttle *Challenger* exploded. It was the Saturday before the Philippines Revolution was to overthrow the U.S.-supported President Ferdinand Marcos, and the Reagan administration had still not taken a position on the problems in America's former colony.

The congregation of St. Paul of the Shipwreck was primarily Filipino, though that day there were many outsiders as well, both black and white Americans. Jackson began: "We're here to celebrate the wall of Marcos come tumbling down. We've been in touch by phone constantly with Mrs. Aquino, and she should be acknowledged soon as head of state. Clearly America has the chance today to be on the moral right and with the majority."

The orator continued, employing his famous rhyming technique: "Now we're gonna see a real thrilla in Manila. It says that love is more powerful than hate. The blood of the innocent has power. The human race is not the nuclear race. The shuttle crew was a 'rainbow in the sky,' America at its best."

He concluded by leading his own chants, with the crowd of more than six hundred enthusiastically following: "We're going to put America back to work. We're going to be free. I am somebody. I am somebody. Down with Marcos. Up with Aquino."

Jackson's speech was followed, as it would be time and again in the 1988 presidential campaign, by an appeal for money. On that day it was for his interim-campaign organization, the Rainbow Coalition. He let his Coalition chairman for Northern California, the Reverend Dr. Howard Gloyd, make the appeal: "It's hard to hear Reverend Jackson and not get excited. He's a man with a mission. The Rainbow Coalition is here to stay."

Afterward, at an ad hoc news conference in the parish hall, Jackson replied to the standard question: whether he would be running again for President in 1988. He said: "It's premature to declare a candidacy. But if we'd've done differently in '84, we would've started earlier. How we did was the will of the people."

Earlier that Saturday in San Francisco, Jackson had revealed more of what he believed people wanted from him: "Moral and economic regeneration. People live not by bread alone. They need motivation and atmosphere. People like a leader."

Jesse Jackson was such a leader. He was rapidly becoming the most famous American in the world, although there was little recognition of him then from the American establishment. The American media hardly ever covered Jackson's endless activity at home, but, occasionally, he would get attention with some foreign adventure. At home in America, however, he was building his machine and creating his myth.

As with other myths, his, too, would be founded on biographical events, facts that would gradually be embellished by him and the people who watched and heard and followed him, and by those who wrote about him. Taking his "biodata," Jackson would later ask his aides to write "preferred biographical introductions" for his speeches. These would be prepared, scripted introductions to be given out to anyone who might have the honor of introducing him to an audience.

In 1988, one such "introduction" began: "Jesse Jackson is a leading candidate for the 1988 Democratic presidential nomination. Mr. Jackson is uniquely qualified to be nominated and elected President of the United States of America. He has spent his entire lifetime as a leader, organizer and advocate for justice and peace and economic development in America and the world. He has achieved a well-deserved reputation as an activist for social and economic change, a successful negotiator, a master mediator, a defender of the poor and disadvantaged, a consummate organizer and manager of nationwide organizations. Jesse Jackson's name is known around the world because of the leadership role he has taken at home and abroad."

Between the glowing introductory first paragraph and the final introduction bringing the star, Jesse Jackson, onto the stage, the key points of his life would be enumerated. There would be several versions, long or short, and some facts included or not, depending upon the audience. Jesse Jackson himself would proudly boast of his humble origins: "I am the descendant of slaves. I was born out of wedlock, of a teenage mother. My mother was a maid and a beautician, and my adoptive father, who gave me his name, was a janitor. Though I was born in the slum, the slum wasn't born in me."

Jesse Louis Jackson was born October 8, 1941, in Greenville, South Carolina. His mother, Helen Burns Jackson, and his grandmother, Matilda Burns, are still living there. His adoptive father, Charles Henry Jackson, a post office maintenance worker, died in 1980. Jesse Jackson and his only wife, Jacqueline Lavinia Brown, were married in 1964 and now reside in Chicago. The Jacksons have five children.

Jesse Jackson grew up in the South under the laws of segregation and early became a leader in this nation's civil rights movement. In 1959, he graduated from Sterling High School, then the all-black school in Greenville. He was a star quarterback and, also, president of his school's chapter of Future Teachers of America.

In his first year of college, Jackson accepted a football scholarship to attend the University of Illinois in Urbana-Champaign. Afterward, Jackson liked to say that there he soon realized that the coaches had no intention of letting a black play quarterback on a team on which whites also played. That explained his leaving the next year, he said, because he had decided that it would be better for him to attend an all-black college where he would have a chance to play quarterback. But, years later, journalists investigating Jackson's past have reported that university records revealed that the quarterback for Illinois that year was a black, Mel Meyers. Also, it was reported that Jackson actually left Illinois after being placed on academic probation during his second semester, according to the late Ray Eliot, then head football coach at Illinois.

The next year, Jackson transferred to North Carolina A&T State University in Greensboro, North Carolina, where he became the star quarterback. While a student at A&T, Jackson participated in the beginnings of the sit-in movement, which began in Greensboro in 1960. Three years later, Jackson was elected president of his student body, and graduated with a BA degree in sociology in 1963.

Jesse Jackson would boast in 1988 that he had had twenty-five years of experience in Democratic politics. The same year he graduated from college, Jackson attended his first Young Democrats convention and has been active in the party ever since. That year he also went to work for the Democratic governor of North Carolina, Terry Sanford. Over the years, Jackson personally organized and led a national drive to register Democrats across the country. In both 1984 and 1988, he registered more new voters than any other presidential candidate. Jackson claimed that it was his efforts in voter registration, enlisting two million new Democratic voters, that succeeded in bringing a Democratic majority back to the U.S. Senate in 1986, including, coincidentally, the election of his former boss, Governor Sanford, to the Senate.

Jesse Jackson also had years of experience as a political organizer and orator. After college, he attended the Chicago Theological Seminary at the University of Chicago for two and a half years. In the spring of 1965, he dropped out of the school six months before his anticipated graduation in order to take a full-time role in the civil rights movement, joining Dr. Martin Luther King, Jr., in the voting rights march in Selma, Alabama. In 1968 Jackson was ordained a Baptist minister, and he has remained a freewheeling minister within the National Baptist Convention. Years later the Chicago Theological Seminary conferred an honorary doctorate degree on its former student Jesse Jackson.

Jesse Jackson was at the center of the major civil rights organizations of the sixties—the Congress of Racial Equality (CORE), the Southern Christian Leadership Conference (SCLC) and the NAACP. He participated in the successful civil rights campaigns to adopt public accommodation bills, to enact the voting rights act, to win open access to housing and to achieve admission to all American schools. Jackson worked closely with Dr. King for the last three years of King's life, and he was with King in Memphis when the American civil rights leader was slain. In these public introductions Jackson would not want anyone to mention the controversy over his self-aggrandizing behavior immediately after King's assassination—although he could not deny that at that time he had set his sights on inheriting King's mantle as the leader of American blacks.

In 1967, Dr. King had appointed Jackson to serve as executive director of Operation Breadbasket. It was a civil rights program to find more jobs for blacks in bakeries, milk companies and other firms having heavy minority patronage of their products. It was the economic arm of SCLC, Dr. King's organization. Despite Jackson's pushiness, which had offended many SCLC members and often worried King himself, Jackson had impressed King with his skill in organizing Chicago's black ministers to support Operation Breadbasket. King had decided to put Jackson in charge of the operation with a mandate to expand it into a national program. Jackson held that position until 1971 when he broke away from SCLC to found his own organization, PUSH.

Ever since the assassination of Dr. Martin Luther King, Jr., in April 1968, tension mounted constantly within SCLC between Jackson and other members of the late leader's organization. There was bitterness that Jackson was trying to seize control but was not the rightful heir. The year after King's murder, *The New York Times* had proclaimed Jackson "probably the most persuasive black leader on the national scene," and *Playboy* billed him as "the fiery heir apparent" in an interview spread across nineteen pages. In April 1970, *Time* put Jesse Jackson on the cover of its special issue on black America.

In December 1971, SCLC's board suspended Jackson temporarily for "administrative impropriety" and for "repeated violation of organizational discipline" because he had failed to get permission from SCLC before organizing trade fairs for black businessmen. Jackson decided it was time for him to leave SCLC and go out on his own. He resigned the same month and declared: "I need air. I must have room to grow."

Jackson immediately called together a dozen black celebrities, including Roberta Flack, Aretha Franklin, Carl Stokes and Richard Hatcher, to meet at New York's Commodore Hotel and endorse his plan to start his own organization. His new national civil rights organization, PUSH, was launched with Jacksonian fanfare on Christmas Day 1971. The acronym PUSH first stood for "People United to Save Humanity" but soon became "People United to Serve Humanity." Its goals were similar to Operation Breadbasket's —boosting minority employment and minority businesses. An affiliate organization, PUSH for Excellence, or PUSH-Excel, was founded to improve ghetto schools and to promote educational advancement for minorities.

It was during his years as the head of PUSH that Jackson began his schools campaign—flying around the country, inspiring students with his oratory to develop self-esteem and self-discipline. With him as their inspiration, thousands of young people took pledges to say no to dope, long before any other American leader was discussing drugs, to turn off their televisions and study. Jesse Jackson knew that these young people, black and white, rich and poor, would become America's future voters, and he knew, as he often acknowledged later in his presidential quests, that he could inspire them enough so that they would never forget the day Jesse Jackson had come to their schools years before when they were children or teenagers. Those youths who saw and heard him once became part of the charismatic leader's vast political network reaching into every nook and cranny of America. In this way, Jesse Jackson began creating his stardom.

It was then, during those years with PUSH, that he started leading the school chants that later became a trademark of his presidential campaigns: "I am somebody . . . I may be poor . . . but I am somebody . . . respect me . . . I am somebody . . . My mind . . . is a pearl . . . I can learn anything . . . in the world . . . down with dope . . . up with hope . . . nobody will save us . . . for us . . . but us . . . I am somebody" etc.

In addition to his education efforts, Jackson also used the organization to negotiate with major corporations to hire and promote minority workers. Through Jackson's own verbal powers of persuasion, and also sometimes with threats of boycotts by blacks, PUSH succeeded in the early 1980s to negotiate agreements, called "covenants," with such firms as Burger King Corporation, 7-Eleven

Stores, 7-Up, Coca-Cola Company, Southland Corporation, Adolph Coors and Heublein Corporation. Some of the companies felt the negotiations had been conducted in the most positive manner, but others later reported that Jackson's method was threatening and heavy-handed. Jackson simply viewed it all as more signs of his success as a diplomatic negotiator and national leader. But Jackson's problems with PUSH lay not in his flamboyant successes in schools and in business negotiations—they arose from the questions raised about his ability to manage the organization, both administratively and financially, while at the same time flying high as a charismatic leader in the limelight.

Jesse Jackson had never held an elective office by the time he ran again for the Democratic presidential nomination in 1988. But he believed that he could point to his leadership of PUSH for more than a decade as a sign of his administrative and managerial abilities. Yet, contrary to that belief, it was because of Jackson's management (or flawed management) of PUSH that he later came under the most critical scrutiny during both his 1984 and 1988 presidential campaigns.

Over the twelve years between his founding the organization and his first run for the presidency, PUSH and its affiliates succeeded in obtaining more than $17 million in federal grants as well as private and corporate donations. It was one of the few organizations attempting to promote minority business enterprise, and for many years the donors simply overlooked its flaws, especially in administration and accounting. Jackson himself, as the leader of the organization, continued to spiral upward in national attention by virtue of his oratorical skills and ingenuity. But the organization itself, left without his oversight while he flew around the country and the world, floundered dangerously along with little attention to where and how the vast funds were spent.

In an interview with the *Los Angeles Times,* which was one of the many news organizations that investigated Jackson's management, one PUSH official described the way things were run back at the Chicago headquarters: "While Jesse was flying around the country, things in Chicago were in absolute chaos. We stumbled from one crisis to another . . . [Also] Jesse didn't always have the best and brightest people running things. The key staff people were put there on the basis of their loyalty to him, not on their ability. Loyalty, absolute loyalty, was always the most important thing to him, not whether you could do the job." Later, staff members in both of Jackson's presidential campaigns reported the same chaos and lack of managerial skills in contrast to his showy charisma.

Finally, after numerous audits by the U.S. government, in the autumn of 1988 PUSH-Excel agreed to pay $550,000 to the federal government to settle longstanding civil claims of more than $1.1 million sought by the Justice Department. Previously, Jackson had described the problem as simply an argument between accountants. Many believed it should have proved an embarrassment for Jackson, but by then little notice was taken of the brief announcement.

Jesse Jackson first launched his candidacy for President of the United States in November 1983 and ran as a Democratic candidate in 1984. That year he won 21 percent of the total primary and caucus votes and 11 percent of the total delegates at the Democratic convention in San Francisco. Jackson did not like to be reminded that his first campaign was tarnished by his use of the epithet "Hymie" to describe Jews and his continuing association with the anti-Semite Louis Farrakhan, the Nation of Islam leader.

During that 1984 campaign, Jackson ventured overseas on two successful peace missions. At the beginning of the year he went to Syria and negotiated the release of U.S. Navy pilot Lieutenant Robert Goodman, whose plane had been shot down over Lebanon. Later that year Jackson obtained the freedom of forty-eight Cuban-American prisoners held in Cuban jails. At the same time, in an effort to ease church-state tensions, Jackson succeeded in getting Fidel Castro to go to church for the first time in decades. Over the years Jackson has offered peace and justice plans for Central America, South Africa and the Middle East.

Throughout the 1984 campaign Jackson talked about his Rainbow Coalition and afterward he formally established the National Rainbow Coalition and became its president. It was founded as an alternative to the shift to the right within the Democratic Party that began taking place after President Reagan's landslide reelection and the defection of many traditional Democrats to the Republican Party. The Rainbow Coalition was headquartered in Washington, D.C.

In October 1987, Jesse Jackson launched his second campaign for the presidency of the United States. At the beginning of 1988, he was listed among a Gallup poll's ten men in the world most admired by Americans, trailing only Pope John Paul II and President Ronald Reagan. In the Democratic presidential campaign, Jesse Jackson was the runner-up to the nominee, Michael Dukakis. At the Democratic National Convention in July, Jesse Jackson vowed to continue campaigning for the party and especially for the interests of his constituency.

During the four years between the 1984 and 1988 campaigns, Jesse Jackson labored incessantly to build a vast political network and grass-roots machinery that would serve as the foundation for his remarkable 1988 presidential campaign. During most of that time this indefatigable politician was not noticed by the American media or the political establishment, who had written him and "his followers" off as irrelevant fringe elements in the American political system. They were wrong. Jesse Jackson was building toward a phenomenon that eventually the media could not ignore.

Jackson did not hide his activities from those who would listen. "Farmers who supported Reagan two years ago have now signed on with our Rainbow Coalition. We've been building infrastructure. People say: 'We know they have a good idea and they have mass appeal,' but the test is organization, and we're building it now."

And on February 22, 1986, the day I spent with Jackson, as I watched the enthusiastic responses he elicited everywhere he went, I had the sense of discovering a secret. The secret was that there were a lot of people out there in America, all across the country, who were unhappy with Reaganism and who were eagerly reaching out with hope to Jesse Jackson. Something was happening in America in the mid-eighties, even if the media had not yet made it a reality.

The goal of his organization was to bring together all the disparate groups in America into one brightly colored coalition. In the winter of 1986, Jesse Jackson was already trying to expand his base from a predominantly black staff and constituency. And there were a number of white Americans, including farmers, blue-collar workers, even so-called rednecks and many liberals left over from the sixties, who were interested in what he was saying.

I was among those whites. Earlier that month I had returned to America, on vacation from my work as a foreign correspondent in the Middle East. I hadn't lived in the States for ten years, and I hardly recognized the country, now enshrouded by Reaganism. Yuppies, a new term I had to be taught, were coming into power. Everything I'd left behind in 1976, the year Jimmy Carter was elected President, seemed lost.

For those of us who had come of age in the sixties, all we had worked for appeared to have been forgotten in this new Reagan era. The only politician in the mid-eighties who seemed courageous enough to address the important issues was Jesse Jackson. Those of us, black and white alike, who had grown up in the South and struggled to make the civil rights movement succeed felt that Jackson was among the few national leaders trying to keep alive the vision of an integrated United States, a rainbow nation.

Much of my adult life had been spent living and working in the Third World. I served as a Peace Corps volunteer in Kenya in the late sixties. Later I worked as a social development planner at the United Nations. Also, I had worked on a doctorate in social anthropology and had spent two years conducting doctoral fieldwork in the Republic of Maldives in the middle of the Indian Ocean. For the past decade I had worked as a reporter covering events in Asia, Africa, Europe, the Middle East and the Pacific.

I had first met Jesse Jackson in Syria in late December 1983, when he came to win the release of the captive American pilot Lieutenant Robert Goodman. I had been on assignment in Syria as *Newsweek*'s Cairo bureau chief and correspondent for the Middle East. For seven years, from 1979 to 1986, I covered the Middle East for both *Newsweek* and ABC News.

Reporting on Jackson's successful, whirlwind visit to Damascus was one of my most memorable stories. He came and conquered a place and a situation and, more importantly, a leader, President Hafez al-Assad, who had sent many American negotiators away in failure after other diplomatic missions. On that occasion, I had accompanied Jesse Jackson and the freed U.S. hostage on their triumphant flight back to America on January 3–4, 1984, and had immediately returned abroad.

But from abroad I continued to follow Jesse Jackson's career. I was absolutely fascinated by this extraordinary man who reminded me a lot of many of the other world leaders I had been covering regularly overseas. While Jackson had impressed me in many ways, one thing that stayed with me was that special look in his eyes. I had seen a similar look in the eyes of a few other world leaders— Muammar el-Qaddafi, Yasir Arafat, Walid Jumblat, Pope John Paul II. It's a focused, driven look that combines charisma with vision, sexuality with power and, potentially dangerous, ambition. Like some of those other leaders he resembled, Jesse Jackson had an uncanny sense of the dramatic.

Watching him from afar over the next two years, I knew, however, that Jesse Jackson's charismatic power reached far beyond simply his instinct for the dramatic. Feeling like an alien in my own country, I wondered why other Americans, especially reporters like myself, were not picking up on what this man was doing. Even by 1986, Jesse Jackson was so globally popular that I was sure that if he were running for President of the world, he would win. Yet in America that seemed impossible. After living years abroad in places where I had ceased to be aware of people's skin color, I was shocked to find racism still rampant in my own country.

While I was home during that cold winter of 1986, when the space shuttle exploded and the millions of homeless were left to freeze, I decided to contact the Reverend Jackson. I was curious about what he was up to two years before the next presidential campaign. I was always looking for a story and was hoping he was planning some new foreign foray that would provide me with a scoop.

As I followed him during February 1986, I saw how he sensed a need across America that he would tap. I had previously observed his remarkable negotiating talents abroad, and now I could see his unique talents for capturing the imagination of his fellow Americans. I also gained a firsthand appreciation for his unusual abilities in political strategizing. For a foreign correspondent like myself, it was exciting to be observing such a leader in such close proximity. But our meetings that winter ultimately led me down a different path with Jesse Jackson, and not overseas, as I'd expected.

"How would you like to be the press secretary for a presidential candidate?" Jesse Jackson leaned back on the sofa and grinned at me.

I thought about half a second and then replied: "I've always wanted be press secretary to a special President. So a specially interesting presidential candidate would do, too."

We were then talking in Jackson's suite at the Howard Inn near Howard University in Washington, D.C. He had just got out of bed and was wearing his white terry-cloth bathrobe. The night before, he had phoned me around midnight to come meet him at seven in the morning to talk. As usual, he hadn't been ready when his guest arrived.

By the time I was finally ushered into his large suite at about 8 A.M., his top aides were with him. His new aide-de-camp, Kgosie Matthews, a South African lawyer from London, was moving quietly about the room collecting papers and gathering up clothes to send to the laundry.

When I showed interest in his suggestion, Jackson turned to the other two in the room—his current press secretary, Frank Watkins, and his foreign policy adviser, Jack Odell—and he mused out loud: "That could make a real good combination. Right? A black presidential candidate from South Carolina with his white female press secretary from North Carolina. We're already looking ahead to Super Tuesday." And he laughed and looked at all of us for approval.

On Tuesday, March 8, 1988, Super Tuesday, that unique day in the whole campaign season, twenty states would hold primaries and caucuses. And most of those states were Southern or bordered on Southern states. It was the region where the majority of American blacks lived, and in some states they even represented a majority of the electorate. Jesse Jackson had been preparing himself for this mega-contest day since 1984. He believed he had a chance of winning it and thence putting himself out in front in the Democratic presidential race. In the South it would appear to be a real coup for a black Southern male presidential candidate to have a white Southern female as his top aide, his press secretary.

The proposition was vintage Jesse Jackson. It appealed to me for national historic reasons and more. A direct ancestor of mine had been Andrew Jackson's law partner and, as his campaign manager, had sent Jackson to the White House. That ancestor was among the largest slaveholders in the South. What irony. I was proud that we in our generation had come so far. The idea was also intriguing to me for its modern, global implications—following a presidential candidate from my first meeting in the ancient Syrian capital to crisscrossing America in a U.S. presidential race. It appealed to my sense of history.

However, I was still on vacation on February 22, 1986, as Jackson campaigned in the San Francisco area. I was just visiting friends and decided to spend the day following Jackson around on the stump. He delivered five different speeches and held organizational meetings throughout the day.

He spelled out his goals loud and clear for the relatively few who were listening that day: "Ours is not just one season's work. We're building a fifty-state, 435-congressional-district organization. It's a Rainbow Coalition for 'justice at home, peace abroad.' We're building a coalition toward the year 2000, not just till 1988."

"Our Rainbow Coalition is moving towards becoming the 'Loyal Opposition,' " he continued. "What we said in 1984 was called naïve, too leftist, and now it's the status quo. Our vision—humane priorities at home and human rights abroad."

Jesse Jackson told the people around him that day a lot of things that revealed his philosophy and direction. He described "American politics" as "really about those macho boys, the white males—looking like Kennedy and acting like Reagan. They say the fifty-three percent population's women, sixty percent poor, Hispanics, blacks, Indians don't matter."

Jackson's gift for speaking ex tempore was evident that day. En route from the Catholic church back to the AME Church for a Rainbow planning meeting, his San Francisco Rainbow chairman, Eddie Wong (who later became Jackson's field director in his 1988 campaign), suggested that he stop to speak to a meeting of San Francisco's Asian community at Christ United Church. February 22 was the "Day of Remembrance" for the 120,000 Japanese-Americans who were interned in the United States forty-three years earlier.

Jackson immediately assented, and with minimal briefing, he delivered an ad-lib speech, recalling his own experience as similar to that of Asian-Americans: "Just as we look back today and say, 'Never again,' I recall how Marvin Kalb asked me, 'Are you black or are you American?' . . . The very idea that anyone could ask that is like saying to you, 'Are you Japanese or are you American?' We must say, 'Never again.' "

The Asian-American commemorators clapped and cheered wildly as Jesse Jackson walked out through the church, shaking every hand proffered and kissing whoever got close enough to him. Jackson was the only person of note from outside their community who had bothered to come and share in their "Day of Remembrance."

Back at the black Bethel AME Church, in the parish office of the Reverend Dr. Howard Gloyd, the chairman of his Rainbow Coalition in Northern California, Jackson divulged part of a blueprint which for the next two years would be the foundation for his '88 presidential campaign.

"In '84 we went through the experience of an exhilarating campaign, but we were all spirit and not much body. We need both ministers, who were our original base, and politicians, but now we need politicians more so we're not labeled some kind of fringe.

We've got to expand the Rainbow Coalition. Broadening our base is the right thing to do—mathematically, morally and politically."

He gave his detailed ideas about how his first Rainbow Convention should be organized: "If you invite Hart, Gephardt and Biden, they can't turn you down. Programming and rhythm are important. Everything needs finesse. It makes people and the press look at the situation differently. It can make us look formidable."

As in most of his planning and staff meetings, Jackson was the primary speaker and strategist. He went on: "Our backbone was preachers. The role they play in the convention must be substantial. We can't take them for granted. Their having a prominent place is very important.

"But we also have to have the stars. The rainbow has to be a happening," the great stage manager elaborated. "We need the glitter. *People* magazine wants the stars there. The primary transmitters of our mass culture are the movement artists. We must be sure they're there."

As usual, the Reverend Jesse Jackson ended the meeting with a prayer. Everyone present joined hands, and there was a powerful feeling of a real rainbow formation.

Later that night, across the bay at the Mission Safe for the Homeless, Jesse Jackson did not pass the hat. It was the weekend after days of torrential rains in Northern California had added more people to those left homeless after more than five years of Reaganomics.

Jackson's last event that Saturday night was one in which he appeared to be most at home—at a shelter for the homeless in East Oakland. There were lots of blacks in the audience, and Jackson moved almost hypnotically into old-time black evangelical rhythm.

He tailored his oratory, including his cadence, tone, vocabulary and subject, to the audience present, in the style he knew was his best. For blacks, it was familiar and appreciated. For whites, it was exotic and exciting. For everyone in the audience, Jesse Jackson's oratory, especially this traditional preaching style, was profoundly moving and perhaps at times threatening, frightening to certain nonblacks.

He began slowly, following traditional practice, and cited religion: "Religious experience teaches us to reach out and defend the poor. You measure character by sharing and caring. Jesus said: 'Inasmuch as you've done it to the least of these my brethren, then you've done it to me.' "

Then he moved directly to himself as a twentieth-century Jesus, the modern bringer of hope and compassion. "We come to disturb the comfortable and tell you you haven't done enough. We come to say, 'Put hope in your veins, not dope.' I understand the rejected and am making them the cornerstone.

"Those who are homeless and hungry can redeem our society. You know what it feels like to have no mailbox, no address. Even the birds have nests, even the foxes and snakes have homes. When a man has no home, his mind is blown.

"We must believe in our people." He was preaching louder and faster now. "There is nothing more basic in the world than being somebody's. There's power in love. Love lifts."

Then Jackson the teacher: "We have three options when our backs are against the wall . . .

"You can surrender. But don't. Don't give up your vote. Even the homeless and the hungry can register to vote." By now members of the audience were punctuating his every line with shouts of "Give 'em hope, Jesse," and "Teach us, Jesse."

Jesse Jackson continued, rolling his lines right off the refrains: "You must use what you've got and do your best. Don't put dope in your veins. Don't get drunk. Don't have babies out of wedlock, all because your back's against the wall."

Jackson pulled the experience of his rejected audience right into his own: "I was called a bastard. I am an adopted child. Our backs were against the wall. I understand 'back is against the wall.' "

And he ended with the line he would use time and again to inspire his audience and remind them of where he'd come from: "Just because you're born in the slum, it doesn't mean the slum is born in you."

The next day I was planning to accompany Jackson on another tour, but early that morning I got a call from my bosses at ABC

Radio News instructing me to rush back overseas. I was to go to Manila to be the roving radio correspondent for Asia.

I left and soon returned to Cairo to prepare to move to Manila when in April I was told first to go to Libya. Later, Jesse Jackson's press secretary, Frank Watkins, told me: "The next time we saw you was on ABC Television reporting live from Tripoli the night the U.S. bombed Libya. We knew then you weren't available for the time being."

The morning after the bombing of Libya, I received a call from the foreign editor at National Public Radio offering me a position as diplomatic correspondent in Washington. It seemed a good time for me to come home and become reacquainted with my own country after working abroad for a full decade. Later that summer of 1986, by then working in Washington, I interviewed Jackson for stories I was doing about his Southern Africa initiatives.

I reported that Jackson's efforts were pushing the Reagan administration to open more lines to the black states of Southern Africa. I had several very reliable sources in the State Department, USAID and the National Security Council, all of whom had confirmed that Jackson's trip to Southern Africa had prompted an acceleration in Reagan's aid plan. The Reagan administration responded angrily and publicly denied it, even though officials privately told me that the details of my story were accurate and precise.

I did not hide the fact that I thought Jackson was a phenomenon that the U.S. foreign policy establishment and the American news media could not ignore, but both the State Department and my foreign editor at NPR criticized me for suggesting that more attention should be paid to him.

For over a year and a half, the establishment media continued to dismiss Jesse Jackson and his work. No one, they said, with any knowledge of the American political scene could take the man seriously.

The polls in the autumn of 1987 showed Jesse Jackson running first among Democratic presidential hopefuls for the 1988 nomination. For months he stayed at least ten points ahead of the other top contenders—at that time, Massachusetts governor Michael Dukakis and Illinois senator Paul Simon. But that substantial lead was discounted by the media and the Democratic establishment.

Jesse Jackson was black. He also had a type of personality that appeared to many to verge upon the fanatic and, certainly, at times demagogic. Thus, the political analysts wrote him off as "unelectable." But they hardly ever acknowledged that it was perhaps more his somewhat frightening personality, rather than his race, that actually turned many people, especially the establishment, away from him.

"Jesse Jackson: What does he really want?" became the stock dismissal.

Jesse Jackson gave his basic, unequivocal answer to that question in the very beginning of the 1988 presidential campaign. On October 24, 1987, in Raleigh, North Carolina, Jackson officially announced his candidacy for the Democratic presidential nomination.

"I want to be elected President of the United States of America," the unlikely candidate announced.

But the media once more responded with the taunt: "What does Jesse want?"

The media's headline question became the catchphrase for Jesse Jackson's 1988 campaign. Later, it reflected the establishment's continuing amazement and increasing discomfort at being thrown off guard by the Jackson phenomenon.

The oft-repeated question infuriated Jackson, especially in the first months of his campaign, when it seemed no one in the media or political establishment took his candidacy seriously. Over time, however, Jackson could at least laugh sardonically when a reporter called out: "What do you really want?"

Jesse Jackson believed he was more qualified than any other candidate to be President in 1988. Even losing the race for the Democratic nomination did not change his wish and he intended to run again in four years.

There were, of course, other things Jesse wanted to achieve, other goals, but they were all secondary or tangential to the first goal. Born an illegitimate child, he does yearn for legitimacy. He does seek respect. He would have settled for the American vice presidency on the way to the top. He did want to be acknowledged as Martin Luther King's heir in leading black America. But all of those he could achieve on his way toward his ultimate and not yet abandoned goal—President of the United States of America.

2

ORGANIZING
THE RAINBOW
STAFF

"I see the face of America—red, yellow, brown, black and white," Jesse Jackson would say to almost any group he addressed. "We are all precious in God's sight—the real rainbow coalition." It was his ideal vision.

At the national level, Jesse Jackson wanted to establish a great multi-hued coalition, and on the micro level, he believed his own staff should reflect that diversity. His public rhetoric and espoused ideals, however, often did not meld with the more limited, less than impartial way he dealt privately with people and, in particular, the ways he used his own staff.

Jackson had spent years developing perhaps the most extensive grass-roots political network in American history. Now he needed to create a framework at the top. He needed to provide his one-man band with a formal organization. Always before, he had functioned as his own team owner, coach, quarterback, center, running back, wide receiver, tackle and even cheerleader. The only roles for his staff were perhaps as water boys and mascots. But he knew he needed to change, at least temporarily.

In 1984, Jackson had miraculously finished third in the race for the Democratic nomination, despite the almost universally acknowledged disorganization of the campaign itself. Jackson maintained that his performance was a singular success because it was a model of cost-efficiency. It was actually Jackson's charisma and message that propelled the movement.

But Jackson did hear the criticism and the complaints that he ignored "the work that needs to be done in the trenches." Some talked about his abusive treatment of the staff, pointing out how he would verbally attack them in public, always criticizing, never complimenting them for their work. Reporters who followed Jackson's 1984 campaign unanimously described it as chaotic, the most mismanaged, disorganized campaign they had ever covered.

"Jesse Jackson came out of 1984 having learned what a presidential campaign is supposed to look like and knowing he needed a better structure if he wanted to run a better campaign," Democratic political consultant Ann F. Lewis explained. A former political director of the Democratic National Committee, Lewis became an adviser to Jackson in late 1987.

"Keep your eyes on the goal, and don't get sidetracked by the enemy," Jesse constantly reminded himself out loud by reminding his close aides in the early months of the 1988 campaign. To observe Jackson was soon to be aware that he was a shrewd and calculating political tactician and strategist. Every move he made was aimed toward the ultimate goal.

Jackson's first major reorganizational tactic was to name Willie Brown, Speaker of the California Assembly, as his national campaign chairman. Brown had been one of the many key black politicians who had supported other Democratic candidates in 1984, candidates they thought had a real chance to win. Jackson had been active in state and national politics for more than twenty-five years. The rejection had galled him, but now he set about relentlessly to woo Brown. In his usual manner, Jackson began telephoning Brown every chance he got, from every stop along his itinerary throughout the country. And Jackson's method—phoning and meeting Brown numerous times—finally succeeded. Speaking from his Sacramento office soon after his appointment, the veteran politician Willie Brown announced to the staff: "We're building an infrastructure to relieve [Jackson] of the day-to-day responsibility of running his campaign. . . . He has literally been a one-man operation, and if anyone would ever really report the story, they would see that Jesse Jackson is a phenomenon. There is just no single national candidate who has ever done, or could do, what he has done."

At the top, Jackson had a powerful black politician in place; his deputy campaign chairmen were a black, former mayor Richard Hatcher of Gary, Indiana, and a Hispanic, former governor Toney Anaya of New Mexico.

Jackson also knew he needed acceptable whites in key staff positions and as advisers to demonstrate that his constituency was not only the black and underprivileged core. The position of campaign manager should, at least initially, be filled by a white male to give credibility to Jackson in the eyes of the "white macho establishment." Jackson began looking around.

The problem was, Jackson himself couldn't conceptualize what a real campaign manager would do, since he had always been his own campaign manager. By late 1987 he had already asked half a dozen men—the black lawyer Ron Brown, Mondale's former campaign manager, Bob Beckel, and New York City political leader, Basil Patterson. No one wanted the job: Jesse Jackson had never taken orders from anyone.

Since 1969, one of Jackson's chief aides had been Frank Watkins, a white man about his own age, known in the inner circle as Jesse's alter ego; Watkins was a thoughtful, compassionate, white Church of God minister, but to the public he was nearly invisible. Watkins was self-effacing and had learned, through experience never to expect a word of thanks from Jackson for anything, not even for having written Jackson's speech for the 1984 Democratic convention. Frank had served so long as right-hand man, makeshift campaign manager and press secretary that putting Watkins in a key position would not advance the Jackson image.

A few whites, such as Watkins and Carolyn Kazdin, had been with Jackson since 1984, but he had always kept them out of the limelight. Kazdin, who was Jewish, had been actively involved in grass-roots rural organizations since her days in the Peace Corps in the late sixties. She was a hardworking organizer for Jackson, but she always stayed behind the scenes, and Jackson did nothing to encourage her to appear publicly.

Yet Jackson knew, finally, toward the end of 1987, that he would have to give a few staff members some visibility—the minimum necessary to show the media that he was opening up his organization. This part of his game plan conflicted, however, with an intrinsic aspect of Jackson's modus operandi. Jesse Jackson always liked to appear to be the only one running his show. The aides who had survived over the years were those he'd kept very much in the background. They had learned that Jackson simply did not want them to be seen out front.

In addition to promoting whites, Jackson acknowledged that he needed Jews in order to overcome a major obstacle to success in the 1988 presidential race. The Jewish vote was important, and he had been seen as anti-Semitic ever since his use of the term "Hymietown" in reference to New York City in the 1984 campaign. He wanted the national media to see that he had solid Jewish support at the core, as well as Southern whites and women. At the same time, he knew he must keep his traditional black constituency happy by not appearing to be running over completely to the white side. It would be a delicate balance.

Early in the autumn of 1987, Jackson asked Robert Borosage to take over as his campaign manager. Borosage was Jewish, had been director of the left-wing Institute for Policy Studies in Washington, D.C., and had worked with Jackson during the '84 campaign. A tall, handsome man in his mid-forties, a graduate of the University of Michigan and Yale Law School, Borosage had a confident manner around Jackson that made him seem like a buddy. That appealed to Jackson, who sought a sense of camaraderie with white men. Borosage turned the job down, however, saying he would rather come on later as chief policy adviser, thus forgoing the satisfaction of massaging Jackson's ego with praise while at the same time pumping him with ideas and facts that Jackson could incorporate into his own mental computer.

Jackson then turned to Gerald J. Austin. Not only was he Jewish but he also had on-the-ground experience in the real world of politics. A native of the Bronx in New York, the forty-four-year-old Austin had spent nearly two decades in Ohio running successful political campaigns, including those of Governor Richard Celeste. He was also a wizard at making political commercials for TV and radio. Gerry Austin was straight-talking, tough-talking and not afraid to order Jackson around when necessary, even if he didn't have the "good ole boy" approach of Borosage.

In October 1987 Austin was flown out to California to meet Willie Brown. "Much to everyone's surprise," as Austin later put it, they "got on instantly." Brown immediately sent him off to travel with Jackson for a few days' testing. Within a day, Jesse was calling Gerry his campaign manager—before they had even officially sealed the deal. That was perfect Jackson style. He never liked to go through an official process of appointing, hiring or firing. He liked such things to just happen, and if he could get people to work for him a short time without pay, so much the better.

Gerry Austin took over as campaign manager in November and immediately began to put some order into the Jackson organization. The chaos prior to his arrival had existed largely because Jackson never sat still long enough to deal with it. And no one else had dared. Austin did. He strategized, he hired, he gave out assignments, he saw to it that money came in and that the staff were paid and bills taken care of. He made essential day-to-day and long-range decisions that had previously been brushed aside while the one-man show stayed on the road in constant motion.

But it was hard for Jackson to accept Austin in authority. In late December, at the first staff meeting Jackson attended after Austin assumed his new position, Jackson said: "Well, things are a little better organized now that Gerry is here as the administrator." Jesse didn't even realize he was insulting Gerry by calling him that.

That same month Austin organized the overnight move of Jackson '88 campaign headquarters from Washington, D.C., to Chicago. Jesse had had the idea, and Gerry had concurred. It was strategic and symbolic. Chicago was Jesse's hometown, had been for twenty-five years. It was the center of the country, where many of Jackson's constituents—workers, farmers, urban and rural poor—came together. It gave the Jackson campaign a unique address, not the usual Washington, D.C., political base; so in the first weeks of the new year "Jackson '88" was installed on the third floor of 30 West Washington Street in downtown Chicago.

At the same time, Gerry Austin began immediately to organize the staff. When he'd come in, a number of staff positions were already filled, but because of the lack of organization, many had no title and only vague notions of their responsibilities. It took Austin to impose some order on what already existed. He found that the staff was comprised mostly of blacks and other minorities: Yolanda Carraway, a black woman who had worked on Mondale's '84 campaign, ran Jackson's Washington, D.C., office; May Louie, an Asian-American woman, ran the New England operation; Eddie Wong, another Asian-American, had been brought in from San Francisco to be the campaign field director; the Reverend Willie T. Barrow, a black woman, headed up PUSH for Jackson; Ron Daniels, a black male, ran the Southern operation; Dr. Armando Gutierrez, a Hispanic, ran the Texas campaign; Tyrone Kreider, a black minister, coordinated the students campaign; Pam Smith, a black woman, had come from the Portland, Oregon, Rainbow Coalition to run the communications office at Chicago headquarters; Danette Palmore, a black woman, was in place as Austin's personal assistant; Mary Washington, another black woman, was Jackson's personal secretary at headquarters; and traveling on the road with Jackson were two young black males, Kgosie Matthews and Bill Morton. Besides Austin himself, the only whites in key positions were Watkins and Kazdin and the treasurer, Howard Renzi.

Austin set to the task of creating and filling other key positions, mainly with white males. Mark Steitz, formerly a top domestic policy adviser to erstwhile presidential hopeful Gary Hart, would come on board in late January as Jackson's traveling issues director. Frank Clemente, former director of Jobs for Peace, would serve as issues coordinator in the Chicago headquarters. Steve Cobble, formerly with ex-Governor Toney Anaya in New Mexico, came on to coordinate Jackson delegates.

Frank Watkins was eager to leave his longtime post as press secretary, a job he'd always loathed, because he maintained he couldn't stand the press. He wanted out in 1988, as he had two years earlier when we'd all talked. And in early December, just after the unexpected death of Chicago's mayor, Harold Washington, it seemed as if there might be a suitable replacement for Watkins—Washington's former press secretary, another white male. But just as Austin was on the verge of naming him the new press secretary for the campaign, blacks in Chicago let it be known they believed he favored white reporters and disapproved of the appointment. Austin dropped the idea immediately, and the campaign staff acted as if the offer had never been made.

I didn't know about any of this, but ever since Jackson had announced his '88 candidacy in October, he and his new campaign had been on my mind. I wondered whether I ought to contact Jesse again about my working for him. We hadn't discussed it for nearly two years, since I had gone back overseas. The only times I had seen him since then were when I was interviewing him for National Public Radio. I had lost contact with his people and didn't know what his staff needs were in late 1987. At the time, I was working as media adviser to Senator Terry Sanford of North Carolina.

Then, almost serendipitously, on December 15, in Washington, D.C., I happened to meet with Democratic political consultant Ann Lewis. I told her about the conversation I'd had with Jackson two years earlier about the possibility of becoming his press secretary. "If you're at all interested, you ought to get hold of them again," she advised. "His campaign is really shaping up in an interesting way, especially now that the new campaign manager, Gerry Austin, has come on board."

Immediately after Christmas, Gerry Austin phoned to say they wanted to talk with me as soon as possible.

Meanwhile, Jesse Jackson kept up his whirling dervish pace of campaigning across America. He talked by phone constantly with Austin to advise, suggest and approve his organizational and strategic plans. But he himself never stopped campaigning and collecting personal human-interest stories for his vast anecdotal repertoire.

Just before Thanksgiving, Jackson had flown to the Persian Gulf to try his hand at bringing peace in the long-raging Iran-Iraq war. It turned out to be his last overseas foray until after the summer political convention. Jackson knew that he couldn't risk leaving the domestic home front during the 1988 campaign. But at least the trip gave him more firsthand experience to try to use as proof of his foreign policy expertise.

That trip was interrupted, however, by the death of Chicago's first black mayor, Harold Washington. Jackson rushed home on Thanksgiving to attend the funeral and, more importantly, to be present at the succession negotiations. He knew it was even more important to look like a peacemaker in his adopted hometown, the late Mayor Richard Daley's Chicago, than in the far-flung Persian Gulf. Chicago would be critical in the Illinois primary, in which Jackson would have to contend with another "native son," Senator Paul Simon.

On Christmas Day, Jackson and his family spent some of the day visiting and comforting prisoners in the Cook County jail. Jackson would later relate in his campaign speeches how his family never exchange Christmas presents but customarily spend that day visiting the rejected in jail. Jesse would cite that time and again in his campaign speeches, "The cost of a scholarship to the Cook County jail is ten times more than a state college scholarship."

In early January, Jackson visited two other important sites that would also provide regular anecdotes for his repertoire. In McAllen, Texas, on the Mexican border, he saw workers in a field who had no access to plumbing, who were paid far below the minimum wage and whose children were laboring instead of going to school.

Also while in McAllen, he learned there were very few guards to protect the United States against the vast amounts of drugs coming over the border. A few days later he visited a Coast Guard ship off Florida, and he learned that spending for the U.S. Coast Guard was being cut by $100 million. For months, Jackson could throw this in the face of the Reagan administration. His constant traveling was more than simply campaigning for Jackson; his being in touch with people provided useful stories to cite as critical examples of the many changes needed in America.

But on Monday, January 11, the American media weren't paying much attention to the Jackson campaign. Early that morning I flew to Chicago and went to the new Jackson headquarters to discuss the press secretary's job. People in the office seemed in a bit of a daze from the recent move, but were all very friendly and eager to get to work.

Everything about the new headquarters then gave the appearance of a fly-by-night operation. I couldn't help wondering whether I could bear to work in such a disorganized operation in which the man at the helm seemed always to be flying by the seat of his pants and improvising according to whim. I thought back to my very first meetings with this remarkable man, Jesse Jackson. I remembered those dramatic days in the ancient Syrian capital.

It was Friday, December 30, 1983. Jesse Jackson's arrival in Damascus, Syria, seemed superficially like just another stop on the American campaign trail—with cameras, reporters, local dignitaries waiting at the bottom of the steps pushed up to the airplane. But he strode down the stairs from the commercial Lufthansa aircraft into a scene that was far from usual in this tight police state.

It was a cool desert night in the ancient heart of the Middle East, the region of the world that has long stymied and plagued American Presidents and statesmen. Only the day before, the Syrian Defense Minister had declared his nation at war with the United States.

Jackson, always a private citizen without official portfolio, had come to Syria to do what the President of the United States, Ronald Reagan, and his State Department had failed to do. He had come to win the release of a U.S. POW, Navy pilot Lieutenant Robert O. Goodman, Jr., a black American. It was a big gamble, but Jesse Jackson announced on arrival that he had come "to break the dead-lock in Syrian-American relations" and he had "high hopes for arranging [Goodman's] release." Goodman had been taken prisoner by Syrian troops after his A-6 jet was shot down over Lebanon during a raid on December 4, 1983.

Jesse Jackson waited it out, in good Middle Eastern style, but in his own style he managed to orchestrate photographic media events every day. He accepted the many cups of tea and coffee proffered. Daily he waited for summons to meet various officials until he eventually got to the President on Monday. In between, he held meetings with the ecumenical leadership of Damascus—Catholics, Protestants and Muslims. Accompanying Jackson in his traveling party were several American ministers, including the Islamic leader Louis Farrakhan.

On New Year's Eve, he attended a reception dutifully given him by the American ambassador. Then he paid a visit to the quarters of the U.S. Marine embassy guards during their New Year's Eve party.

Then on New Year's Day, when no Syrian officials would see Jackson, he managed to fill his day on his own. He met with the head of the Palestine National Council and other leading Palestinians and Lebanese and visited a Palestinian refugee camp outside Damascus. Later, he made an unusual appearance at the very ancient Greek Catholic church and delivered a sermon in honor of World Peace Day.

Finally, on Tuesday morning, January 3, 1984, the word came that the Syrians would hand over the U.S. POW, not to the American ambassador directly, but to Jesse Jackson, the maverick diplomat-negotiator.

The Syrians, however, wanted to make the presentation as quickly and quietly as possible and just end it. They weren't interested in the American media the way Jackson was. But Jackson succeeded in stalling long enough to be sure that all the reporters and camera crews reached the Foreign Ministry before he arrived to receive Goodman. I rushed straight to the ministry as soon as I got the tip-off, but I ended up having to wait more than half an hour even though my taxi had left after Jackson's limousine.

I learned later how he'd managed the delay. A photographer friend of mine who had followed Jackson said they had circled the city of Damascus several times before approaching the Foreign Ministry. Obviously, Jesse had realized the media needed time to get there, and he'd managed to persuade his drivers to give him another tour to buy that time.

I was on both flights when Jackson took Goodman home to the States. The first was on a U.S. Air Force cargo plane sent to Damascus from Germany. And the second, which was a real coup for Jackson, was on President Reagan's own Air Force One. On board, I was granted a one-on-one interview with Jackson, but I learned in the course of it what most reporters discover: he seldom says anything that he hasn't said before, even repeated many times publicly.

Jackson did say that night, in describing his successful mission to Syria: "Moments in history are served up when unusual things happen. This is such a moment. Saul's course [St. Paul's conversion on the road to Damascus] changed the history of the world. I have a sense now we are on the cutting edge for change in the Middle East. It is the paradox of a military man shot down in combat and then used for peace."

Also on that flight home, I noticed something else, the significance of which I wouldn't realize until years later. Jackson spoke about the book he was then reading and how important he felt it was. The title was *The Search for Common Ground,* and the author was a black theologian, Howard Thurman. The impact of that book on Jackson's thinking would not become obvious until 1988, when his call for seeking "common ground" became a major theme of his second presidential campaign.

The next day in Washington, D.C., Jesse Jackson accompanied Lieutenant Goodman to the White House. President Reagan welcomed them both at a formal ceremony in the Rose Garden. It was the closest Jackson had been to the White House in that decade, but Jesse savored the feeling.

Four years later, as I sat in Jackson's '88 campaign headquarters waiting to talk to his top aides about my working as his press secretary, I recalled my overall impressions of covering that story. There was constant confusion, even chaos. That was usually the case in covering the Middle East, but I recalled being surprised that this American and his staff also operated in such a disorganized fashion.

I remember feeling sorry for his press secretary, then a sweet, well-meaning black woman. Later I learned, from Frank Watkins, who took over as press secretary in the '84 campaign, that she had suffered a nervous collapse immediately after that trip to Syria. I realized then that probably Jackson didn't even want a real press secretary but felt he had to tolerate some figure with that title.

Frank Watkins came out to welcome me. A husky blond with a receding hairline, he was wearing a nondescript open-necked shirt and corduroy trousers.

Watkins had been serving as Jackson's press secretary ever since early '84, and from our meeting in 1986 I knew he couldn't stand the job.

Watkins and Jackson were about the same age, and though white, Watkins was an ordained minister from a similar background of poverty. They had been together for nineteen years, and Jackson consulted him constantly for political readings of almost any situation. Frank was candid about his position: "Working with Jesse is doing what I want. I never expect him to thank me. When it ceases to suit my purposes, then I'll leave."

That day in Chicago I immediately noticed that Frank seemed more relaxed than when I'd met him two years ago. He smiled broadly. "My old job of press secretary is open now, and we need to fill it fast."

Frank explained: "As you probably realized, I always hated that job, and I hated the press. But you're from the press, so you can likely cope with the work better. Now I'm going to be full-time political director, doing what I really like."

There was no doubt that he had the appearance of a freer man this year. I acknowledged that I was very interested in the job and let him continue.

"The problem is," he went on, "you'll find it really frustrating because Jesse likes to surprise everyone, including his press secretary and others close to him. It can often be very embarrassing for you."

"I already figured that's how it could be to work with Jesse," I responded. "When I first met him in Damascus and was covering his mission there, I realized that his press secretary had no access to him and never knew what was happening ahead of time. We journalists just learned to go straight to Jackson himself. It made for a lot of confusion. That's not how I'd want to be perceived. I'd want to discuss that with Jesse before taking the job."

Frank warned me that day in Chicago: "I have to be honest and tell you, Liz, it can be really frustrating, even for someone like myself who's known him for years. He thrives on doing his own thing and trying to surprise not only the press but people like me. Sometimes it can hurt. You gotta be prepared for that if you take the job."

Frank went on: "At least you know you can handle the nonstop travel, since you've been a foreign correspondent, especially in the Middle East. Being on the road with Jesse is as grueling, maybe more so, as you know.

"Look, the truth is, Jesse doesn't even know what a campaign manager should do, and he certainly doesn't know what a good press secretary should be doing," Watkins continued candidly. "Jesse is used to thinking he's playing all those roles himself."

Frank was really straight in laying out the situation for me. It would have been an understatement for me to say the job sounded like a challenge.

Just then, the campaign manager, Gerald Austin, walked up and introduced himself to me. Tall and slightly portly, he wore a dull gray suit. He was red-faced with gray curly hair above a long forehead. He didn't give much of a smile, but he seemed quite affable. I later learned that, although he seldom smiled and often appeared gruff, he was a sensitive and warmhearted tough guy.

Gerry Austin had grown up in a poor Jewish family in the Bronx, where his father had been a laborer and a bodyguard for Paul Robeson. On Gerry's desk in Columbus, Ohio, was a photograph of the great actor and Austin's father standing behind him. The picture was taken in 1949 at a rally in Peekskill, New York, just before violent racial clashes erupted. Gerry was five then, but years later he still recalled riding home from the rally with his mother and sister on a bus that was attacked by angry demonstrators.

Thirty-nine years later, Gerry Austin was in Chicago working as the campaign manager for the first black presidential candidate. He suggested to me that we go out for lunch to discuss the job.

We said goodbye to Watkins and left the office to walk around the windy corner for lunch at Mayor's Row restaurant. As I settled down to my Reuben sandwich and Gerry to his tuna fish, both of us sipping Diet Cokes, Gerry said: "Look, this is going to be the most exciting campaign this year."

I agreed, but up to then I had figured it would last only up to the convention. But Gerry began to convince me that it was truly in the realm of possibility that Jackson could go on beyond the convention. America was changing enough so that people could actually contemplate his being the Democratic nominee and ultimately President.

Austin continued: "Before I took this job, I traveled a few days last October with Jackson to see how we got on. After I saw him in action a few times, I began to think: This guy can go all the way. Jesse Jackson can be elected President. And that's the way I'm now running this campaign."

Then Gerry explained quite candidly that they could use a white woman in a visible position to round out the rainbow appearance of the campaign staff. He explained that at the moment there were only two young black men traveling with Jackson all the time, and that didn't look good in the pictures. Also, he acknowledged that so far most of those he'd hired had been white males. So he said they were glad I had come along, a white woman, a professional and the best-qualified applicant. But he said that I would need an assistant and that, though it would ultimately be my choice, he would want me to hire a black woman, and they already had a candidate, Delmarie Cobb, lined up for me to interview.

Austin then suggested that I go meet Jackson somewhere that week and travel with him for a few days to see how we got on together on the road. I said I'd already traveled a little with him before and felt confident I could handle it.

Back at the office, Jesse was calling from Florida. Gerry told him I was there and handed the phone over to me.

"Why don't you come meet us tonight in Miami," Jesse said immediately. He expected people to drop everything and go wherever he needed them. I explained that I had to go home first for a long-standing doctor's appointment. "But I'll meet you Wednesday night in Jackson [Mississippi] and then go on with you to Iowa. I'm really looking forward to working with you, and I'm awfully excited about the campaign."

"Okay, whatever you have to do, but come fast," he said.

Jackson then hinted again, as he had two years earlier when we'd talked about my being his press secretary, that he would be glad to have a white Southern woman in his entourage. "We've got some real problems down here in the South, and I can use you. So hurry. . . . Give me back to Gerry now."

It was nearly midnight when Jesse Jackson finally showed up at the hotel in Jackson. It was Wednesday, January 13. I had flown into the Mississippi capital a couple of hours earlier and had been waiting in the lobby of the Holiday Inn Downtown.

On the way into the city from the airport, my taxi driver, a young black, had told me how excited the people of Mississippi were with their new governor. Ray Mabus, a thirty-nine-year-old white liberal, had been inaugurated that day. The cabdriver explained that Mabus had been elected by both blacks and whites who were eager to develop a new Mississippi. They all had high hopes that he would bring industry and education to the state. That black driver was much more turned on to the promises of his new governor than he was to the Jackson campaign.

Suddenly, the Secret Service agents in the hotel began moving toward the door and talking into the radios in their sleeves. The Reverend Jackson was on his way back to the hotel from dinner. A dapper black who gave only the name Wyatt was in charge, and he indicated that they would decide what to do with me once they got the signal from Jackson himself.

When he entered the hotel Jesse marched up to me and gave me a greeting kiss, "Welcome, Ms. Liz. It sure is good to see you. We're really in need of your help on the road." The handsome man, dressed in a dark suit, still looked neat and energetic after an exhausting day of campaigning across several states in the South.

At that time, there were only two other staff members traveling with Jackson—both young black men, Kgosie Matthews and Bill Morton.

Kgosie Matthews, a thirty-one-year-old South African with a British law degree, had been Jackson's chief aide-de-camp ever since the two met in London at an anti-apartheid conference in 1985. For nearly two years, it was essentially only Kgosie who accompanied Jackson everywhere on a daily basis. Kgosie always seemed gruff and wary until he got to know you, and then if he accepted you, he was a very sensitive, gentle man. Though only thirty-one years old, he was almost bald and always sported mod-style British suits with huge shoulder pads across his slight, wiry frame.

Bill Morton, a handsome young American, had joined Jackson the past October. Only twenty-seven years old, Bill came from Colorado and had worked on the Gary Hart campaign as an advance man; after it collapsed, Bill found work with Jackson. A graduate of Georgetown University, Bill exuded a preppy air, with thin horn-rimmed glasses and Brooks Brothers suits, button-down collars and rep ties. Bill had become Jackson's "trip director," meaning he was supposed to coordinate everything concerning the daily trip with the head office and the Secret Service and hired limousines and local officials. Although the division of labor was never clear to anyone, not even to Bill and Kgosie at times, it was essentially that Kgosie handled all Jackson's personal affairs on the road and Bill his public movements.

That night Kgosie gave me a greeting kiss, and Bill gave me a friendly welcome and introduced himself. For a while, we were Jackson's core traveling team.

On seeing the welcome Jackson gave me, the Secret Service men finally nodded acceptance of me. I was given the go-ahead to move freely with the candidate and go in and out of his suite. The next day the Secret Service gave me the little red-and-gold metal pin that would give me Secret Service clearance for months. The four of us went up to Jackson's suite. The Secret Service stood guard outside, as they would do throughout every night. Bill and Kgosie went immediately to work. Kgosie pulled scraps of paper with messages from the brown leather briefcase that contained a portable phone. He went into Jesse's bedroom and began placing telephone calls from the room phone.

Bill pulled out the schedule for the next day and started going over it. Jesse walked in and out of the living room of the suite. Now clad only in an undershirt and his trousers, he would change the television channel and then go back to the bedroom to make other phone calls. Jesse Jackson's use of the telephone as a political tool was extraordinary. Late every night, then again early in the morning before most people were awake and then throughout the day whenever he saw a phone, he would make calls, discussing ideas, wooing potentially powerful supporters, summoning or ordering movements of friends, family, staff and other minions.

In between his activities that first night, I made small talk, waiting, I'd thought, for him to discuss my job. Finally, Jesse said that he was going to bed and that we would talk in the morning. We hadn't discussed the job at all. It was about 1:30 A.M., but he told me to come to his room about 7 A.M. and brief him on the news. The next morning when I went there on time, after having had a full Southern breakfast with Bill Morton and a few reporters, Jackson was still in bed and sent me away. I would have to brief him at the last minute in the limousine en route to the Governor's Mansion, the first stop of the day.

This was the beginning. It looked like the usual full day on Jackson's schedule—meet with the new governor, Ray Mabus, in the antebellum Governor's Mansion, address the state legislature, speak to the students at Mississippi State University, open the JJPC '88 (Jesse Jackson Presidential Campaign '88) state headquarters, have lunch with the state campaign staff. In the afternoon we would fly from Mississippi to Des Moines, Iowa, for an address the next night to the students at Drake University, and then we would begin preparing for the Iowa debate on Friday night. It was then less than three weeks until the Iowa caucus, the nation's first in the long list of primaries and caucuses for 1988. After that, the New Hampshire primary and Super Tuesday on March 8. Then on to the New York primary on April 19, the California primary on June 7 and finally to the Atlanta convention in July. Jesse Jackson was running all the way.

In the next few days Jesse Jackson added members to his team, and we were ready for the first long stretch of the season.

3

THE IOWA CAUCUS

"We meet at the crossroads, a point of decision. Common ground." Jesse Jackson would start and end his 1988 campaign the same way, carrying the same themes.

Early on and then again much later, in his speech at the Democratic convention, he would compare America to another, ancient melting pot. "Take the city of Jerusalem, an intersection where many trails met, a small village that became the birthplace of three great religions—Judaism, Christianity and Islam. Why was this village so blessed? Because it provided a crossroads where different people met, different cultures, different civilizations could meet and find common ground."

"Now again we meet at a new crossroads, a point of decision. We are meeting to find common ground," the Reverend Jackson would explain to the voters in Iowa.

Iowa, the geographical center of the United States, a crossroads, had become the first "point of decision" in the long presidential campaign season. Since 1972, it had become the tradition that candidates first had to devote almost excessive attention to this small, relatively liberal, Midwestern farming state. With a population of 2.8 million, only approximately 200,000 would brave the bitter winter cold to cast their oral votes in the town-meeting-style caucus on February 8.

Jackson's confronting the Iowa voters also represented a special "point of decision." Iowa's population was predominantly white, middle-class and Protestant. Only 2 percent of the population was black or Hispanic. Iowa was such a "lily white" state that many people there had never even seen a black person before Jesse Jackson appeared among them.

A year before, Jackson had come to Greenfield, a small town in rural Iowa, to meet real Iowa farmers, the backbone of the state. Their first meeting was an instant love affair. Jackson decided to make his state campaign headquarters in this unlikely place. All the other candidates, both Democratic and Republican, based their Iowa operations in the capital, Des Moines.

The all-white town of Greenfield had served as Iowa's Ku Klux Klan headquarters in the 1920s. Jesse Jackson's first visit there was on the night of the Super Bowl in 1987. It certainly hadn't started as a propitious time for a strange black politician to come to this quiet hamlet where almost everyone wanted to be at home watching the game between the New York Giants and the Denver Broncos. The schedulers had realized too late that the speech had been set for the same time that night at the United Methodist Church, and so they had just kept it on the schedule.

Jackson had just left a black church in Des Moines when he set forth over the fifty miles to the unknown Greenfield. It was cold outside, about fifteen degrees, and already dark. Jesse was catnapping, as he often did between locations on his political stump. Suddenly, he recalled, his car was stopped by a sheriff's car on the outskirts of Greenfield. It made him a bit nervous when an excited officer shone a flashlight into the back seat and then began shouting, "They're here! They're here!" Then the sheriff pointed his lights at cars parked all along the road and shouted, "They're here! And the church is a mile away!" When Jesse told the story later, he remarked that he had never seen anyone, especially a policeman, so excited before.

Finally, the Jackson car got to the little church. The crowd was too large for the parish hall, where Jackson had originally been scheduled to speak at a cooperative dinner, so they had moved to the church sanctuary. Jackson delivered one of his great soul-inspiring speeches from the pulpit, and thus began the special relationship between him and this unlikely community in rural Iowa.

Afterward, Jackson and about twenty townspeople met and conferred at the house of a local lawyer, Jay Howe. Then and there they decided to make this town Jackson's state campaign headquarters for the country's first political caucus in 1988. Jackson himself was overwhelmed by the outpouring of support and interest that the people of Greenfield gave him that night and over the following months. Later he would describe the scene: "There was an emerging sense of a deep and abiding reunion. Lot of romance in it. People were trying to say so many things, like they wish they had done this a long time ago."

Jackson's decision was symbolic. He and the people of Greenfield had met and found common ground. He supported them, and they supported him. In 1987 they had eaten together, celebrated the new year together, and now he was back again, this time for the first caucus of 1988. Later he would promise to come again the next year to celebrate all their successes of the past.

It was breakfast time on a bright, cold Saturday morning, January 16, on the Iowa farm when the Jackson entourage (staff and press corps) arrived. By Iowa standards, however, it wasn't that cold, with temperatures a little above zero. Jesse wore only a green-and-yellow quilted vest over an open-necked white pin-striped shirt.

The host farmer Tom Hoy ushered Jesse straight to the dining table. It was placed at the end of the living room next to the open kitchen, set apart only by a counter. The scene in the room was striking—Jesse Jackson and five white farmer menfolk, all sitting down at the table while the farmers' womenfolk (wives, girlfriends and daughters) stood cooking and serving up the food in the kitchen. The male farmers talked only with Jesse, ignoring the women in the kitchen. Jesse and the hosts all ignored the members of his staff, who were forced to stand near the table in the same room because it was too cold to wait outside. The men started by talking about the weather. Then they soon got into the havoc Reagan's farm policies were causing them. Jesse said he had come to offer them help.

The whole scene was like a tableau I had seen before in other countries, but for heartland America in 1988, it was almost anachronistic. There I was, I mused, in my "advanced" home country, the United States of America, working for a presidential candidate, and the situation was the same as I had observed many times in African and Arab countries, where the ruler sits and eats with his male hosts while the women serve and the ruler's staff stand idly by, hovering near the table but ignored.

I turned to Carolyn Kazdin, Jackson's brilliant campaign organizer for Iowa (also in 1984 and later in other states in 1988), and I could tell she was thinking the same things. I remarked: "It reminds me of scenes I saw when I was in the Peace Corps in Africa." She expressed a similar sense of *déjà vu.* Twenty years before, we'd been Peace Corps volunteers at the same time in different countries—she in Brazil and I in Kenya.

The real irony came an hour later. First, during the barnyard speeches, in which Jackson and some of the farmers addressed neighboring farmers. They stood on large block-shaped bales of hay stacked to make platforms. One of the two women who spoke commented that it was an insult that they were allowed to speak only at the end and treated almost as incidental. Jackson wasn't pleased that she had aired her annoyance in public.

Then, after the speeches, Jackson called a meeting of all the farm women and his female staff members. He said: "It's time to organize the rural women here and to bring them together with urban women across America. We need to find common ground." He instructed Carolyn to organize just such an event for the next weekend.

The paradox was that while Jesse believed in his idea and believed that he was striving to end sexism in America, he hadn't noticed the blatant sexual segregation at breakfast. When I said: "It's a good thing that woman had the courage to speak out about it," Jesse retorted: "No, it wasn't a good thing this morning, not in the middle of my rally."

January 1988 was only the third time that the United States had honored the birthday of the black civil rights leader Martin Luther King, Jr., with an official holiday. His real birthday was January 15, but this year it was commemorated on Monday, the eighteenth. Jesse Jackson started talking about it weeks ahead in his speeches, and especially on the weekend before the holiday. And on the actual holiday, Jackson made a flying stop in Memphis, the city where King had been assassinated nearly twenty years ago on April 4, 1968.

That day Jackson talked about how King had spent his last birthday, and how Jackson had been among the disciples who shared it with him in January 1968. They spent the morning meeting and planning the direction for the Poor People's Campaign. They were at King's house in Atlanta. Then King's family joined them, and someone brought in a birthday cake. "It was a happy birthday," Jackson concluded. "The Reverend Dr. Martin Luther King spent it the way he liked best, working and relaxing, with his family and his staff and friends."

Jesse Jackson was very careful now to tell anecdotes only of the living King, not of his assassination, for that day of assassination had been followed by years of bitterness among King's followers, mostly directed against Jackson. These were all too painful for Jesse, and although he remembered the week before, the day itself, the next morning and the years of angry words, he didn't like to talk about them.

There have been so many accounts that many people remain puzzled about the facts of those hours surrounding the assassination. From all of them, though, one story seems to survive as the most factual. A week before King's death, Jackson had publicly opposed the leader during a staff meeting. This was not acceptable. The other aides, like Andrew Young and Ralph Abernathy, who also had aspirations to inherit his mantle someday never openly opposed King. The twenty-seven-year-old Jackson felt no hesitation in asserting himself. That day King appeared to have reached his breaking point with young Jesse, and as he was leaving the room, he turned on his disciple, who was trying to follow him to discuss their point of argument. King was reported to have said: "If you are so interested in doing your own thing that you can't do what the organization is structured to do, go ahead, but for God's sake, don't bother me."

A week later, on April 3, the night before King's assassination, the two men had another argument. According to David Garrow's biographical account, based on accounts by SCLC staffers, King was again openly displeased with Jackson. Garrow wrote that on that last night "King again berated Jackson . . . he said, 'Jesse, just leave me alone' . . . Jackson responded, 'Don't send me away, Doc. Don't send me away.'"

The next evening, on April 4, Martin Luther King, Jr., was preparing to leave his Memphis hotel to go to a big rally. Most of his aides were milling around downstairs waiting for him. Jesse, along with Andy Young, was among those standing in the courtyard of the Lorraine Hotel under King's balcony. Suddenly, the leader appeared and summoned Jackson: "I want you to come to dinner with me." That was interpreted by all present as his signal that he wanted to patch things up with Jackson. Reports put that exchange at 5:59 P.M.

Jackson was then reported to have called up to King that he wanted to introduce a saxophonist, Ben Branch, who was visiting from Chicago, where Jackson now made his home base. King was then heard to call down to the musician: "I want you to play my song tonight, play 'Precious Lord.' Play it real pretty."

It was at that instant, at 6:01 P.M., that a shot pierced the evening and ended the friendly laughter. Dr. King lay slumped in a pool of blood, his feet dangling over the balcony. Ralph Abernathy, who was already upstairs with King when the assassination occurred, grabbed the body of the slain leader and held him in his arms.

Below, in the courtyard, Jackson and others plunged to the ground and stayed there until they thought it was safe to get up.

Abernathy called down to the Reverend James Bevel, also from Chicago, to run over to the church where King had just spoken and try to calm the panicked people. Bevel asked Jackson to join him, but, according to Bevel, Jackson answered: "Man, I'm sick. I got to go to Chicago and check into the hospital. This has really shot my nerves." Bevel said: "All right," and left Jackson there.

Then the television crews started arriving. Jackson was still there and started ordering the other disciples: "Don't talk to them." Then, according to several reports, Jackson himself began telling the TV reporters: "Yes, I was the last man in the world King spoke to." Then he flew to Chicago.

For years afterward, the general media account, usually nonattributed, of King's assassination would describe King as speaking his last words to Jackson and then would say that the young disciple Jesse Jackson cradled his slain leader in his arms awaiting the arrival of the ambulance. This account has always infuriated other SCLC staffers who were present. They maintain that the media got their story from Jackson himself but that it was not at all true.

The next morning, much to the surprise of King's other disciples who had remained in Memphis, Jesse Jackson appeared on NBC's *Today* show. He was still wearing the tan turtleneck he'd had on the night before when King was killed, and now he was claiming that it was smeared with the blood of the leader. The other disciples were horrified to watch him perform in such a way, before their beloved King's body was even cold.

Jesse's "blood of King" story has plagued him ever since. The other disciples and the leader's widow, Coretta Scott King, have never forgiven him for seizing the moment and using such morbid symbols to promote himself so quickly after King was assassinated.

Jesse himself, deep down inside, regrets that he behaved in that way because he knows it created rifts that have never been mended. He himself has even told different people different things about how he got the blood on his shirt. First, he said he was holding King's body, whereas others there say he never touched it. Later, he said the blood was sprayed everywhere, which other witnesses have denied. Several witnesses have suggested that Jackson smeared the blood on his shirt before leaving the hotel to catch a plane out of town. Jackson has said that he was still wearing the shirt the next morning when the *Today* show telephoned because he was so distraught that he just never took it off.

Whatever the truth, it is clear Jackson regretted the controversy, if only because of the bitterness it had caused within the black community. At the beginning of his 1988 campaign, he considered the subject closed, and he wanted others to forget it. The problem was that those closest to King would never forget it. Jesse's behavior then represented to them the real Jesse Jackson—the impulsive, egocentric, dangerously selfish person. Jesse himself believed it represented an immature side of him that he had now grown beyond. And he hoped he would be able to succeed so well with other Americans whose cause he represented that the opinion of King's widow and disciples would become irrelevant. In many ways, he would accomplish that goal in 1988.

It was now January 18, 1988, and the nation was observing the birthday of Dr. King. Jackson reflected that day and throughout the week on the progress that had been made since his death twenty years before, and he talked about what more had to be done. Jackson believed his presidential quest was the pursuit of King's dream.

Sunday night, January 24, in New York City was an important night at the start of Jesse Jackson's 1988 campaign. Gloria Steinem, longtime feminist leader, and Shirley Chisholm, former member of Congress, threw a fund-raising rally in his honor. Chisholm was black, and Steinem was Jewish. Both contributed significantly by putting their names behind Jesse Jackson for President, but at that time the media were not reporting much about Jackson's campaign.

January 24 was also the first night I went officially on the road with Jackson as his paid press secretary. Previously I had been traveling with Jackson unofficially, as was his custom, so that we could get a sense of working together. I was excited about the prospects. I told Jackson: "I believe we can turn the media around, and soon they'll realize how important your campaign is. They'll come running soon and start covering us."

That night a lawyer for Columbia University, who came to hear his speech, remarked: "But people predict Jesse won't get more voters than he's already got now." I said that wasn't true, that more people would come forward for Jackson. And she then asked: "Who new, then?" I said: "People like you, who'll decide he's the best candidate."

The rally was held on West Forty-third Street at the union hall of AFSCME (American Federation of State, County and Municipal Employees), New York's largest union. The union president, Stanley Hill (who was state co-chair along with Manhattan Borough President David Dinkins), was giving his personal adviser, forty-one-year-old Carol O'Cleireacain, time to work as a policy adviser to Jackson. Ever since earning her Ph.D. from the London School of Economics thirteen years earlier, O'Cleireacain had been specializing as a public finance expert for the union. That same night, the equally personable and bright thirty-one-year-old Mark Steitz, former adviser to Gary Hart, also joined the staff as the traveling issues director.

Late that night, when we'd all moved into the gaudy new Grand Hyatt Hotel on Forty-second Street, I went by Jesse's suite to see if he needed me or had any instructions for tomorrow. The Secret Service let me into the room automatically, but I knew immediately I had interrupted a private meeting. Jackson confirmed this, but he graciously introduced me: "Liz is going to be our new press secretary."

In the room were Marian Cosby, comedian Bill Cosby's wife, Simon & Schuster's editor-in-chief, Michael Korda, and others from the publishing company. They were talking with Jackson about his long-projected autobiography, which seemed increasingly valuable to Simon & Schuster in view of Jackson's present standing in the polls.

A very beautiful black woman with nearly all-white hair around a young face, Marian Cosby, along with her husband, was a longtime friend and supporter of Jackson. She was in that meeting, however, because she served as a personal adviser to Jackson. She often helped him with Personalities International, Inc., the private speaker's bureau for Jackson and his family which he'd set up after his 1984 campaign.

Jackson then told me to return at about 7 A.M. to brief him on the news. It became our usual routine: I would get up at 5:30, watch the morning network shows, listen to National Public Radio and read six newspapers. In New York, of course, it was easier to get hold of the major newspapers than in many other places. I would then sit in the living room of his suite and call the news into the bedroom, where he was dressing. Sometimes he would wander out with only his underwear on. And in between portions of the briefing, he would have his personal aide, Kgosie Matthews, place phone calls for him. Bill Morton would come in to get his bags and tell him the schedule for the morning. It was all very casual, though focused and not necessarily relaxed.

On Monday night, January 25, there was to be a debate in Boston. In the early days of the 1988 presidential year, there was a debate almost every week for the Democratic candidates. This one was in Massachusetts, in Governor Dukakis's home state, in Boston's historic Faneuil Hall. Even with a snowstorm and its being on Dukakis's home turf, no one thought to decline the invitation of the sponsoring organization, the *Boston Herald*.

That night in Boston, there was not yet a leading candidate, and none thought Dukakis would prove a chief competitor. Rumor had it that so very few people in Massachusetts liked their governor that it was unlikely he would be able to endear himself to the nation. Jackson took special note that night of the angry gay and lesbian demonstrators chanting against Dukakis outside the hall. Dukakis had evoked their ire by passing a state bill giving priority in child adoption to married heterosexual couples over homosexuals. Jackson was always on the lookout for second-class citizens: his constituency.

Often before the debates, the Democratic candidates would meet together in a single holding room. In those early days, the other candidates shared a kind of camaraderie that seemed to exclude Jackson. He was the different one. The media weren't taking him seriously, though they acknowledged he was a great debater, the best of the lot in the opinion of most audiences. But several of the candidates acted as if the media's ignoring the odd man, the rabble-rousing, black preacher, validated their leaving him out of their network. It was clear that most of them did not take him seriously.

At the beginning, only Bruce Babbitt and Senator Paul Simon seemed to make true efforts to include Jackson. Babbitt, the former governor of Arizona, had worked with Jackson before and shared many of his views. Later, Gary Hart became friendlier to Jackson when he realized that he would have to drop out of the race and recognized that many of his constituents would become Jackson's.

Senator Paul Simon, who likewise shared many of Jackson's political views, was also friendly to Jackson. He was a senator from Jackson's home state, Illinois. Simon later wrote in a *New York Times Magazine* article: "The most fascinating personality in the campaign was the Rev. Jesse Jackson. Jackson made a major contribution by seeing to it that the less fortunate were not forgotten." And he added: "I like to believe I helped in that also."

Simon went on to explain what he saw as Jackson's contribution, which came out especially in the national debates with other candidates, "His instinct for the right phrase, the quick response that makes national television, and the crowd-pleasing dramatic gesture marked him as the real professional in appealing directly to an audience; compared to him, the rest of us were amateurs."

The holding room for the candidates that night before the debate in Boston was a large trailer. As we entered with Jackson, it was noticeable that the other candidates had been laughing and sharing jokes with one another, but they became somewhat ill at ease when the Jackson contingent walked in. Our faces must have looked tense because we could sense that Jackson himself felt uncomfortable in the midst of this white men's locker room.

The de facto host, Michael Dukakis, immediately spotted our unease. The usually reserved Governor Dukakis remarked to us: "Why do you all look so serious? Smile."

After the Boston debate, there were two weeks before the voting in Iowa. Jackson felt he could spend most of the last week there, but already he was thinking ahead to the South and Super Tuesday, March 8, more than six weeks away. It was the big one, and Jackson expected it to be his watershed.

The decision was made. We would spend most of the coming week campaigning across the South. First, from Boston to Washington, D.C., to talk to the newspaper executives of Morris Communications, a Southern-based news service. At first, some of his aides attempted to prevail upon him not to meet this "bigoted" group. I disagreed, and Jackson finally met them on January 26, at their special forum, "Quest for the Presidency," held at the Willard Hotel.

As Jackson started to talk to them and argue his case, he soon found he enjoyed it. He then set about to woo them; he wanted this organization that had long catered to rednecks and the white Southern middle class to start printing his news. From the day of that meeting, Jackson put CEO William S. Morris III on his phone sheet.

Early each morning when I would go to Jackson's room to brief him on the news, he would instruct me to place calls to Mr. Morris, or to whoever was in the head office in Augusta, Georgia. Jesse would then just talk a while with them, telling them about his ideas for the New South and how he thought he could win Super Tuesday. Within a couple of weeks, Morris had dispatched his Atlanta bureau chief to cover Jackson almost on a regular basis through Super Tuesday.

That last week of January turned into a whirlwind tour, like all the preceding weeks. It was typical for Jackson, but now he was pushing himself to the limit, with no time for any rest. Often he would deliver five or six speeches in a day and hold press conferences after each one. In between those events, Jackson would be phoning contacts all over the country. That same day, January 26, from Boston and Washington, where he addressed the Morris meeting, it was then on to George Mason University in Fairfax, Virginia, to the state capital, Richmond, to the university town of Charlottesville, ending up after midnight in Raleigh, the capital of North Carolina.

The next morning as Jackson opened the state campaign headquarters, he had me hold his hand while he cut the ribbon. And on television, he made a point of citing my mother, "Miss" Marie Colton, who happened to be a North Carolina state legislator.

It was useful copy for the Jackson campaign in North Carolina that I had formerly worked as a media adviser to Senator Terry Sanford. Jesse's first job had been in Sanford's office in Raleigh when he was governor. Jesse was furious that Sanford and other Southern senators had refused to support the Jackson candidacy and instead picked their "white boy," young Senator Albert Gore, Jr. Jackson himself took full credit for Sanford's and other Southern Democrats' being elected to the Senate in 1986—because of the two million black voters he had registered in the South. Jackson took it as a betrayal by Sanford, but diplomatically he told the press that day: "In politics, you usually end up going full circle and bumping into the same people again from another direction."

All that day, January 27, was spent in central and eastern North Carolina. From Raleigh we flew to Wilmington and Greenville, and finally very late to Houston, Texas. The next day we were all over Texas, from Houston to Austin to Fort Worth and Lubbock.

By then, Jesse was sick and exhausted, but he hated to admit it. He usually just kept on going, but over the past twenty years he had been hospitalized at least six times, for what was usually described as exhaustion. When asked, however, he would deny the hospital stays were all for exhaustion but rather were sometimes for bronchitis or just a regular checkup.

Also, Jackson had sickle-cell anemia trait.

About two million black Americans, or eight percent of the black population, carry the abnormal gene of sickle-cell trait. Sickle-cell anemia occurs when two copies of the gene are inherited. In 1987 a *New England Journal of Medicine* article by an expert, Dr. Louis W. Sullivan of the Morehouse School of Medicine in Atlanta, reported that "all available evidence suggests that sickle-cell trait is a benign condition that, with rare exceptions in special circumstances, has no adverse effect on health."

A doctor was called in to the suite at Houston's posh Four Seasons Hotel. Jesse stayed on the telephone most of the time while the doctor was trying to examine him. He told the candidate that he should rest before he collapsed; however, Jesse didn't want to interrupt his schedule. Finally, after much deliberation and long-distance discussion with Gerald Austin, Jesse agreed to cut off from campaigning for at least a day. It was time finally for him to take a break and go home to Chicago. It was typical of Jackson to push himself to the brink of exhaustion and then have to stop, a little while, but never long.

Austin then told Pam Smith in the Chicago communications office to tell inquiring reporters that "Jackson was suffering from exhaustion and was taking a break." Jesse became furious when he heard this the next day, and on the Learjet enroute back to Chicago he called Austin to attack this report coming out of campaign headquarters. He said: "This is not the story we'd agreed on. [The media] are always eager to put me in my coffin, so they should never be told I'm exhausted. I'm going home to see my family and attend an old friend's funeral."

Jesse Jackson never enjoyed sitting still very long. About half a day of rest was the maximum he could take. Even then he would usually spend his time politicking on the telephone or having people come to visit him in his bedroom to talk strategy. His strategizing was endless, his energy boundless. His mind never stopped working. He was one of those lucky people who simply didn't need much sleep to keep going at a frantic pace for weeks—until he would drop for a day and then bounce back again.

By Saturday, January 30, Jesse was eager to be back at work, and Austin persuaded him to hold an inner-circle staff meeting at Jackson '88 headquarters. The trip home to Chicago turned out to be useful for Jackson and the staff. It was the first opportunity since the core traveling team had been put together that he and Gerry

Austin were able to meet with both the traveling staff and the key people in headquarters. We were all summoned that afternoon to meet at the Jackson house at 4:30 P.M.

The Jackson house is located on South Constance Avenue in Chicago's well-to-do, semi-integrated, though mostly black neighborhood on the South Side of town. Earlier in the century it had been a fashionable white section, until the whites moved to the northern suburbs and the upwardly mobile blacks slowly began trickling into the area. The Jackson place was a large, rambling white stucco Tudor-style house with stained-glass windows. A small front lawn separated it from the wide, quiet street just west of South Shore Drive.

Inside, the spacious rooms were fairly dark, and the decor was enhanced by Victoriana and artifacts the Jacksons had collected on their travels abroad or received as gifts. Mrs. Jackson's well-publicized hatboxes and half-refinished antiques were placed around the rooms and in the large central hallway with its wide staircase going to the upper floors. In the dining room to the right of the entry hall was a long lace-covered table and heavy wooden chairs. Over the fireplace in the living room was a huge portrait of the young, revolutionary Jesse Jackson wearing his dashiki of the sixties. It made him look like Che Guevara.

Jesse's wife, Jackie, was there to greet us when we arrived after passing through the Secret Service security check on the street. I had met her before, recently in Washington and previously in Ethiopia. Jacqueline Jackson, a short, sexily plump woman, was vivacious, friendly and, as always, in charge. She directed the visitors into the large living room to the left of the open entry hall. She seemed used to such meetings, with people, many of them strangers, coming in and out of her house.

I assumed that, being in the small core circle, we were all on a first-name basis. Pam Smith, who ran the communications office in Chicago, went in before me and greeted Jackson's wife as "Jackie" and in turn was greeted by her with "Hello, Miss Pam." I followed suit, and said, "Hello, Jackie." Gerry Austin had only that afternoon referred to her as Jackie.

A few minutes later, as we were all milling around the living room waiting for the meeting to start, Jackie summoned me from the hallway: "Ms. Colton, could you come here a minute, please." I went.

Then, quite sternly and coldly, she addressed me with a surprising reprimand: "Ms. Colton, you should understand that I don't appreciate being called Jackie by someone like yourself. You are to call me Mrs. Jackson in public. If we get to know each other, then what you call me in private may be different, but never in a public meeting like this. We have worked a long time and hard to get to the point that we were addressed properly as Mrs. Jackson, not by our first names. That's all, but I hope you understand now."

I was shocked and felt hurt. I could see that she was treating me differently. I had spent years learning to act grown up enough to address other adults in America by their first names, and it had taken me a long time to relax enough to do that. Now I was being told that she considered me ill-mannered.

I held back tears at the unexpected reprimand from a woman about my own age with whom I had expected to have a rapport. I apologized profusely and made my way back to the circle of chairs in the living room.

Fortunately, about a week later, she and I had the opportunity to spend a couple of days together in Iowa, and I felt we established bonds of friendship then. I realized that her initial rebuke was part of a tough façade she felt she had to establish before she could get to know me. We talked about our lives and our views on marriage and life and pain and happiness. We never discussed her initial rebuke to me, and when we were alone together in a van or a hotel room, I would call her Jackie. But in public I was careful to refer to her as Mrs. Jackson.

Mrs. Jackson is a strong woman. She has been the foundation of her family, raising five impressive, well-behaved, bright children while her husband has spent most of his time away from home. But she and Jesse Jackson have a firm marriage that has grown over the years, with many ups and downs. His unusual career path has added both difficulties and strengths to their marriage, but in the end it has survived, twenty-five years by 1988, probably because they both wanted it to and both maintained their own independence while dependent on the foundation of their marriage.

Jacqueline Lavinia Davis Jackson was a coed at North Carolina A&T State University in Greensboro, when Jesse transferred there in his sophomore year. Already known in college as a leftist, she was actively involved in the civil rights movement in Raleigh. Jesse and Jackie first got to know each other when he went to her for advice about a term paper: "Should Red China be admitted to the United Nations?"

She recalled that her first impression of this new student was that he "was a bit too fast, a bit too full of himself" for her taste. But she admitted that she, too, was pretty full of herself. Born March 17, 1944, she was the daughter of migrant farm workers in Florida and had been smothered with attention by her mother. She described herself when she entered college: "I was pompous and vain. Anyone who sat with me was just very fortunate. Big lips, nappy hair, the whole bit, yet I thought I was the loveliest, most exciting person in the whole world—and still do to a certain extent." And that was still the air she exuded.

She said that Jesse was her first real boyfriend. When she got pregnant, they got married in 1962, and their first child was born six months later. They never made a point of hiding that fact. Jesse Jackson, in his usual style, viewed the situation as a victory. He would say: "We got married and established family security. We broke the cycle."

Jesse graduated in the summer of 1963. He had the opportunity to go on to law school at Duke University, but he decided against it; instead, he accepted a Rockefeller Foundation grant to attend the Chicago Theological Seminary, for he had always wanted to be a preacher. He and his young wife and child moved to the big city of Chicago, and they never left. It became their home.

Jackie dropped out of college to begin raising her family, but she never stopped educating herself or her children. The five children came in the first twelve years: Santita (Sandy) Jackson, born July 16, 1963; Jesse Louis Jackson, Jr., March 11, 1965; Jonathan Luther Jackson, January 7, 1966; Yusef Dubois Jackson, September 26, 1970; Jacqueline Lavinia Jackson, September 28, 1975.

Anyone who observed her family knew that it was she who was educating her children while her husband stayed on the move. He became their godlike ideal—the great father figure, but at home it was their mother who kept it all working calmly in the midst of the chaos created by Jesse's style. Now in 1988 she adamantly protected her house as her family's home, not to be invaded by hordes of staff and reporters.

Jackie lived her own life, and sometimes even would defy Jesse's orders to join him at a particular place. Once in Iowa she decided to stay in Des Moines rather than fly all over the state with her husband. At the Cedar Rapids private air terminal, Jesse grabbed a pay phone and called her at her hotel: "You're shitting on me. I need you with me now." He listened, and then again: "You are violating me. You're not supposed to be staying in Des Moines. I need you to go along with me. We're supposed to be together." Jackie didn't show up finally until four days later but only stayed overnight to appear with her husband the next morning, February 5, on the *Today* show.

Jacqueline Jackson always appeared self-confident. She often proudly boasted: "I don't care what people say. They always say whatever they think anyway, and you can't stop them. They like to say I'm an alcoholic because I have a drink now and then. Or they say I'm a lesbian because I'll hold hands in public with a woman friend. I don't care. I just live my life the way I want."

That includes helping her husband immensely. "Just because we're not together all the time doesn't mean we're not the best kind of partners. We are," she would say. "A lot of people don't understand my relationship with my husband because they can't understand what partnership can mean. It doesn't mean I have to worry about him, be jealous all the time and chase him all over the country. I do my own thing, but we're completely together." She has traveled all over the world, often in advance of Jesse, sometimes carrying messages for him, and usually talking with women leaders to learn what's really happening in a country. Jesse Jackson often proudly referred to his wife's work and travels as great contributions to his campaign.

That January evening at home in Chicago, Jesse himself seemed relaxed. He was wearing blue jeans, a blue sweatshirt and sandals. He looked a bit flabby in his jeans, and even as early in the campaign as January, he was showing the effects of not exercising.

On the table in the middle of the living room was an empty bottle of champagne, but it was ignored. Jesse didn't usually drink, though Jackie did, but that night none of us had anything to drink during the four hours the meeting lasted.

As with most meetings conducted by Jackson, he dominated it and did almost all the talking. In those days, I simply marveled at his leadership ability, whether in a small group like this or in huge crowds.

Assembled was Jackson's current core staff. His staff would continuously change, according to the leader's needs. That night, the group included those Jackson then said would be taking us through Iowa to the high point of Super Tuesday and finally "on to the White House." There were Gerry Austin, Mark Steitz, Kgosie Matthews, Bill Morton, myself, the scheduler Gary Massoni, Pam Smith, Eddie Wong, Steve Cobble, Willie Barrow, and two black Chicago businessmen, Cirillo and Leon Finney, who would run Jackson's Illinois campaign.

Jackson talked about the group as potentially running the White House. He said: "We're living in a very delicate fishbowl. It stands to reason they're looking at us, considering whether Gerry can be a President's chief of staff, or Liz the press secretary, or Mark the policy adviser, or Bill and Kgosie doing something in the White House. We need rhythm. We need extraordinary discipline." The two blacks listed in that group, Bill Morton and Kgosie Matthews, were furious at the time that he couldn't think of specific jobs for them but listed the whites.

Later Jackson added, as if he'd realized he had only mentioned whites in specific positions: "The press will try to play race games on us. We've already learned that *Newsweek* is trying to dream up a story with the preconceived thesis that my staff is all white now.

They're wrong. We're the inner circle here. We've got the most well-rounded staff in the history of American politics."

Jackson went on to explain how much we had gained from being underestimated. He said the media and political establishment would have to come to him. "We're number one because we're number one thinking."

That night Jackson laid out his plan for how his daily schedule should be constructed. Every day between 7:30 and 9 A.M., there should be a leadership breakfast with "prestige endorsers" attending, followed by a press conference. Then we should get to a local school, where Jackson could win the hearts of America's future voting population. Then another press conference. Around noon, there should be a "point of action," something newsmaking and photographic—at a plant gate, at a farm auction, riding a tractor, steering a ship. That would also be followed by a press conference. Then there should be a big rally about 7 P.M., in a school or civic auditorium—no more churches, he said—and out by nine o'clock. That was Jackson's ideal, but in reality he would also usually slip in several more events.

Steve Cobble, the numbers man on the campaign, who counted states, districts and delegates, suggested that Jesse hit several, ideally three, media markets in one day. It was a way to get massive publicity without having to pay for it, which was important since the Jackson campaign at that point didn't have the millions other candidates had for advertising.

Cobble's idea was that you spend the morning in one city, where the news of Jackson's visit would be broadcast in that state and neighboring ones. The next stop would be beamed out to other states. A third stop for the day would spread the message into yet more states. And the "point of action" on the day's schedule would make the national news. It was a good game plan. It just meant that Jackson and the traveling team would have no rest for months.

Another idea that Jesse came up with, after talking with me about the power of radio, was the notion of a "radio blitz." It dovetailed perfectly with Cobble's multi-media-market scheduling strategy. The other candidates were putting all their money into television commercials, but Jackson realized he could get very powerful, free advertising by being on the radio all the time. The idea was to make phone calls early in the morning to radio stations in other media markets, often those where we would be going the next day so we could have advance publicity.

I would call and offer to put Jackson on the phone for a live interview right then and there. Jesse could then get in five or six interviews from his hotel bed before he even left for the first formal event of the day. The radio stations loved it. Most were ecstatic to get a call from Jesse Jackson's press secretary offering a live interview with him. Many stations, especially black ones, would use the tape with Jackson's voice over and over for days. It gave the campaign incredible mass advertising that the other campaigns didn't catch on to for months. They were so programmed into thinking television that the power of radio had eluded them.

The morning after our Chicago strategy meeting, we all flew into Iowa. It was Sunday, January 31. This week would be the last before the season's opener—the Iowa caucus on February 8. Jesse Jackson was disciplined and ready. He would remind those of us who were with him: "You win great races in the starting blocks."

Jesse seemed calmer than usual, purposefully in control of himself and his team. "Maintain steadiness," he would urge, talking as much to himself as to the four or five of us usually around him.

Jackson played the role of coach and quarterback all the time, but at this point it was in a caring way. Wherever we went that week, whether driving around Iowa in luxury vans or making a day trip to Kenosha, Wisconsin, to support the Chrysler workers or flying in our newly leased DC-9 for the first time on an overnight swing to New Hampshire, Jesse was coaching himself and his team. The payment for the DC-9 lease had come from campaign contributions and federal matching funds. Gerry Austin had determined that priority spending should go to transportation first and TV commercials after.

Then Jesse would explain again, usually repeating himself daily for emphasis, what he meant by "maintaining steadiness," in the context of the Iowa caucus. "Number one: People keep receiving us. Number two: They sense something is going on. Number three: We must stay free from flaps. We must stay consistent, play conservative. If we can get out of Iowa intact, that will be victory. Let the media come to us. There's reason to believe we'll get double digits [percentages of the vote at 10 or above]. That's a victory. But we can't talk now openly about our predictions or expectations. Let them learn how our message is getting across, and then they'll come to us eventually."

Jesse Jackson was determined to stick to the issues, not to get involved in personality fights. "It's our message that people are listening to: Save the family farm, save jobs, save the environment, save the family, reinvest in America, down with drugs, up with hope. That's what we're saying. That's what people want to hear." He repeated it everywhere he went.

And in Iowa, that first unlikely state, where most voters were white and middle-class, the people did respond to all these messages. They were especially concerned about saving their family farms. The Reagan administration's farm policy had progressively driven many from their traditional farming activities. Reagan had made farming an unprofitable profession. Iowans in general wanted to keep jobs from leaving their state. They wanted to save their environment from destructive national farming policies and acid rain coming from elsewhere. They wanted to preserve their family units, which had traditionally been the backbone of their solid Midwestern life. They wanted the U.S. government to reinvest in America and not abroad. They wanted to keep drugs out of the country, away from their children. They wanted to give their children hope. And to many who heard Jesse Jackson, it seemed that he was the only candidate who was seriously listening to their concerns and talking about those issues.

That Sunday, January 31, was overcast, gray and very cold. Much of the Iowa landscape was covered with snow. Jesse was a bit up and down that day. In the morning he was relaxed aboard the cramped propeller plane we flew from Chicago's Midway Airport to

Cedar Rapids, perhaps because his wife, Jackie, was accompanying him. But then later we realized she'd left and gone off on her own to Des Moines. Jesse phoned her later in the afternoon from the Cedar Rapids airport to berate her for deserting him then.

That was the day the Jackson presidential campaign had decided to raise money in churches across the country. The move was very controversial, but Jackson defended the decision, saying that for a long time it had been in churches that his people were found and it was there that traditionally they had contributed to a variety of causes. In Liberty, Iowa, an hour's drive from the Cedar Rapids airport, the Hispanic priest of St. Joseph's Roman Catholic Church turned his pulpit over to Jesse Jackson, and then later, unabashedly, allowed him to collect campaign funds in the church hall under the sanctuary.

Later that afternoon we took off from the Cedar Rapids airport in the small prop plane en route to Burlington for another rally, but the aircraft developed serious engine problems and we had to turn around. Jackson took off in a small jet with Mark Steitz, who by then on the road had become known as "Jesse's security blanket." All day long, Jesse would call: "Steitz, Steitz. I need Steitz." And Mark would run over to calm the candidate with jokes and detailed information on policy issues for use in his speeches and in the debates. The rest of us drove northeast to Dubuque on the Mississippi River.

That night there was a mini-debate for the Democratic presidential candidates in Dubuque, but Jackson ended up missing it because of the aircraft trouble. While we waited for Jackson to meet us at the Dubuque airport, the other candidates passed through the terminal on their way from the debate to other destinations in Iowa. When Jackson finally arrived, Bruce Babbitt was still waiting for his flight, and the two went to a corner for a private tête-à-tête. Of all the candidates in 1988, Jackson probably got on best with Babbitt. They had a lot in common politically, and each respected the other.

In those early days of the campaign, before the first caucus, when there were still seven candidates, Jackson used to place calls to them as he traveled along. Sometimes he would say to Kgosie Matthews or Bill Morton, who were the ones to carry Jackson's brief-case with the portable phone as well as the invaluable phone book he kept: "Get Simon on the phone" or "Get me Gary" or Bruce Babbitt or sometimes Richard Gephardt. He said he called them, often just before a debate, to "keep in touch with them. It's a way to throw them off guard." Sometimes one of them would agree to praise the other or ask particular questions of the other in a debate. Jackson could get along especially with Hart and Babbitt and Si-mon. Jesse would always reach to fix Senator Simon's bow tie when he saw him. He felt that Gephardt was more aloof and thought he was constantly stealing his ideas.

As for the other two candidates, Governor Dukakis and Senator Gore, Jackson had the least time for them, and they in turn for him, apparently. Strangely, in those early days, Jackson didn't anticipate that Dukakis would become the chief opponent. Perhaps it was because he couldn't imagine that such a little man could get far. It was Gore he saw as his chief opponent, at least looking ahead to Super Tuesday and the South, but Jackson didn't like to acknowl-edge that and refused to appear on the same television talk shows with Gore. The Tennessee senator also rankled Jackson by his su-percilious manner toward him. Whenever they were in the same place together, they both gave off uneasy vibes.

The next morning, Monday, February 1, as soon as I went to Jackson's room, at the Dubuque Inn, he announced that he thought we should go to Kenosha, Wisconsin, the next morning to stand with the auto workers at the plant gate. He'd been mulling it over since last Thursday afternoon when in Austin I'd relayed the news to him that Lee Iacocca's Chrysler Corporation was closing down its plant there. Jackson told me to get Steitz so we could all plan the trip before we proceeded with the Iowa itinerary for the day. I reached the mayor of Kenosha and the president of the UAW local there, and Jackson told them his plan and asked them to invite him there. Steve Cobble would fly there right away to set it up for Jack-son's arrival the next day.

Then we proceeded on the Iowa schedule, driving from Dubuque to Elkader, to Oelwein, to Vinton and finally to Waterloo. We traveled in a couple of vans then. Jackson's had a television set, a plug for his portable telephone and space for five of us behind the front seats, where two Secret Service men sat. Those days were almost jovial, with Jackson always strategizing, thinking out loud. Sometimes he napped, and we ate boxed meals in the van. The handful of traveling press followed behind in a less comfortable van.

The next morning we flew from the little Niederhauser Airport in Waterloo in a Learjet to Racine, Wisconsin, the nearest airport to Kenosha. From the Iowa waiting room, I had tried to reach Chrysler president Iacocca for Jesse, but he was reportedly unavailable, tied up in a conference elsewhere. Jackson spoke to his assistant and warned him that we were on our way to Kenosha. Much to the disappointment of the hardworking Iowa staff of Jackson's campaign, much of the schedule for that day in Iowa was scrapped. Later that afternoon Jesse persuaded both the mayor of Kenosha, Eugene Dorff, and the UAW local president, Ed Steagall, to fly back with us to Iowa for a show of solidarity with Jackson at the Teamsters rally in Des Moines. That entailed getting another plane for the staff bumped out of the Learjet, but there was no argument Austin could put up on the phone since this was the kind of political statement Jackson loved making.

The Wisconsin primary would not be until April, but Jackson was always thinking long-term. Also, as he said, it was a national issue, and it was Jesse Jackson's aim always to be seen "at the point of challenge," standing at the plant gate with the locked-out workers or at the courthouse with the farmers when their farms were being auctioned. The entire event was a classic "point of action," photogenic and newsworthy, that Jackson wanted to have in every campaign day. But the national media gave scant attention, if any, to Jackson's disappearing that day from the Iowa campaign and jetting off to Wisconsin. Indeed, the national media paid little attention at all to Jackson during the Iowa campaign. No one took him seriously yet. Jackson wasn't electable, they maintained.

That night Jackson kept his appointment in Indianola, Iowa, at Simpson College, where George Washington Carver, the former slave who became a scientist, had first studied. Jackson received the

G. W. Carver Award. While he was speaking, giving much the same speech we so often heard, a couple of his chief aides imitated his lines and cadence backstage. Jackson seemed unaware that this often happened while he was out front, but some onlookers appeared shocked at their open mockery. The noise from their jocular imitation possibly was heard in the auditorium.

That night only Kgosie and I accompanied Jackson, along with the Kenosha mayor and the UAW president, to Winterset. The motel was tiny, and the other staff members just dropped off. Jesse was angry, though, when he learned that Mark Steitz, upon whom he had become so dependent, had decided to stay behind in Des Moines. The next morning, Wednesday, February 3, after attending a fund-raising breakfast at the American Legion hall in Winterset, where schoolchildren came carrying American flags to welcome the presidential candidate, we drove back to Des Moines, then on to Newton and back again to Des Moines.

Jackson was scheduled to address the New Hampshire legislature the next day. Late that Wednesday afternoon we again departed Iowa, this time in the campaign's newly chartered DC-9 "Sunworld" jet. There were so few newspeople accompanying us then that we and the Secret Service just seemed to rattle around in the big aircraft. We arrived in Manchester so early, at 7 P.M., and had no event for a change, that for once we all got some rest. It was welcome, and Jesse especially showed the positive effects of his rest the next day. Some of us actually managed to have a sit-down dinner in the restaurant at Manchester's Holiday Inn West.

That night a new staff member, Jeff Griffiths, joined us. He was a tall, gentle black man in his forties, who had a withered arm from an earlier machine accident. But he'd overcome his handicap and learned to do radio, using both hands. He was to be our radio technician; he would record Jackson's speeches and feed them out to radio stations, mostly black stations, across the country. It turned out to be a difficult task because the entourage would often leave a site before Jeff could get the wires rolled up again, or sometimes he would be left because he was out of earshot in a room where he managed to find a phone. When he had time, he would also record news spots himself, then cut them and send them out with Jackson sound bites for radio systems, which would then feed them into local stations across the country.

At 7:45 the next morning, Thursday, February 4, I went in to Jesse's suite to see if he wanted to make some radio calls, according to our new plan. There was a snowstorm up north, and it looked like we might not be able to fly there for a rally later as planned. It was decided we would spend the morning in the hotel before going at midday to the state capitol in Concord. Jesse stayed in bed for the next couple of hours and gave long-distance interviews to grateful stations across Iowa. In between placing calls for him in his bedroom, I managed to meet with the key New Hampshire staff and begin mapping out our media strategy for that state the week before its primary. For a change, we had room service for the rest of us, too—coffee, orange juice and croissants. Jesse was so relaxed that he didn't seem to mind everyone else also going at a calmer pace.

Jesse was calmly incensed about a *Newsweek* story that week alleging that his staff was mostly all white now. He told me to get him on the telephone with the magazine's top editor, Richard M. Smith, who used to be my boss when I worked there. But I wasn't allowed by Jackson to speak to Rick, just to his secretary, and then for almost an hour Jesse lambasted the stunned editor, who would have had morning meetings to attend, but he couldn't get the irate Jackson off the phone. Jesse told me to take notes from the conversation and then write a letter repeating what he'd said. Later, I did that, using Jackson's own words, but he was never happy with it, even though it was exactly in the language he'd used on the phone and told me to copy.

Very late that night we returned to Iowa, having to land in Moline, Illinois, the nearest airport to Davenport, Iowa, across the Mississippi. We got little sleep, though, since we had to get up at 5 A.M. in order for Mr. and Mrs. Jackson, who had met her husband finally that night in Davenport, to appear on NBC's *Today* show at six in the morning (seven Eastern Standard Time). Davenport had the nearest NBC affiliate on Jesse's itinerary where the Jacksons' interview could be aired live that morning. The show's host, Bryant

Gumbel, interviewed them for only one segment, and I was told to phone the top producer at the *Today* show and complain that Vice President and Mrs. Bush had been given two segments. I reached Cliff Kappler, an old colleague of mine from our days in the London bureau, and he gave the NBC response—there was more news related to the Bush interview because he had just that week come out of his broadcast altercation with CBS anchorman Dan Rather.

Then, for the second straight morning, and perhaps the last, we were able to relax briefly before rushing through the rest of the day. It was because Mrs. Jackson was there. After the interview, she insisted that, since we had a little time, we all go back and have a seated breakfast in the dining room of the Ramada Inn, where we'd spent the night and where the rest of the staff was waiting for us. Jesse had me jumping up and down from the table, however, to set up radio calls for him from the nearby pay phone. But Mrs. Jackson managed to force her husband to stay seated. She said: "He needs me to make him civilized from time to time. Otherwise, he would never stop and sit to eat." That was true. It was a rare occasion on the campaign trail that we ever ate sitting unless we were on the plane or in a car or bus.

Then we drove to Iowa City, where Jackson spoke at two high schools—City and West. From there we went on to the Cedar Rapids airport. Jesse wanted me to go back to Des Moines to begin setting up the radio blitz for the last couple of days of the Iowa campaign and also to begin planning ahead for the next stretch after the Monday caucus. Jackson and the rest would fly to Oakland and San Francisco for the day for a special fund-raising dinner. They would fly back to Des Moines that night. I was frankly relieved to be able to stay behind. It also meant that I was able to spend the rest of the day with Mrs. Jackson, getting to know her as we drove back to the capital. Jeff Griffiths was with us, too, and the three of us relaxed and got to know each other finally, along with a black woman volunteer named Verna who'd come all the way to Iowa from Los Angeles to help the Jackson campaign.

Also, for the first time I was able to take a couple of hours off to have dinner with an old colleague and friend, NBC's longtime political correspondent, Garrick Utley. Over salmon at Des Moines's Savery Hotel, I talked about how I believed Jackson would last and become a central candidate. Garrick told me how he remembered Jackson back at the 1972 Democratic convention—coming up to newsmen and offering to give interviews.

The Jackson team that went to California didn't get back to Des Moines until nearly dawn on Saturday, the sixth. So I waited until 10:30 A.M. before going to the Jackson suite in the Holiday Inn South, where we were all staying. Jesse was already up, wandering around in a robe over his underwear.

Overnight two of the Jackson children, seventeen-year-old Yusef and twelve-year-old Jackie, had flown in to the Iowa capital to join their parents. They had slept on the sofas in the living room of the suite. Both were in exclusive private boarding schools—Yusef at St. Alban's in Washington, D.C., and Jackie at the Fay School outside Boston. (I had already met her a couple of weeks earlier, the night Jackson participated in the Boston debate.) Yusef was a senior and a star football player, and just at that time was deciding to accept a football-academic scholarship at the University of Virginia in Charlottesville to start the following fall of 1988.

The other two boys, twenty-two-year-old Jesse Jr. and Jonathan, who had just turned twenty-two the month before, would be showing up later. The eldest child, the twenty-four-year-old daughter, Santita, was studying at Howard University in Washington and wouldn't be coming that weekend to Iowa but would meet up with her father later when he would be going through there.

All five Jackson children never failed to impress people, not only when they first met them but continually. Each was polite, bright, alert, gentle, independent. None was pretentious or egotistical about being a child of Jesse Jackson. They helped both their parents and were always smiling and kind to the people and staff and reporters who swarmed around their father. Even after hours of being with them, one always came away with the most positive feelings about each of them. Observers always remarked that it was a rare family of politicians or celebrities about which one could say all the children had turned out well.

There was something remarkably cozy about those last days in Iowa. We all then felt a sense of being part of a family. Jackson was still the head, but he was relaxed, at ease then. Looking back to those days, it was obvious the changes started taking place a few days after the Iowa vote when Jackson began returning to his taut, anxious, perhaps defensive state as we moved closer to Super Tuesday and beyond. But then the family atmosphere of the Jackson suite that Saturday morning seemed to embody the feelings we all had at the time. We were a family.

At 3 P.M. on February 8, caucus day in Iowa, Jackson held his last strategy meeting before the polls closed. We convened in a small conference room at the Des Moines airport's private Elliott Terminal. We were on our way from a rally in the western part of the state to a live interview at CNN's studio in downtown Des Moines. From there we would go to Iowa State University in Ames and finally on to the "victory party" in the headquarters town of Greenfield.

Jesse began: "Our victory is in expansion. But there is a chance we will break the double-digit sound barrier. That will be a big deal, and it will throw a certain kind of light and daggers our way. We must prepare now to be careful. We must always show self-control."

Jesse then turned from the negative aspect of success to the positive side. "First, the plus side of the victory, though, will be money. We must turn the news story into a commercial appeal. *Ebony* has nine million readers. There's immediate fund-raising potential through Mr. Johnson [the owner-publisher of the major black magazines *Ebony* and *Jet*]. And black radios and Percy Sutton.*

"We must get the message out that we need money. Then we'll be translating success into votes and money. Even in what we say tonight at the celebration, we can add: 'And if we had money to go with our message, then we can have real success.' Six thousand black elected officials are to be targeted with a one-page letter: 'Our crowd don't need no term paper.' And phone calls immediately to two hundred top donors," he said no one in particular. Jesse often

---

* Percy Sutton was politically powerful and owned radio stations in New York.

talked out his plans without giving the assignment to anyone who could actually carry it out. The word would somehow get to the right person to implement some of the plan.

"Second, there's the Rainbow—the Iowa piece of this," he reminded the staff. "As we fold up this carpet, capturing this constituency, we need to cement it, not just black but others, programming them all into our computer."

Then he concluded: "Then there's damage control we have to think of for tonight—what to say, not to say. We must have a clean, confident, clear message. We're all in the same pocket. It must be consistent with that spin. Now, let's go—on to CNN, to Ames and to Greenfield."

That night the Jackson campaign had a "victory party" with the people of Greenfield, Iowa. It was held at the still being renovated "Old Hotel" on East Iowa Street. There weren't many television cameras, and only the Chicago TV stations were there to do live interviews for their nine o'clock news shows.

At that point in the counting, it looked like Jackson would place fourth in the field of seven and could possibly hit double digits at 10 percent. It was a victory for the Jackson campaign, whether anyone outside Greenfield was watching or not. Jesse's victory speech told a tale on the night of that first caucus that he would be able to repeat and build upon over the months ahead.

He began: "Greenfield and Adair County allowed America to win tonight a great victory—allowed our people to be great. In a time of tension, Greenfield was the oasis in the desert, a source of hope and joy and love. We've sought to pull together urban workers and rural farmers. We watched the people come to grips with race. We've come to grips with old walls and pulled them down. We'll never be apart again. We the people will win."

The people of Greenfield cheered. Jesse Jackson had become their hope and symbol. He'd put them on the map. He went on, as many wept with the emotion of the night: "People have been on TV crying about our campaign. The tears represent hope. We've worked with the people. We've built a political organization. We now have a different political coalition.

"Tonight is the league opener—one game down, forty-nine more to go. I'll be careful to take your message everywhere and on to the White House," Jackson promised the people of Greenfield. "We're going to make America better. Greenfield is a source of hope for America tonight. Let's keep hope alive."

As it turned out, Jackson finally won only 9 percent of the Iowa vote, not double digits, but it was higher than anyone had predicted. It was first in Iowa where Americans began to show they had the capacity to be color-blind. Later, after the Iowa caucus, Jackson would say: "The untold spiritual and psychological story of Iowa is that we were received well. No racism greeted us, and the numbers prove it."

4

THE
NEW HAMPSHIRE
PRIMARY

"Common ground. It takes two wings to fly. Whether a hawk or a dove, you're just a bird, living in the same environment, the same world. The Bible teaches that when lions and lambs lie down together, none will be afraid, and there will be peace in the valley. Lions eat lambs. Lambs instinctively flee from lions. Yet even lions and lambs find common ground. Why? Because neither lions nor lambs want the forest to catch on fire. Neither lions nor lambs want acid rain to fall. Neither lions nor lambs can survive nuclear war. If lions and lambs can find common ground, surely we can as well, as civilized people. The only time that we win is when we come together."

Iowa was over. It was early Tuesday morning, the ninth of February. New Hampshire was next, in a week, with the nation's first primary. And Jesse Jackson would keep pumping his same message:

"Save the family, save family farms, save jobs, save the environ-ment, keep drugs out, keep jobs in, reinvest in America, down with drugs, up with hope. We, the people, will win." Depending on the state, he would add or emphasize special notes for the different voters. In Iowa, he had concentrated on farms and plant closings. In New Hampshire, he would focus on the environment and jobs. But unlike most other candidates, Jackson refused to dump any part of his message just because he had left the place where it was most important. That morning he said to all of us: "We'll keep hammering away at economic violence and drugs and clean air."

At 6:45 A.M., just at sunrise, our vans pulled out of Greenfield, Iowa. All of us had spent the night in houses of the hospitable townspeople. The staff had then met in the early morning at the state headquarters and then had gone to collect the Jackson family at the farmer's house where they'd stayed. Jesse's wife, Jackie, and his daughter Jackie got in the van with him. He then called to Mark Steitz and me to join them. He wanted to talk strategy. In those early days, Jesse was planning the long race ahead with "a mea-sured gait," as he would often say.

The final caucus count wasn't in yet, but Jesse felt comfortable saying he'd got 10 percent of the vote. And that was something. It showed that whites would vote for him in a state where 98 percent of the population was white and middle-class. A tenth of the elec-torate had liked and bought his message. Jesse said: "Our constitu-ents' appetites have been whetted by our showing in Iowa."

He'd placed fourth, after Gephardt, Simon and Dukakis, in a field of seven candidates. He beat three others, Babbitt, Hart and Gore. As Jackson kept telling people: "Iowa's only the first game of the season. There's no way to know that early who'll be playing in the World Series."

The media that morning had taken little notice of Jackson's re-markable showing in Iowa. The night before, ABC News, the only network to have requested a prime-time interview with Jackson, had sent word in the middle of his victory speech that he wasn't wanted after all. Instead, ABC anchorman Peter Jennings would interview Albert Gore, Jr., who hadn't even campaigned in Iowa, and was that night in Atlanta, preparing for Super Tuesday, a month away. Jesse was furious when I told him about this, and he planned to phone Peter Jennings and ABC president Roone Arledge as soon as possible.

That morning on the Op-Ed page of *The New York Times,* A. M. Rosenthal, the former executive editor, wrote in his column that a job would have to be found for Jackson, and he suggested that he be made the national "drug czar." On our way to the Des Moines airport, I told Jackson about the column, which Carol O'Cleireacain had read to me earlier on the telephone. It seemed rather condescending to make such a suggestion the morning after the Iowa caucus, as if Rosenthal and the *Times* already considered Jackson a noncandidate but because he was black and special some job would have to be found as a sop. Jesse recognized that it was a backhanded compliment, but he also immediately pointed out that we could look at the positive side and take it as recognition that he had become the national leader in the fight against drugs. Jesse picked it up and ran with it, as he often did with media remarks that began as slights. Within months, the term "drug czar" and acknowledgment of Jackson's leadership in this field were part of political reporters' vocabulary.

At the Des Moines airport, Jackson was greeted by reporters who had come for the news conference we'd announced earlier, inasmuch as no networks had asked Jackson to appear for morning-show interviews. The news that day was all Gephardt for the Democrats and Dole for the Republicans, with the preacher Pat Robertson's remarkable showing also eclipsing Vice President Bush.

Jackson summed up his Iowa showing this way: "We had the least money, the smallest staff and the least media coverage. Yet we did well." But very few reporters were paying attention.

At 9:25 A.M., having left the friendly farms of Iowa, we were flying to Washington, D.C., where I had arranged for Jackson to meet with the editorial board of *USA Today.* Ever since I'd joined Jackson's staff, I'd been arguing that he needed to start meeting with the editors of the major news organizations. He had to establish collegiality and put his ideas out in front of them and not just to their reporters, who would never have the clout to get him the kind of big coverage we were envisioning. Jesse liked the idea, but other members of his staff had earlier discouraged him from meeting with such establishment boards. Among reporters, Jackson's staff, except now for me, was viewed as the most negative and antagonistic toward the media. Finally, however, Jackson was going to go with his own instinct and meet the editors face to face to establish a more personal and cordial relationship.

When the plane had landed and finally stopped on the tarmac at National Airport, Jesse ordered the traveling press to deplane. He wanted all the staff to stay on board for a little meeting. There were about ten of us.

Jackson also invited Mike Cheers, the reporter for *Jet* magazine, to stay with us. He had been covering Jackson for years and was usually treated as if he were staff. He had, in fact, briefly worked as Jackson's press secretary the previous autumn. Other reporters remarked upon Cheers's special insider treatment, but none dared print it. There was little doubt that Jackson believed any black newsperson owed allegiance first to being black.

We gathered around the leader and listened. Jackson directed me to take notes, and then he began: "Now that the 1988 presidential campaign is officially underway, we will all need to maintain a common spirit. We've come through hostile terrain and survived.

"We're now living in a very amplified fishbowl because we will be viewed as possibly running the Western world. From now on, staff members can have no personal life. We must be careful. People will be assigned to destroy us character-wise before they try to physically," Jackson warned us, pausing to look at each one.

"The media will try to magnify dust particles in our campaign and make them into logs. But we must remember that we have the most broad-based campaign. There was great meaning in Iowa. In spite of the media blitz against us today, we now know that Jesse Jackson's support is real.

"Now we have to move on to the next contests. We need to think of new strategies. For example, Liz has a media strategy that we'll begin to follow, and Gerry is working on a new fund-raising strategy. Our campaign has many brain cells that should focus on the one month left to go before Super Tuesday. Now let's have a prayer."

Jesse Jackson had us—his motley staff and members of his family, Christians, Jews, Muslims, atheists—all join hands along the aisle and across the plane seats. Then he prayed for all of us and our campaign. I was moved. We all were.

Then, at the end of the prayer, Jesse turned into a football coach, exhorting: "Okay, let's go—on to Super Tuesday." In those early days, he made us all feel part of an exciting, trailblazing team. He was the captain and the star, and we felt constantly in awe of his brilliance.

Limousines met us at Butler Aviation, the private air terminal of National Airport in Washington, D.C., and we were whisked off to the *USA Today* building in the nearby suburb of Rosslyn, Virginia. We were early arriving at the modern, new skyscraper, perched next to the twin building of the parent company, Gannett.

The view across the Potomac from the *USA Today* offices was spectacular: the Washington Monument, the Kennedy Center, the White House, the Lincoln and Jefferson Memorials, and the Capitol in the distance, all spread out below the windows. It seemed the whole, majestic capital of the United States was in easy grasp.

Jesse was still relaxed and seemed pleased we were early because it gave him time to make some phone calls, talk plans and leaf through *The Washington Post* and *USA Today*. He called Yolanda Carraway, the black woman in charge of his Washington campaign office. She was organizing a fund-raising reception for later that afternoon.

Jackson also talked casually with his old friend D.C. representative Walter Fauntroy, who had come across the Potomac to meet him at *USA Today*. Fauntroy, like Jackson, was an ardent supporter of statehood for the District. Fauntroy was one of the people Jackson consulted on a regular basis, and sometimes Fauntroy would join Jackson on his travels.

John Seigenthaler, *USA Today*'s editorial director and another

Southerner, stepped forward to greet Jackson. Seigenthaler, who had started as a reporter and ultimately became editor-in-chief of the Nashville *Tennessean,* had been among the first Southern opinion-makers to support John F. Kennedy in 1960, and he had become a member of the Camelot circle. But like many of them, Seigenthaler returned home when Kennedy was assassinated.

Then in 1982, when publisher Allen H. Neuharth founded *USA Today,* in the face of much ridicule from the media establishment, he had called in Seigenthaler to help. And ever since, John Seigenthaler had been commuting weekly between his hometown, Nashville, and Washington, D.C.

Seigenthaler was now in charge of the editorial pages, and every day he ran a full-page interview with someone of note. Either the interview would consist of a synopsis of a question-and-answer session with someone like Jackson visiting the editorial board, or it would be conducted by the chief interviewer, Barbara Reynolds. Two years earlier, I had approached Seigenthaler about my doing an interview with Jackson, and at the time he had remarked: "He won't ever appear before our editorial board because Barbara Reynolds is in charge of our interviews." Reynolds had written a biography of Jackson in the seventies, and the subject had not been pleased with the result.

Reynolds happened to be considered Jesse Jackson's nemesis. As a *Chicago Tribune* reporter, she had at first been an ardent admirer of Jackson. Over time, however, after covering him for five years, she had become disillusioned and wrote a biography of him in 1975. She and her publisher immediately began to receive threatening phone calls, and her book publicity party was subsequently canceled. Within days of its publication, Jackson managed to have copies of the book removed from most Chicago bookstores. What had been most offensive to him was her rehashing the story of the King assassination and Jackson's questionable behavior afterward. Jackson never forgave her for washing that and other dirty linen again in public. She always accused him of demanding that black journalists give their allegiance first to being black, not to their journalistic code.

Barbara Reynolds was there for the meeting. Jackson's eyes took in her presence as we entered the large conference room with John Seigenthaler and other editors. There were about forty editors and reporters from all over the newspaper. Jackson was visibly nervous and his eyes were darting around the room. Bob Borosage, who was still working at the Institute for Policy Studies and advising Jackson at the same time, had come along to brief him and keep him calm with facts.

This was his first major editorial board meeting; he was doing it against the advice of some of his aides, and there was Barbara Reynolds, ready, it seemed, to pounce on him with her usual questions about the aftermath of the King assassination.

She said she wanted to know why he had claimed to be the last person King had spoken to and then had rushed off to Chicago to appear on television the next morning and brag about his role while the corpse was still warm. She contended, as she had in her book, that other witnesses disagreed with his account.

Jackson looked nervous, and his eyes flashed angrily, but he managed to calmly deflect her questions: "Barbara, I believe I've answered these questions sufficiently before, and I don't think we need to go over them again." She couldn't get him to budge. The matter was closed, to the public at least, as far as Jackson was concerned.

Jesse insisted to the editors of *USA Today,* as he would to other newspeople throughout the campaign: "The media should be covering substance and not personality. Focus on my message and direction."

Jesse took this occasion to excoriate the media in general for categorizing him as only a "preacher" candidate, along with the fundamentalist Pat Robertson. It made good copy, but Jackson pointed out it still was degrading. "You like to say that we have 'followings,' while you give other candidates the dignity of having 'constituencies.' That's not right," he told them.

For months, the media had been downplaying the seriousness of the campaigns of the Democrat Jackson and the Republican Robertson by referring only to their "reverend" status. Later in February, *People* magazine wrote about Jackson and Robertson: "They are the odd couple of this campaign season, two brothers of the cloth pursuing new career opportunities, two Christian soldiers who have suspended the search for lost souls to campaign for the leadership of the great and various American flock."

The day Jesse was speaking to *USA Today* was only one day after Robertson's surprisingly strong showing in Iowa and Jackson's own mid-field placement. Not that he had any sympathies for Robertson's political viewpoint, which was on the far right with the so-called Moral Majority, but Jackson did empathize with him in the maltreatment he received from the media.

At the end of the session, in informal conversation, one editor remarked to Jackson: "You're a lot different from when you came here four years ago. It seems you've done some maturing."

Jesse blinked. He thought it unlikely the same remark would have been made to a white candidate, but he handled it deftly, as he would when the same remark was made later by editors of other news organizations. He responded: "I hope I have matured in four years. We all should keep growing." He was determined throughout this campaign to show he had self-control and remain cool in the face of any assault. That was the resolution he had made to himself at the start of 1988.

The next day *USA Today* printed a color picture of Jesse Jackson on the top inset of their front page and ran excerpts of the editorial interview on their Op-Ed page. It was a good start for the editorial board plan.

The New Hampshire primary was only a week away, on February 16, Jackson didn't expect to do spectacularly there, but he did hope to achieve another decent showing, proving again that a black could garner votes in another nearly lily-white state. His goal was to get the media to notice and report that story.

But ever since Iowa was over, Jackson's real focus was on the South and Super Tuesday. On Super Tuesday, March 8, there would be the mega-election of the entire primary season in which voting would be held in almost all the Southern states on the same day. Jackson had to keep reminding himself to pace himself, for there would be a few other contests before that huge play-off. He refused to be like another Southern candidate, Albert Gore, Jr., who was putting all his energy into Super Tuesday.

The main contest in New Hampshire was expected to be between the victor in the Iowa caucus, Dick Gephardt, and the governor of neighboring Massachusetts, Michael Dukakis. It was conventional wisdom, based on history, that the winner in the New Hampshire primary would be the party's presidential nominee. In early February, Jackson didn't believe that either of them would be the major competitor in the South. There were rumors already that Dukakis's campaign chest had more than ten million dollars and some of that money was beginning to flow across the South, but to Jackson and others then, "the little Greek from New England" wasn't expected to be the major threat.

Jackson and the media believed that his chief opponent in the South would be young Albert Gore, Jr. And Jackson was bothered by the knowledge that Gore had decided to focus completely on Super Tuesday and from there move full steam ahead nationally. Gore's strategy was to sweep the Southern states, and thus he spent most of his time touring the South while Jackson and the other candidates stumped in the Northern and Midwestern states where early polls were held. But Gore was also pouring hundreds of thousands of dollars into television advertising in New Hampshire and elsewhere outside the South.

Jackson's first inclination was to pay only lip service to the New Hampshire primary. He was persuaded, however, that it would be wise to make a few more appearances there before the voting and also to be present in New Hampshire on election night. Rather than appear to be chasing Gore, who was busy in the Southern sunshine, Jackson would demonstrate that he was serious about his campaign being a "marathon" and "a fifty-state decathlon." By staying in New Hampshire he would prove his goals were national.

Jackson's vacillating about how much time to spend in New Hampshire created the usual confusion about his campaign schedule. There was an ongoing debate within the small staff circle about scheduling, to remedy the chaos that resulted from the constant changes. Jackson insisted on approving every point up until the last moment in the always overfilled day. But even when a program was decided upon, his impulsiveness and incorrigible tardiness contributed to an ever-changing schedule.

Gerry Austin acknowledged, without hesitation, that "getting control of Jesse Jackson's schedule" was his biggest headache during the '88 campaign. He admitted that there were "hourly" scheduling meetings, which drove him and the staff crazy, but he learned to put a good face on the chaos by giving a stock explanation to reporters: "There's a reason for all this. Jackson has a brilliance about scheduling, and he always wants input. Plus, he just flat out knows more about it than anybody else, and he has an incredible memory. So if we go into Oklahoma, he wants to add a stop in Ada because he remembers three people there who were for him in 1984."

Certainly this was true—that Jesse might know more about most places than anyone else because he had been traveling up and down and politicking all around the country for at least a quarter of a century, and his memory was remarkable. But the scheduling issue reflected another problem. He could not delegate. He loathed the idea of allowing anyone to sign off on something. He was either too much a micro-manager like President Jimmy Carter or sloppily hands-off like President Ronald Reagan. Scheduling in general was a strategic point Jackson should have dealt with, but ultimately it occupied too much of his time.

Jackson continuously surprised people with his brilliant insights, things he saw that no one else noticed. On Saturday, February 13, the League of Women Voters held one of its Democratic debates at St. Anselm College in Goffstown, New Hampshire. It was the weekend before the first primary. The Democratic candidates, all men, had come to take part, and the moderator was a man, Edwin Newman. The only woman to participate at all was the LWV president, who simply made welcoming remarks and introduced Newman. For nearly an hour the moderator posed different "issue questions" to each candidate. But something was wrong and no one noticed, at least not until Jesse Jackson pointed it out in his concluding remarks. He said: "There's something wrong here. There has not been one question or comment about women and their special issues, yet this is a League of Women Voters debate." He was right, and everyone was shocked.

Such demonstrations of concern for women gave people the impression that Jesse Jackson was not a sexist. And he wasn't in his public positions. Jesse genuinely believed he was a true supporter of women's rights, but his rhetoric didn't match his personal treatment of women.

On the 1988 campaign, on the road, the few female staff members were fully aware that they were treated as second-class citizens by Jackson. But what happened there, as must have also happened on other candidates' staffs, was that most of the women simply bit their tongues and didn't complain. The reason must have been that they were so grateful to have been allowed to get even that close to power for the first time that they didn't want to say anything to jeopardize their jobs. There were so few women in such positions that they knew Jackson, or probably any other candidate, would simply find a replacement if they complained too much.

There was something else, too, that could never be discussed. Despite his noble efforts to hire women and have them work on his staff as professionals, Jackson, nevertheless, and not unlike most other candidates in 1988, looked on them ultimately as sexual objects. And if they didn't play that game, then they would be criticized until they left or they just kept taking it.

Jesse had been a notorious womanizer in his early days. For years, there were rumors about his affairs with such famous singers as Nancy Wilson and Aretha Franklin, but it was the black singer Roberta Flack with whom he had his longtime friendship—in 1973 she recorded a passionate love song entitled "Jesse"—and they have remained close friends over the years.

But during the '88 campaign Jackson was usually discreet. His wife's standard remark about whether she cared about his affairs was: "You know what goes on during these campaigns—it's life. But nobody comes into my bedroom."

The bottom line was that Jackson's womanizing, however slight it might have been by 1988, was not really an issue. His core constituency, the blacks in America, didn't really care, and especially if the white media should begin to attack him for it, they would throw their full support behind him. But even the major news organizations, which had research teams to ferret out dirt on such candidates, were not able to pin him down regarding his extramarital affairs. Jesse Jackson's "womanizing," if that's what it could be called, would hardly be likely to bring him down, and the news media finally seemed to realize that and leave it alone.

But one problem that was still very much with him in New Hampshire was the issue of his relations with Jews. In those early days of the campaign, New Hampshire reminded him the most of the excruciating days in 1984 when the controversy over his mindless racial slurs, his alleged anti-Semitism, nearly derailed his campaign and had plagued him ever since.

Jackson and the American Jewish community had a history of conflict. In 1979, Jews had been enraged by a photograph of Jackson embracing PLO chairman Yasir Arafat during a trip the black American made to the Middle East. Later in the same year, it was disclosed that his organization, PUSH, had received a $10,000 check from an anti-Israel Libyan diplomat. And during his 1984 presidential campaign, there were newspaper reports that the same organization had received $200,000 in contributions from the Arab League, the confederation of twenty-one Arab nations and the PLO. In his response to criticism from Jewish leaders, Jackson said they were applying a "double standard": "If the Arab League can contribute to Harvard and Georgetown and other institutions of higher learning, can they not contribute to the PUSH Foundation?"

Earlier, in January 1984, Jackson had referred to Jews as "Hymies" and to New York City as "Hymietown." He had made the remarks to Milton Coleman, a black reporter at *The Washington Post,* in a conversation which began with his frequent line to fellow blacks: "Let's talk black talk." Jackson had mistakenly assumed that Coleman would honor their black brotherhood rather than report a story. It wasn't until three weeks later, on February 13, that the slurs appeared printed in a *Post* story entitled "Peace with American Jews Eludes Jackson." Buried far down in the article was the line: "In private conversations with reporters, Jackson has referred to Jews as 'Hymies' and to New York as 'Hymietown.' "

It took the *Post* several days to pick up on its own story, which editorial writer and U.S. political expert Michael Barone furiously pointed out to his editor, Meg Greenfield. Leonard Downie, then deputy national editor, and later managing editor, was called in to check on it, and he concluded that Jackson used these terms for Jews all the time. But Barone blasted out an editorial on February 18 denouncing Jackson's language as "ugly . . . degrading . . . and disgusting" and demanding that Jackson produce an explanation and apologize. The *Post*'s vitriolic attack on the black presidential candidate concluded by saying that Jackson's language was "not typical, we think, of the way any large number of Americans usually talk and certainly not of the way they want political leaders to talk."

The bombshell had dropped. The national media went wild with the story, and Jesse Jackson became enraged. His campaign manager at the time, Arnold Pinkney, described Jackson as changing drastically under the pressure. Frank Watkins said that Jackson "disintegrated." He first vehemently denied he'd made the remarks. Next, he counterattacked, accusing Jews of a conspiracy to derail his campaign. The black reporter, Milton Coleman, allegedly received a number of threatening phone calls, even some death threats. He was labeled by Jackson supporters as a Judas to his own race. The management of the *Post* found it necessary to provide security protection for both Coleman and his family.

Then on February 25 in Chicago, Jackson's longtime ally, the Nation of Islam leader Louis Farrakhan, an outspoken anti-Semite, came to Jackson's defense and, in so doing, put a further hex on Jackson's career. Farrakhan, standing next to Jackson, viciously warned Jews: "If you harm this brother, it will be the last one you harm." Jesse Jackson stood by unnaturally silent.

Louis Farrakhan had already become anathema to many whites

in general and Jews in particular. His brand of Islam, proclaiming supremacy for the blacks, sent chills down the spines of most whites. Over the years, Jesse Jackson had been close to Farrakhan for politically symbiotic reasons. Farrakhan's people had for years served as physical protectors of Jackson before he was ever entitled to national protection from the Secret Service as a presidential candidate. Also, Jackson had long needed the support of the radical Black Muslims before he went national and began soliciting the support of white Americans. By then, however, he felt he couldn't sever his old ties with Farrakhan and his supporters. Likewise, Jackson believed, and was frequently reminded by other blacks, that it would be viewed as giving in to whites for him to cut Farrakhan off completely. Thus, Jesse Jackson, when he became a national political figure, was trapped between two demands. His hope was that most people would realize that he no longer kept company with Louis Farrakhan but that he had a strong sense of loyalty that wouldn't allow him to cut the man off completely.

But in February 1984, Farrakhan's threat and Jackson's silence fanned the fire worse than ever. Jackson's few white advisers, like Frank Watkins and Barry Commoner, urged him to apologize, while many blacks, including Jackson's wife, urged him not to surrender to the Jews' "Stop Jesse" campaign. Jackie raged against the double standard in the press and said: "I've heard many Jews refer to Washington as 'Chocolate City,' " and she pointed out that nothing was said about that.

On February 26, Jesse Jackson had flown to New Hampshire to try to pick up the pieces of his campaign before the primary voting. That afternoon at the University of New Hampshire in Durham, he finally agreed with Watkins and others that he must do something to appease the outraged Jewish population of America. But he also knew that it wasn't only Jews who were incensed. White liberals were abandoning his campaign. They didn't want any part of it if this was how he talked and behaved.

Finally, Jackson attempted to atone. That evening, February 26, 1984, he marched to the front of Temple Adeth Yeshrun in Manchester, New Hampshire. Later he said he felt like "Daniel in the lions' den." He stood before an audience of national Jewish leaders in the synagogue. He asked their forgiveness, but he was angry with humiliation as he read his prepared confession: "In private talks we sometimes let our guard down, and we become thoughtless. It was not in a spirit of meanness, an off-color remark having no bearing on religion or politics . . . however innocent and unintended, it was wrong."

Grim-faced, his voice tense, the Reverend Jackson went on to add that he was amazed "that something so small has become so large that it threatens the fabric of relations that have been long in the making and must be protected."

Then, standing before this council of Jewish leaders, he vehemently denied that he was anti-Semitic. "I categorically deny allegations that there is anything in my personal attitude or my public career, behavior or record that lends itself to that interpretation. In fact, the record is the exact opposite."

But many Jews would never accept this public atonement. They simply didn't trust him. They suspected him of being a preacher who was a closet bigot, not only toward them but also toward other whites. Jesse Jackson had made too many "casual remarks." He'd been thoughtless too often in conversations. And then there was Louis Farrakhan, even more anathema than Jackson, and Jackson wouldn't denounce him.

Jackson never seemed to understand, neither then in 1984 nor later in 1988, the extent of the mainstream Jews' fear and distrust of him. All he could think at the time was that he was glad to be leaving New Hampshire, where he'd had to endure such pain and humiliation. But the memory of 1984 stayed with him and in 1988 he knew he would be equally relieved when the New Hampshire primary was over and he could move back to the South, where he felt much more at home.

Jackson did not have any illusions in 1988 about the votes: New Hampshire was Michael Dukakis's neighboring state, and it was a foregone conclusion that Dukakis would take it (and he did).

But Jackson wanted to demonstrate that "ordinary people are gravitating to our message," even in New Hampshire. And so he organized a "Rainbow Express" whistle-stop train tour in New Hampshire's lake district. It took place on a glorious, sunny winter day, Valentine's Day, February 14. A blizzard two days earlier had left the landscape a winter wonderland as the train, laden with camera crews and Jesse Jackson, rumbled along from Plymouth to Laconia to Tilton to Concord. In addition to staff and reporters, there were also about one hundred paying supporters who rode along on the train.

Jesse was in his element bundled up in a U.S. Olympic Hockey sweatshirt and addressing the crowds at the rally organized at each stop. When the train was moving, Jackson would wander up and down the aisles talking with his supporters or giving interviews to the journalists. This, he said, was the kind of "point of action" he would like to have every day. It was the first major event of his campaign to get widespread national television coverage, and so the surprise was that instead of reliving the humiliation, it seemed he was on his way to fulfilling the beginning of his media dream.

On February 16, Jesse Jackson surprisingly placed fourth out of seven candidates in the New Hampshire primary. He didn't hit double digits. But, as in Iowa, he showed he could run well even in a state with a nearly all-white population. The afternoon of the primary, we went into Boston for another well-received editorial board meeting, this time at *The Christian Science Monitor.* That night, as the votes were coming in, Jackson gave a round of interviews that far exceeded anything in Iowa. And the next morning, again in contrast with Iowa, where there had been no invitations for morning-show interviews, Jesse Jackson appeared on three networks. It was a good send-off for the flight South later that morning, Ash Wednesday, February 17.

5

THE
MINNESOTA
CAUCUS

"Common ground. America is not a blanket woven from one thread, one color, one cloth. When I was a child growing up in Greenville, South Carolina, and Grandmama could not afford a blanket, she didn't complain and we did not freeze. Instead she took pieces of old cloth —patches—wool, silk, gabardine, croker sack—only patches, barely good enough to wipe off your shoes with. But they didn't stay that way very long. With sturdy hands and a strong cord, she sewed them together into a quilt, a thing of beauty and power and culture. Now we must build such a quilt.

"Farmers, you seek fair prices, and you are right—but you cannot stand alone, your patch is not big enough. Workers, you fight for fair wages, you are right—but your patch of labor is not big enough. Women, you seek comparable worth and pay equity, you are right—but your patch is not big enough. Women, mothers, who seek Headstart, and day care and prena-

tal care on the front side of life, rather than jail care and welfare on the back side of life—you are right—but your patch is
not big enough. Students, you seek scholarships, you are right
—but your patch is not big enough. Blacks and Hispanics,
when we fight for civil rights, we are right—but our patch is
not big enough. Gays and lesbians, when you fight against discrimination and a cure for AIDS, you are right—but your
patch is not big enough.

"But don't despair. Be as wise as my grandma. Pull the
patches and the pieces together, bound by common thread.
When we form a great quilt of unity and common ground,
we'll have the power to bring about health care and housing
and jobs and education and hope . . . We, the people, can
win."

Jesse Jackson was exhilarated that Wednesday morning of February 17. With Iowa and New Hampshire behind him at last, he was
free to focus on the South. In between, there would be other New
England elections, including the Maine caucus on February 28 on
and Vermont's primary on March 1; both were states he had already
been to, albeit briefly. There was no point in spending time in Massachusetts, because the governor, Michael Dukakis, was another
Democratic candidate. Other than blitzing the South for the next
three weeks, Jackson would need to make only a few side trips, to
Minnesota and South Dakota, where primaries would be held on
February 23.

As soon as the standard press conference was over at the Stead
Aviation Terminal of the Manchester airport, the flying Jackson
team took off from snow-covered New Hampshire; it was 8:45 in
the morning aboard the chartered DC-9 jetliner. The candidate was
in a strategizing mode and wanted to talk plans and his vision for
the New South.

We couldn't compete financially with the overflowing treasure
chests of the two chief opponents in the South, Senator Gore and
Governor Dukakis, but we had a chance to win if we could mobilize
Jackson's vast network of contacts throughout the region and im-

plement a media strategy that didn't call for the money required for television commercials. The Jackson headquarters in Chicago—or often Jesse himself—would call the local contacts wherever we would be headed, and they in turn would organize our meetings. Like the staff itself, which was not highly paid, most people working for the Jackson presidential campaign were serving out of a sense of mission and commitment.

Appropriately, the first destination for Jackson's jet was Tallahassee, Florida, the second most important state in the South in terms of population and, consequently, delegates. After Tallahassee, the team would fly that night to Texas, which electorally was the most important Southern state. In between, there would be stops in Alabama, Arkansas and East Texas, all in the same day.

Today's schedule, Jackson pointed out, would be a model for the campaign's new "multi-media-market strategy." Hovering around Jesse's seat on the plane, several of us pored over an AAA map of the United States that I carried in my briefcase. The first stop was the Florida capital, Tallahassee, from which news of Jackson's noonday visits would be carried out by radio and through newspapers all over Florida and into nearby Georgia and Alabama. The next stop, Mobile, would beam out throughout Alabama and into Mississippi, New Orleans, southern Louisiana and east to Pensacola. The third stop that day, in Texarkana, Texas, was planned geographically to hit not only that state and Arkansas, where the airport was located, but also neighboring northern Louisiana and Oklahoma. We spent three to four hours in each city. That night we would arrive late in Dallas, but the late news and the morning papers would pick up Jackson's arrival. The strategy, then, entailed hitting eight states' local markets and aiming eventually for the national networks to pick up at least one of Jackson's events of the day. The radio stations played sound bites from their Jackson telephone interviews that morning even before he reached town.

As part of the game plan, we had already called ahead from New Hampshire, two days earlier, to the editors of the major newspapers in the cities Jackson would be visiting on February 17. I had reached newspapers and radios in both Tallahassee and Mobile and had been able to put Jesse directly on the lines to them for advance telephone interviews, which were then published in advance of his arrival.

Jackson wanted to focus on his vision for the New South as he flew around the region. Whenever he had been in the South, he had talked about his ideas, but now on this first major day in his Southern campaign, he was ready to refine his points. "We have a lot of ground to cover between New Hampshire and March 8," he said. "We're going to concentrate on our New South Agenda." Jackson mentioned, as he often did, the advice he received from the former Alabama governor George C. Wallace: "Keep your message low to the ground so even the goats can eat it." Jesse was happy to boast that the formerly rabid segregationist had in recent years become Jackson's political friend.

Two nights earlier, from an office at the University of New Hampshire in Durham, we had already had a telephone interview with the *Tallahassee Democrat,* in which Jackson said: "In Tallahassee, my first stop out of New Hampshire, I'm concerned that Super Tuesday not be made superficial. The New South has tremendous new challenges."

The same night in another advance interview by telephone, Jackson had spoken to Adline Clarke of the *Mobile Press-Register.* The next day, the sixteenth, the day prior to his visit, the interview was published. The article reported: "The presidential hopeful said, 'The key to the New South is the quest for economic security for working people. We have a lot of celebration about the New South because we were successful in ending the Old South. . . . Now we must make economic justice and cleaning up the environment goals in the New South.' "

"The South has the richest soil, but the poorest people," he pointed out. Then Jackson listed the sad statistics of the New South: still the nation's poorest region; nearly half the nation's poor children; the highest infant-mortality rate in the country; the greatest number of working poor families—men and women who work all day and, nonetheless, face poverty at night; one in ten Southern workers at only minimum wage; thirteen million Southerners with no health insurance; 20 percent less spent per student on its schools than anywhere else in the United States; 57 percent of the hazardous-waste dumps located in the South.

Throughout the South, in interviews and in speeches, Jackson pointed to the harsh discrepancies between the celebrated New South and the "economic violence" still existing behind the façade. He often said: "A generation ago, we fought to eliminate legal racial violence, and we've made tremendous strides. I grew up in the New South and worked to make it better. In 1984, we registered two million new voters and built a coalition that gave us a Democratic Senate and allowed us to defeat Judge Bork. Now we must end economic violence.

"We see the 'bowls' on television with all the strong football players, black and white, and all the pretty cheerleaders, black and white. And that's a better South. But just behind the Cotton Bowl are the textile workers, and just behind the Sugar Bowl are the cane cutters."

He concluded: "Workers and farmers—black and white—are beginning to find economic common ground. They want fair prices and wages and return of their jobs. They want to stop drugs from coming in and jobs from going out [of the United States]. These are the keys to stabilizing their families. The New South must end economic violence and clean up the environment."

In Tallahassee, he addressed two student rallies—first in the Moore Auditorium at the predominantly white Florida State University and then in the Charles Winterwood Theater at Florida's mostly black A&M University. There he announced his plan, "The Challenge of the New South: A Call for a New Direction." It was essentially a regional distillation of Jackson's overall economic policies.

On the morning flight South, our traveling issues director, Mark Steitz, had been tapping away on his lap-top computer, redrafting Jackson's "New South Agenda" on the basis of the candidate's previous speeches and discussions. It was ready for distribution in Florida. The plan included ten points:

1. Respect the dignity and rights of working families by raising the minimum wage, enforcing safety laws, protecting and expanding the rights of workers to organize, and supporting working families, providing Headstart and day care on the front side of life, not jail care and welfare on the back side. All women must receive equal pay for equal work.

2. We must stop jobs from flowing out of the country. 1.6 million Southerners were displaced from their jobs between 1974 and 1985. We must provide incentives for corporations to stay in the country, enact and enforce strict plant closing legislation—including requiring corporations to repay any subsidies they have received when they shut the plant.

3. We must stop drugs from flowing into the country and protect families. 85% of the drugs flowing into this country comes through the South and only 10% was stopped. We have cut the Coast Guard's budget by $100 million—providing a green light to drug dealers.

4. We must provide health care to all Americans, regardless of their pocketbook or where they live. 13 million Southerners have no health insurance, and rural hospitals are dying.

5. We must provide decent housing. The South has more substandard housing than any other region, yet we cut housing spending from $32 billion to less than $10 billion under Reagan.

6. We must provide good schools. We must double the federal education budget. We must give our children an even start in life, no matter what region they grow up in.

7. We must secure our farms and rebuild rural America. One in seven Southern farmers lost their livelihood between 1984 and 1986. Ensuring a fair price, providing debt relief and returning lost land to restarting, beginning and minority farmers are the solution.

8. We must use our public pension funds to rebuild our infrastructure and rehabilitate our homes. Using a small fraction of public pension funds—federally guaranteed at a fair rate of

return—will allow us to rebuild and expand our infrastructure while providing good jobs.

9. We must protect our environment—three Southern states account for more than half the hazardous-waste dump capacity in the country. We must build a safer and more secure approach.

10. We must empower ourselves politically. The New South will not be built for us—we must do it ourselves. We must build a coalition that can last.

At both universities we distributed Jackson's blueprint for the New South to the local media and the traveling press. We continued to hand out the same plan in the other cities we visited that day and later throughout the South. Unlike most other candidates, who would complain that they had announced something of substance once but it wasn't picked up by the press, Jesse Jackson and his team would continue to talk about the same issues and proposals over and over, and, eventually, someone would report them. We were employing the basic didactic method of repetition. We all felt that, ultimately, Jackson's message, with its continual repetition of the issues, would have to be heard and reported.

That day in Tallahassee a *New York Times* correspondent, David Rosenbaum, joined the still relatively small contingent of journalists traveling with us. He had spent long hours with Jackson in the autumn before other journalists were covering him. Later, he and I had talked fairly often by phone when he was reporting the political story out of Washington and Atlanta and he needed questions answered about the Jackson candidacy. Now his coming on the road with us was considered a sign that the big-time press was taking Jackson's campaign seriously. At that time, however, the media of the country saw March 8 as Jackson's one and only big event during the primary season.

By early afternoon, problems began to mount. First of all, the schedule, as usual, included the notation "lunch and press filing time" for one hour before departing from Tallahassee. But, as usual, no one had arranged for food and there were no special rooms or telephones provided for the reporters to file their stories. Thus ensued a scramble through school offices to find telephones.

In the meantime, Jackson was meeting upstairs in the administration building with local leaders who were already committed to support him. As soon as he decided to leave, the Secret Service whisked him out, without notifying the staff or press, who were working in whatever rooms they could find, most of them out of sight or earshot. Most of us managed to catch up and grab seats in the cars following the Jackson motorcade to the airport, but a couple of staff members who had been working in a distant room completely missed the departure.

Jackson had no patience with delay that day and ordered the plane to leave. His longtime aides looked amazed and remarked that they were particularly surprised since one of the missing was Jackson's current favorite, his thirty-one-year-old briefer, Mark Steitz. Just as the stewardesses were preparing to close the front door of the jet, Mark Steitz, Jeff Griffiths and a radio reporter seconded by Percy Sutton to help Jackson came running across the tarmac.

The men entered breathless and with fear on their faces. Jackson was glaring. Actually, it was a funny sight for the onlookers. Then Steitz, who always had a way with Jackson, finally managed to laugh and turn it into a joke. Jesse lightened up and started talking about the next stop in Mobile. The incident was overlooked, in sharp contrast with Jackson's habit of harboring anger for days, scolding whoever he considered had made a mistake.

On the way to Mobile, we gained an hour with the time change and arrived early. Jackson was going to speak at the Sage Armory at a rally for locked-out employees of the International Paper Company which had been organized by the United Paperworkers International Union and the International Brotherhood of Electrical Workers.

The mother of an old friend of mine drove up from Daphne, outside Mobile, to meet me and to hear Jackson. As she stood with me in the hall waiting for Jackson to start speaking, she was pleased to see that the audience was completely integrated, half black and half white. It was almost always that way in the South when Jackson came to town in 1988. The audiences were much more integrated than elsewhere in the country. It made us feel proud of the changes in our region, all us Southerners.

Skin color didn't matter that day to the members of the audience. They were all workers with the same grievances, and they didn't care if their savior came in black or white if he could help. Jackson would say: "My friends, when they take your jobs away and turn the lights out, it doesn't matter if you're black or white—we all look amazingly alike in the dark."

But the Secret Service didn't seem to be pleased at the wonderful signs of integration visible in the South. From the moment we'd taken off from New Hampshire, they had been warning Jackson and the rest of us that we would have to start being much more careful once we were in the South. It didn't seem that they had any special tip-off; they were just taking precautions based on their historical views of the South. Thus, they had been unwilling to allow Jackson's limousine to linger in Tallahassee to wait for the missing staff members.

And in Mobile they began trying to corral the traveling press, to get them out of the armory before Jackson had even concluded his address and collection of funds. The Secret Service enlisted Bill Morton's aid in rounding up the press, rather than speaking to me about it, because they knew I would defend the media's right to stick with Jackson until the end. Then, I would argue, the press would hightail it to their cars to get in the motorcade to the airport. Any journalist had the right to cover Jackson until his conclusion and then any good journalist would manage to get in the caravan. As Bill went around ordering the traveling reporters to leave while Jackson was still speaking, I became annoyed and told him he shouldn't do that. He said he was doing what the Secret Service ordered. I disagreed with their right to do that. This began a long battle between the media and the Secret Service men with Jackson.

On the plane out of Mobile bound for Texarkana, I asked Bill to join me in talking with Jackson about the problem. Jesse agreed that the press should be entitled to stick with him all along. "They have a responsibility," he said, "to keep a ghoul watch on me." I confirmed this: "Actually, it's true. If something happened to Jesse and a traveling reporter missed the story, then that would be the end of him. He wouldn't have been doing his job of covering Jesse."

It was getting late, and we didn't land in Texarkana, Arkansas, until 9 P.M. By then the flight crew was threatening to spend the night there and not go on to Dallas as planned unless we could be off the ground by eleven. Our staff had been looking forward to having two nights in Dallas, two nights anywhere, in order to get some laundry done, since we usually arrived places around midnight and had to have our bags down in the lobby by six the next morning.

We had to drive over the state line to Texarkana, Texas, where Jesse would address a community labor rally at the Chemical Workers Convention Hall. We all urged Jesse to keep his speech short so we could get out and board the plane that night. Nerves were getting frayed. As soon as we arrived at the hall, the reporters were barred by the local guards from entering a room to use the phone, and once again they were justifiably annoyed because they had no way to file their story. They wanted to know what point there was in their traveling with Jackson if they weren't allowed to stick with him and if they couldn't send their stories out along the way. Understanding their frustration, we arranged to get at least one phone for them to share.

Then I had to go into the hall and start signaling to Jackson, first to give a live interview to the local television station for their ten o'clock news slot, which he did, right in the middle of his speech. The audience seemed to love it because they could watch the news being broadcast live. Then he went back to his speech and to soliciting funds. At one point, as the clock ticked on, I caught Jesse's attention, pointed dramatically to my watch and signaled cutoff. He did, to everyone's surprise, and we managed to take off for Dallas at 10:45 P.M. By the time we got to the huge, but understaffed Loew's Anatole Hotel in Dallas and found that the hotel didn't have reservations for several traveling press and staff, tempers were frayed beyond control.

The Secret Service whisked Jackson straight up the elevator to his suite. While Kgosie put away Jackson's clothes, he immediately got on the telephone, which he always found calmed his nerves. He was beginning to feel the pain of a gout attack coming on, and once it started there was little he could do about it.

Mark Steitz, Jeff Griffiths and I went for a couple of beers in the bar. It was a rare occasion, for we seldom took the time to relax what with arriving late at a hotel, answering calls, catching a few hours' sleep and then leaving. Jeff was upset because Jackson was always criticizing him. Jeff felt he could never do enough right for Jackson, even though the rest of us knew Jeff worked tirelessly. That night Mark told me that he feared Jackson would never want the kind of press secretary I believed one should be and that I should just relax and not expect it. He told me just to stand back and only "babysit" the press, which was what Jackson seemed to want. Mark said he and others believed it was important to have me on the team since it was obvious to them that I had already begun to make a difference in making positive changes and getting things done in spite of Jackson's reluctance to let his press secretary perform as one or to acknowledge her accomplishments. The next day Gerry Austin showed up in Dallas and said much the same thing, but he went further, calling Jackson "a sexist," a fact I would just have to deal with and work around if I wanted to stick with the task, difficult as it was.

At seven the next morning, February 18, I went to Jesse's suite to check in before we left for a homeless shelter at the Dallas Life Foundation. Kgosie Matthews greeted me there with the news that we wouldn't be going to the homeless shelter because Jesse wasn't feeling well and was still in bed. I went downstairs to the lobby and bumped into a couple of local Jackson campaign officials; they told me that the local media would be waiting at the shelter. I went back upstairs and reported this to Jesse, who then decided we should go after all.

Throughout the morning, first at the church-run shelter in Dallas, where Jesse talked with the homeless who were being fed breakfast, and later in Denton at North Texas State University, Jesse's pain apparently increased dramatically. He didn't show it publicly except by curtailing his speeches, but privately he was unusually short-tempered and anxious. He decided to spend the afternoon in bed, surrounded by advisers who had come to brief him for the Dallas debate that night at Southern Methodist University. However, once he was into the debate and the succeeding news conference and media interviews, Jackson's remarkable energy miraculously returned, as it always did when he was engaged in any kind of public speaking.

At six o'clock Friday morning, the nineteenth, we had to bring our bags down to the lobby for loading. The staff's and the journalists' suitcases were always taken early to the plane for checking, usually by electrical bomb detectors and preferably also by trained German shepherds if they were available in the particular city. Then I went to Jesse's room to see if he needed me for a briefing, but he didn't that morning and was still in bed. We had a long day ahead of us. We left for the airport, Dallas's Love Field, at seven. That morning, the same radio reporter who was supposed to be working for Jackson missed the plane again. Jackson was furious and decided to place a call to the reporter's boss, Percy Sutton in New York, as soon as we got to our next stop, Minneapolis. Jackson would ask his friend to send another, more reliable newsman to cover him.

The Minnesota caucus would be the next Tuesday, February 23rd. It wasn't considered critical, particularly because it was a caucus and there weren't many delegates from the state, but it was still viewed as important if Jackson could make another significant showing in another nearly all-white state. For a while the day before, when Jackson was feeling so poorly, there had been some discussion that perhaps he should rest and just miss the Minneapolis debate, the second Democratic presidential debate in two days. But Jesse had balked at the idea of sitting another day and resting in Dallas.

The Jackson campaign's state coordinator for Minnesota was a woman named Kris Blake, and she appeared to be a consummate grass-roots organizer. She met us on arrival and said she believed

Jackson would do very well in next week's caucus. Back in November and January, Jackson had already visited farms in rural Minnesota and also the twin cities. Today it was back to the capital, St. Paul, and its twin city, Minneapolis. The first stop was North High School in Minneapolis. Jackson liked going to a school in the morning; he always got energized by the students' enthusiasm. Immediately afterward, we were whisked across the Mississippi River to a rally with state labor leaders at the Machinists Hall in St. Paul and then back across the river which divided the two cities to an unusual church for a special service.

By the late 1980s, the homosexual community in Minnesota had become a very well-organized minority. The Metropolitan Community Church for All God's Children in Minneapolis was a haven for gays and lesbians, and the church had invited all the Democratic candidates to come and address its congregation. Only Jackson had accepted. (Later, it turned out that Senator Paul Simon's organization learned about this and said Simon would come as well, but by then the church said Simon would have to come another day since Jackson had accepted first for that Friday before the state caucus.)

Homosexuals in America were among Jesse Jackson's special constituents. He was one of the few candidates who dared to reach out to them and accept them as full-fledged members of his organization. He was the only presidential candidate who dared join in the National Gay Rights March on Washington in October 1987. His Rainbow Coalition had a special section for them, called the Lavender Stripe, the color adopted by gays and lesbians as their symbol. Jackson's campaign reached out to every disenfranchised group in America. In this case, the group happened perhaps to be better educated and was thus becoming more organized than others, and Jackson's decision to speak to them and their problems of acceptance in America was bold. On the one hand, they had the power to become a major voting constituency. On the other, many other Americans loathed and discriminated against homosexuals perhaps more than against any other minority.

In Minnesota in 1988, at the time of Jackson's visit, there was an important legal case in progress that had become a national cause célèbre for the entire homosexual movement in America and for civil liberties in general. A lesbian, Sharon Kowalski, was severely injured in a car crash in 1983 and put into a nursing home by her parents. Her lover, Karen Thompson, had been forbidden by Kowalski's parents to visit Sharon and prevented from taking her back to the house they had previously shared in St. Cloud, Minnesota. In 1988, Thompson, a tenured professor at St. Cloud University, was involved in a legal battle with Kowalski's parents. Thompson was fighting to have her female lover's father removed as guardian and replaced by herself or a neutral party. Her cause had gained national recognition with "Free Sharon Kowalski" committees springing up all across the country as a civil rights symbol of the gay movement.

That day in Minneapolis, Karen Thompson was among the speakers at the Minnesota Lavender Stripe Conference in the Metropolitan Community Church. She told her poignant story and appealed for help. Jesse Jackson included her efforts in his speech as a just cause in the American search for equal civil rights for all regardless of race, sex, religion or sexual preference.

Jackson decided that day would also be a good time to announce another of his plans: "Responding to the AIDS Crisis." In his speech, he voiced his compassion for the victims of AIDS and their loved ones. And at the conclusion, we distributed copies of his political plan for dealing with the disease:

I know that many of you are here today because you are concerned about the AIDS crisis and the AIDS hysteria present in many communities. You are tired of an administration in Washington more committed to "humanitarian aid" to the Contras [in Central America] than to finding a cure for AIDS. We cannot allow ourselves to be frightened or intimidated by irrational fears or prejudice or silence in high places. Just as earlier generations of Americans were challenged to develop a compassionate response to typhoid fever, tuberculosis and polio, so must we develop a compassionate response to AIDS. I know that the lesbian and gay community has led the way in this response while the rest of America struggles to catch up. I would suggest that a compassionate response to AIDS entails three components:

One—Effective, preventative education which targets high-risk behaviors rather than stigmatizing certain societal groups. AIDS is not a "gay disease." It knows no bounds of race, class, gender or sexual orientation.

Two—Massive federal funding to research AIDS prevention, treatment and cure.

Three—A national health care system which would include programs of voluntary and confidential testing and counseling to encourage those who may have been exposed to the HIV virus to be tested, and would adequately care for those with AIDS and AIDS-related complexes. Health must never be based on wealth. Every American is entitled to adequate medical treatment.

I want to say a special word to those persons with AIDS who may be here this afternoon. That special word is: "Never give up." Never allow someone else to make your decisions for you or to deprive you of your rights. It may sometimes feel as though you are all alone but you are not. There are those of you who care and together we can meet the challenge of AIDS. We can make a difference.

The gays and lesbians at the church expressed their appreciation to Jackson for coming in their midst and speaking to them. Behind the stage, in the church offices, however, a couple of Jackson's aides made jokes about not daring to use the toilets there. Jackson was oblivious. He was still extremely tired that day and wanted to rest. We left as soon as he concluded his speech and drove back across the river to the Holiday Inn in St. Paul for a couple of hours' rest before that night's presidential debate in the World Theatre in the capital's downtown area. Jesse wanted only a short briefing from his advisers that evening, and then he went to bed exhausted.

Minnesota is the home of the unique Democratic Farmer-Labor Party and a traditionally liberal state. It is also the home state of two of the great liberals of the late twentieth century, Hubert Humphrey and Walter Mondale, now practicing law again in Minneapolis and reportedly preparing to run again for the U.S. Senate in 1990. Mondale was there that night, backstage talking with the candidates: Senator Gore, Governor Dukakis, Richard Gephardt, Jackson, Gary Hart, Paul Simon. When I told Mondale I was now working as Jackson's press secretary, he looked surprised. It was well known that Mondale viewed Jackson's spoiling tactics in 1984 as detrimental to the Democratic ticket of Mondale and Ferraro. It was obvious that night that neither man felt comfortable around the other.

Minnesota's debate was called "We the People" Presidential Forums. That went right along with Jesse's stock conclusion to most of his speeches: "We the people, we the people will win." The Minnesota debate was unique among all the debates that year because the list of issues had been drawn up by citizens at town meetings in Mankato, Duluth, Rochester and Bloomington. Between January 9 and February 3 those citizens had identified the following issues as mattering most to Minnesotans: the federal deficit; arms control; the environment; leadership; foreign policy; employment/unemployment; health care; the farm crisis; social security; meeting the needs of the economically disadvantaged; and education. They were all issues that for months Jesse Jackson, almost always alone among the candidates, had addressed. Exhausted though he'd been only an hour before, Jackson once again rose to the occasion in the debate and talked passionately about all those special issues, so dear to his heart and apparently to the people of Minnesota and to many other silent Americans.

We didn't get out of Minneapolis until late that night because there were two fund-raising receptions Jackson was to attend before leaving. There was some talk about whether we should leave at all that night, for we had been scheduled to fly to western South Dakota, where a fund-raising breakfast would be held in Rapid City early the next morning. South Dakota, whose primary the next week would be held on the same day as the Minnesota caucus, was also a traditionally liberal state. Despite its small population, it would be worth the effort if Jackson could tally up some more delegates. So we decided to go. It turned out to be one of the more hair-raising flights of the campaign, as we hit a blizzard and had to circle Rapid City and the nearby Black Hills for more than an hour until we were finally allowed to land at three in the morning. Even Jesse, who usually believed God was with him, looked nervous on the flight that night.

No one had much sleep that night—even less than usual—as we had to have our bags in the lobby by 6:30 A.M. and Jesse began speaking at 7:10. The fund-raiser was a breakfast meeting of supporters (ranchers, Native Americans and labor leaders) who had assembled in the same Howard Johnson's motel where we had spent the past three hours. It was all over by nine, and we left for the airport to fly to Chicago. There, Jackson, albeit late, addressed an All-Chicago Labor Rally GOTV (Get Out the Vote) in the Great Hall of the large downtown Americana Congress Hotel.

It was now Saturday, February 20. In Chicago that day, my newly hired assistant, Delmarie Cobb, joined our traveling team. She was the younger black woman Austin had told me I should hire if they took me on as the press secretary. He said they'd already brought in too many white males, and they needed a few women anyway, both black and white, at least temporarily.

When Jackson boarded our plane at Chicago's Midway Airport, I introduced him to Delmarie. He gave the greeting that he often gave to women: "How're you doing, babe?" She and I were standing by our seats near the front of the plane, where the staff usually sat just behind Jackson and one Secret Service man who guarded the entrance. (The traveling press and the rest of the Secret Service contingent sat in the back.) Jackson was walking down the aisle toward the rear of the plane, as he usually did before takeoff. He would go back to use the toilet and to say hello to some of the press. He stared at Delmarie, and then, as he began to make his way down the aisle, he tossed a packet of papers at her. It was his style. He often just tossed his coat or papers to whoever was standing nearest him. Delmarie, naturally, hadn't a clue about what to do with them. I explained that he would do that and then later he would ask her where his papers were. The best thing to do was to hand them over to Kgosie, who would go through them and toss out what was trash and save what Jackson might need later.

We were late leaving Chicago. By the time we got to the state fairgrounds in Beaumont, Texas, some of the people waiting to see and hear Jesse Jackson had given up and gone home. But many others had stayed, sitting on the hard bleachers, under hand-lettered signs that read: "The Strike Is Right—Everyone Hold Tight." This was a community rally for the striking OCAW (Oil, Chemical and Atomic Workers).

As in Mobile a few days earlier and elsewhere across the South, the crowd was almost equally black and white. For the past sixteen days, their Local 4-243 had been out on strike against the Mobil Oil refinery, one of Beaumont's biggest employers. And Beaumont, like most of East Texas for the past few years, had really been hurting from the worldwide oil glut. It was a depressed area, and these people were grateful that at least one national politician, this Jesse Jackson, would take the time to show concern about their problems. Again, as in Mobile, it didn't matter to these people of the South what Jackson's color was if he could help them. One local reporter, James Cullen of the *Beaumont Enterprise,* explained: "This is the first time that union people have taken Jackson seriously. In 1984 they thought he was a 'black candidate.' " Now, he said, they believed he was a candidate for everyone, the whole nation and the whole South.

Later, at the Beaumont airfield, Jackson stopped to make some phone calls from the office in the hangar before boarding the jet. Most of the press and staff got on the plane and waited. Inside the building, Gerry Austin, who'd joined us again in Chicago, brought a local white man in to meet Jackson. He was Bruce Hill, business manager for the local pipe fitters' union, and as Austin explained by way of introduction to Jackson, the forty-eight-year-old man had been at the civil rights march in Selma, Alabama, in 1965, where Jesse had also been.

"I marched in Selma," he said.

"Glad to be with you again, brother," Jackson responded.

"Yeah, I was there." Hill grinned. "But on the other side. I marched with the Klan." He was then with the Ku Klux Klan, he explained, but now, twenty-three years later, he supported Jackson. Referring to those earlier times in the South, Hill said: "I was young and full of it. I've changed. Just like a lot of us ole Southern boys. Jesse Jackson is right on the issues as far as the workingman is concerned. He wants insurance for our sick and a good retirement for our old people."

It was one of those vignettes that so often impressed Jackson, and then he incorporated it into his repertoire. Later he would tell the story of the ex-Klansman who came to shake his hand in Beaumont. And Jackson would quote the man as saying: "I just don't want to be on the wrong side of history again."

That night we flew on to Philadelphia, Pennsylvania. It had been another one of those long days—from Rapid City, South Dakota, to Chicago to Beaumont, Texas, and finally ending up in the City of Brotherly Love on the East Coast. But on the Jackson schedule it certainly wasn't atypical.

The next day, Sunday, February 21, there was a huge fund-raising luncheon for Jackson at the Wyndham Franklin Plaza Hotel. It was important because it was then that Jackson finally got the endorsements of some major black politicians who had withheld their support from him in 1984 and until now in 1988. They were Congressman William Gray, Mayor Wilson Goode of Philadelphia and Mayor Melvin Primas of neighboring Camden, New Jersey. (Later in the afternoon Jackson would fly briefly to Newark, New Jersey, to pick up the endorsement of another black politician, Mayor Sharpe James.) The scene at the luncheon, however, was a striking contrast to the integration we'd been seeing across the South. There in downtown Philadelphia, the ballroom was filled with blacks, with only a handful of white supporters present. This was the virtually segregated urban Northeast Jackson would be facing after Super Tuesday.

The next couple of days we were up and down the eastern seaboard—from Philadelphia to Newark, to Augusta and Atlanta, Georgia, to Washington, D.C., and back up to New York City the night of Tuesday, February 23. The schedule finally included some more meetings with various editorial boards, including breakfast at *U.S. News & World Report*'s beautiful new headquarters in Washington and lunch at *The New York Times*'s Washington bureau. As always, at the last minute there was some audible opposition from other staff members who felt it wasn't wise for Jackson to meet face to face with these establishment news organizations. But, again at the last minute, I was relieved that he kept the appointments, though he was often quite late.

In the case of the luncheon on Tuesday, the twenty-third, at the *Times*'s bureau in the Army and Navy Club on Farragut Square, I wondered whether his tardiness canceled out whatever positive effect his discussion later had. What happened was that Jackson's adviser Ann Lewis, who operated out of Washington, had arranged another interview without notifying anyone but Jackson's Washington liaison, Yolanda Carraway. She was so accustomed to Jackson's being late and to everyone's just accepting it—presumably out of gratefulness to see him at all—that she hadn't bothered to tell anyone else, including his press secretary. Lewis wanted Jackson to give an interview to the *Jerusalem Post*'s correspondent, Wolf Blitzer, but she had arranged it for the time when Jackson was scheduled to be at the *Times* luncheon. Neither Jackson nor his Washington office bothered to tell Lewis he already had an appointment at the *Times* for that time.

When I finally found out what was happening, I phoned an editor at the *Times* to say Jackson might be a few minutes late. Jackson himself never bothered to reschedule the Blitzer interview or to apologize for allowing his plans to be changed. The editor, a friend and former colleague from my reporting days, exploded over the telephone at me: "You'd better not let Jesse Jackson be late for this, Liz Colton. We've got limited time, and we don't have all day to wait for him." I responded in extreme frustration: "Look, there's simply a limit to how much I can change Jackson to get him places on time. I'm doing the best I can, but ultimately I can't take responsibility when he changes his schedule without notice." When Jackson finally showed up more than half an hour late, he was oblivious

to the annoyance felt toward him by the *Times* editors and reporters. Instead, he energetically and deftly entered into a verbal duel
with columnist William Safire and felt pleased with the performance.

Late that afternoon when we got on our plane at National Airport, Jackson's aide-de-camp, Kgosie Matthews, wasn't on board. It
wasn't really unusual, since he would often come and go, dropping
off along the way to handle some personal business for Jackson. But
that day other aides whispered that Kgosie was fed up with Jackson's constant criticism of him. Usually he just took it and seldom
talked back, but today he had said he was tired of being treated like
a flunky. A few days later, when Kgosie came back on board, he
simply said that he was upset by some personal matters. Jackson
himself never referred publicly to it.

That night we had to land in Teterboro, New Jersey, and then
drive into Manhattan to the Harvard Club for another fund-raising
dinner. Afterward, Jackson went to the University Club for a private meeting that Vernon Jordan, executive director of the National
Urban League, had arranged with black intellectuals. At eleven
o'clock we went to Rockefeller Center for a late-night television
interview on NBC.

Finally we arrived at our hotel, the Grand Hyatt, but the long
day didn't end then. ABC's *Good Morning America* phoned to ask
Jackson to appear on their show the next morning. This required
several hours of discussion between me and our scheduler and Jackson before it was finally agreed that he would go.

At 6:40 A.M. Jesse and Mark Steitz and I were driven to the ABC
News studio on the Upper West Side for Jackson to go live on *GMA*
a few minutes after seven. We had just learned that Jackson had
placed second in the Minnesota caucus the day before. We had
almost forgotten that the caucus was held yesterday, but there it
was: a major win. But there was hardly anything about it in the
media.

In the middle of the live interview, Jackson decided that he himself would announce the news to America. He had just come in
second, winning 20 percent of the vote, in Minnesota, a mostly

white state. He suggested that when journalists kept saying he was unelectable, they should ask the voters of Minnesota and those in Iowa and New Hampshire who had also voted for him why they had done so.

Later Jackson would tell reporters: "Suppose Hart or Gephardt or Gore had come in second in Minnesota? How do you think that would have been played? Not only did they not give me credit for being able to do it, they could not say I did it. It was almost a well-kept secret." And he would blow a kiss in the air to indicate how his showing in Minnesota had been kissed off by the media. A few days later, on Sunday, February 28, Jackson placed second in another caucus: this time in the "lily white" state of Maine, with 28 percent of the vote. But the media once again took little notice.

6

THE
ROAD TO SUPER
TUESDAY

"We were separated at childbirth because something happened to our parents, and we never really knew who we were. [Jesse Jackson was talking about the blacks and whites of the New South. The analogy, however, came from his own childhood. He and his half brother were separated because of his own illegitimacy.]

"We had never missed each other because we never grew up together. But then someplace along the way, we bumped into each other one day. [Jackson continued the analogy of the long-lost siblings finding one another in the New South.] The more we talk, the more our curiosity is aroused. Then we begin to find that we really have both been adopted, and we start searching for our parents and we find them.

"We find that we are each other's brother, we are each other's sister. . . . And then here we are in this family reunion. This is the New South. This is the heartbeat of the new America."

Many Southerners, whites as well as blacks, shared Jackson's vision and pride in the New South. I was one of them, and my long-held beliefs about what we, as both Southerners and Americans, could accomplish in establishing a free and mixed society had much to do with my eagerness to work in this historic presidential campaign. Interestingly enough, Jesse and I were the only Southerners in our traveling corps, and that heritage gave us a shared bond, often only tacitly acknowledged. But it was always there. We had a kind of kinship that bound us as Southerners regardless of whatever particular personality clashes we might have.

Jesse and I had grown up in different racial and economic circumstances, but we had both been raised to believe that the old system was wrong and that it was our duty to help bring about the necessary changes in our region and country. I remember how, when I was six in the small town of Morganton, North Carolina, and met a young black boy during my walk home from the white primary school, I couldn't understand why we went to different schools even though we were the same age. I would never forget that summer day in 1954 when the historic Supreme Court ruling *Brown* v. *Board of Education* was handed down. That was when the Supreme Court ruled that separate schooling on racial grounds was unconstitutional. I felt frightened by the way the news was announced over the North Carolina radio station, and I said I was afraid there might be another civil war. At the time, we were visiting my grandmother in Chapel Hill, and she and my parents assured me there wouldn't be another war. My grandmother's mother had been born in the South during the Civil War and had been raised in Savannah, Georgia, by her uncle, a General Jackson. Then in 1960, when Jesse Jackson was in college in Greensboro and participating in the first sit-in movement, I was in the tenth grade in Asheville and joined ASCORE (Asheville Students' Committee on Racial Equality) and began working with other high school students, white and black, in the area to move toward integration. When Jesse became a lieutenant in Dr. King's movement in the Deep South in 1965, I was active in the civil rights movement in Lynchburg, Virginia, where I was attending college. And then while

Jackson was heading up Dr. King's Operation Breadbasket, I joined the Peace Corps and went to Kenya to work with black Africans in 1967–69. All those years we two Southerners had followed parallel paths that finally met.

Ever since I had joined the staff of Jackson's campaign, I had had an idea for an event that would symbolize this bond between us and demonstrate how far the South and the nation had progressed over the past three decades. That was for us to go together, as a campaign stop before Super Tuesday, to my hometown. Asheville, North Carolina, where I had grown up, was only sixty-three miles "up the mountain" from Jesse's hometown of Greenville, South Carolina. We had lived in a world of legal segregation. I had gone to the all-white high school in Asheville, and Jesse's football team used to play against the all-black high school in Asheville. Now those two schools were fully integrated into Asheville High School. I wanted to take Jesse Jackson to my hometown and let us tell that mixed student body of 1988 about the changes and show the world how far we'd come.

Jesse liked the idea, too, but it took a while to find a place for it on the campaign schedule. At first, other staff members had opposed it, simply in terms of electoral numbers. The numbers man, Steve Cobble, and the scheduler, Gary Massoni, in Chicago, didn't think it made sense because Asheville had a relatively small black population, only 15 percent, compared with other parts of the South, and they didn't expect western North Carolina to go for Jackson. But Jesse and I argued that wasn't the point, that what was more important was that our going together to my hometown would be a symbolic event that would appeal to the media, a Jacksonian "point of action."

Finally, it was determined that we would go on Wednesday, February 24. For once, it looked like we had a firm date set several days in advance, and I spent a lot of time the weekend before making arrangements over the telephone with people in Asheville, including the school officials and my parents, who were always supportive, as well as Jackson's North Carolina state campaign manager, Bruce Lightner, who was working mostly in the central and eastern regions and had not operated much in the western part of the state, where Asheville was located.

I also notified various news organizations that in Asheville they would probably get a special human-interest story, and more reporters than usual, at that point, came along for the ride on the campaign plane. For the first time, NBC sent a crew of seven, and Garrick Utley included the event the following Sunday in his *Sunday Today* profile of Jackson. *Time*'s Mike Duffy covered the visit, and the following week his article about Jackson, entitled "More Than a Crusade," devoted a whole paragraph to the event: "His trip to Asheville, N.C., last week allowed Jackson to return to a town 60 or so miles from his birthplace and recall how he played segregated football games nearby during the 1950's. Jackson drove home the point by bringing along his white press secretary, Asheville native Liz Colton. Unlike 1984, Jackson repeats over and over that this is not a black struggle. The poorest Americans, he says, are white and female. 'We can't just lift black boats,' he had said to a black audience at Winston-Salem State University last week. 'We must lift all boats.' "

On the morning of February 24, we were still in New York City. I had been up much of the night making arrangements for the *Good Morning America* interview on ABC, and I felt like I was coming down with the flu. At 5:30, when I got up to dress and take my bags down before going to Jesse's room a little after six, I knew I was quite ill and had a fever, but I didn't feel there was much I could do about it.

In Jackson's suite at the Grand Hyatt, while he was in his room dressing, he called to me in the living room and told me to get hold of his mother on the phone. She was at home in Greenville, also up already by 6:30 A.M., and was pleased to hear that her son was calling. I passed the message on that he wanted her to join us in Asheville later that morning. She could get some friends to drive her up—it was only a little over an hour northwest on the interstate now, and they should meet us at the Asheville airport at 11 A.M.

Jesse then came out and spoke to his mother and repeated the instructions. Everything was set, and off we went for our early-morning Manhattan appointments, first to ABC and then to a fund-raising breakfast for minority contractors at B. Smith's Restaurant at 771 Eighth Avenue. Then, a little later than planned, back to Teterboro Airport in New Jersey to board our charter. But then the van carrying the staff and press bags didn't show up for a while, and we had to wait.

By the time we landed in Asheville, it was nearly 12:30, and Jesse's mother and a few friends from Greenville were waiting for us at the airport. The Jackson campaign officials who were also at the airport told me that my parents had been at the school but were now awaiting our arrival at the Quality Inn, where the lunch was being held. Our first stop in Asheville was to have been the high school at 11:20 and then on to a fund-raising lunch downtown at 12:40. We on the staff who traveled with Jackson wondered how the schedulers could envision such tight scheduling ever working even if we'd landed in the city on time, because it was seldom that Jackson himself would ever wind up an appearance and a speech within an hour. That day the students had been waiting nearly two hours in the gymnasium, and finally they'd been told to go to lunch and their next classes and come back later, after Jackson had finished attending the fund-raiser, where working people had gathered on their lunch-hour break.

The Quality Inn was located at 1 Thomas Wolfe Plaza, which was named after and was near the house of that famous Asheville writer, the author of *You Can't Go Home Again.* But there that day in 1988, crowds welcomed this black Southerner from a next-door city, and I felt a warm welcome from friends who'd come to see me with this famous man, to whom they hoped I would introduce them. Walking into the packed ballroom of the Quality Inn, I felt a thrill to see the completely mixed throng of more than five hundred well-wishers, all on their feet applauding Jackson as he and his entourage made their way along a narrow aisle to the head tables set up on a raised platform. It was the same room where five years earlier I had attended my twentieth reunion with fellow graduates of the city's formerly all-white high school.

My parents stepped out from the crowd and waved. They had

Jesse with his father and half
brothers. (COURTESY OF NOAH
ROBINSON, SR.)

Jesse with Dr. Martin Luther King,
Jr., April 1968, on balcony where
King was shot the next day. (WIDE
WORLD PHOTOS, INC.)

Jesse at the funeral of Dr. King, April 1968. (FLIP SCHULKE ©1984/BLACK
STAR)

Jesse and his young wife, Jackie, on Black Easter in Chicago, 1969. (ARNOLD ZANN/BLACK STAR)

Jesse comforts King's widow, Coretta, on first anniversary of Dr. King's assassination, April 1969. (ARNOLD ZANN/BLACK STAR)

Jesse in 1970 as director of Operation Breadbasket in Chicago, then wearing his ever-present symbol—sneakers, about which he said: "I'm a man of the streets, not a man for the office." (FRANKLYNN PETERSON/BLACK STAR)

Jesse, December 1971, as he left a meeting of the Southern Christian Leadership Conference in Chicago just after he'd been suspended for sixty days without pay for what they termed repeated organizational improprieties. (WIDE WORLD PHOTOS, INC.)

Jesse, president of Operation PUSH, July 1972, calling for black unity at sixty-third annual national convention of the NAACP. (UPI/ BETTMANN NEWSPHOTOS)

Jesse, July 1972, at Democratic National Convention in Miami Beach, reaching to shake hands with Illinois delegates after the convention refused to seat Mayor Richard J. Daley and fifty-eight uncommitted supporters. (UPI/ BETTMANN NEWSPHOTOS)

Jesse, September 1972, pensive at Black Expo in Chicago, (FRANKLYNN PETERSON/ BLACK STAR)

Jesse, thoughtful in July 1973.
(JOFFRE CLARKE/BLACK STAR)

Jesse and PLO chairman Yasir Arafat embracing in traditional Middle Eastern style in Beirut, September 1979, when Jackson toured war-devastated areas of southern Lebanon as Arafat's guest. (UPI/BETTMANN NEWSPHOTOS)

Jesse speaks in Rose Garden ceremony at the White House, January 1984, after he'd succeeded in winning the release of U.S. airman Lieutenant Robert Goodman (third from left). President Reagan, Secretary of State Shultz, Secretary of Defense Weinberger, Vice President Bush, and Mrs. Goodman are among those listening. (JOHN TROHA/BLACK STAR)

Jesse with Nation of Islam leader Louis Farrakhan in February 1984 during uproar over Jackson's "Hymietown" remarks. Later Jackson said he dissociated himself from Farrakhan but would not renounce his personhood. (MARTIN BENJAMIN/BLACK STAR)

Jesse making his first run for the presidency, 1984. Afterward, Jackson said that God had not finished with him yet. (DENNIS BRACK/ BLACK STAR)

Jesse getting his Cuban cigar lit by Cuban Premier Fidel Castro in 1984, just after Jackson had negotiated the release of prisoners from Cuban jails. (JACQUES M. CHENET/WOODFIN CAMP & ASSOCIATES)

Jesse puts his arm around former President Jimmy Carter during an impromptu visit Carter made to the Jackson headquarters, July 1984, on the eve of the Democratic convention. From then on Jackson would call on Carter for advice. (UPI/BETTMANN NEWSPHOTOS)

Jesse visiting former Alabama governor George Wallace at the latter's house in Montgomery, July 1987, as Jackson was preparing to announce his 1988 candidacy. Wallace advised him to keep his message low so the goats can reach it. (UPI/BETTMANN NEWSPHOTOS)

Democratic Candidate Forum, October 7, 1987, from left to right:
Senator Albert Gore, Jr., of Tennessee, Congressman Richard Gephardt
of Missouri, Jesse Jackson, former Chairman of the Democratic
National Committee Paul Kirk, Jr., former Governor Bruce Babbitt of
Arizona, Senator Paul Simon of Illinois, and Governor Michael
Dukakis of Massachusetts. (DENNIS BRACK © 1987/BLACK STAR)

The Jackson family, from left to right: Jonathan, Jesse Jr., little Jackie,
wife Jackie, Jesse, Sandy and Yusef. (JACQUES M. CHENET/WOODFIN
CAMP & ASSOCIATES)

Jesse at "victory party" in Greenfield, Iowa, February 8, 1988, after nation's first caucus of the season. (JACQUES M. CHENET/WOODFIN CAMP & ASSOCIATES)

Jesse with Mrs. King in the shot he'd long sought—the two of them laying a wreath at the tomb of Dr. King outside Ebenezer Baptist Church in Atlanta, March 6, 1988. (JACQUES M. CHENET/WOODFIN CAMP & ASSOCIATES)

Jesse with his last two opponents in 1988, Senator Albert Gore, Jr. (left), who would stand on his toes to look as tall as Jackson, and Governor Michael Dukakis (right). (RICK FRIEDMAN/ BLACK STAR)

New York governor Mario Cuomo (center) trying to mediate during bitter days of 1988 New York primary as New York City mayor Edward Koch (left) warned Jews they would be crazy to vote for Jesse Jackson (right). (CHRISTOPHER MORRIS/ BLACK STAR)

Jesse speaking at "Run, Jesse, Run" rally in Birmingham, Alabama, March 7, 1988, on the eve of Super Tuesday. (ROWLAND SHERMAN/ BLACK STAR)

Jesse holds back tears as his tearful wife, Jackie, stands by his side the
night of the New York primary, April 19, 1988, after Michael Dukakis
was proclaimed the victor. (UPI/BETTMANN NEWSPHOTOS)

Jesse delivering his speech at the
Democratic convention in Atlanta
on July 19, 1988. (DENNIS BRACK/
BLACK STAR)

Jesse in hard hat proclaiming his
election promises of "Peace, Jobs,
Justice" at a Youngstown, Ohio,
rally, April 26, 1988. (JACQUES
M. CHENET/WOODFIN CAMP &
ASSOCIATES)

Jesse delivering his speech to the convention hall full of red Jesse placards, July 19, 1988. (RICK FRIEDMAN/BLACK STAR)

Jesse and his wife, Jackie, stand between the democratic nominee, Michael Dukakis, and his wife, Kitty (on the Jacksons' left), and vice presidential nominee Lloyd Bentsen, and his wife, B.A., at conclusion of convention, July 21, 1988. Democrats called this a show of unity; Republicans described it as a new form of "troika" government in America. (UPI/BETTMANN NEWSPHOTOS)

Jesse with his press secretary, Liz Colton, February 1988. (JACQUES
M. CHENET/NEWSWEEK)

Jackson campaigning in Dallas, Texas. (CARL ANDON © 1988/BLACK STAR)

Jesse Jackson at Coe College in Iowa, February 1988. (CHARLES MASON
© 1988/BLACK STAR)

Jackson on Tom Hoy Farm near Des Moines, Iowa. (DENNIS BRACK
© 1988/BLACK STAR)

Jesse with his mother, Helen Jackson (left), and his grandmother,
Matilda Burns (right), October 1988, as he announced his candidacy for
the presidency in Raleigh, North Carolina. (JACQUES M. CHENET/
WOODFIN CAMP & ASSOCIATES)

President-elect Bush
and Jesse Jackson, after
luncheon meeting,
December 1, 1988.
(RICH LIPSKI/
WASHINGTON POST)

brought along my eight-year-old niece, Elisabeth. Her parents were out of town, but her grandparents had taken her out of school for the day so she could experience this historic moment. It was certainly something she would never forget. I pulled them along in the crush of people behind Jackson—his mother, staff, Secret Service, reporters, campaign officials—and I took them forward to introduce them. Pleased as he always was to have an opportunity to hug a child, especially a white one, for photographs, Jesse lifted little Elisabeth and gave her a big hug, which she returned. For weeks afterward, her mother later told me, she went everywhere repeating Jesse's chant that she learned listening to him that day: "Who are you going to vote for? Jesse. Who're you going to vote for? Jesse. JESSE JACKSON."

That day, as always when he was in the South, Jackson talked about his dream of a New South in which there would be economic as well as racial equality. He said: "Beyond the challenges of race is the challenge to end economic violence, to fight for economic justice. . . . It's not black versus white; that's the old agenda. It's barracudas versus small fish."

His speech, as in so many other places, was applauded throughout, and often briefly interrupted by calls of "Amen" and "You tell it, brother." In the tradition of the old black preachers, Jackson would halt rhythmically at these punctuations which seemed only to add to his fervor. Behind the white cloth covering the table where he stood at the podium, his taut legs would flex at the knees as part of the rhythm and breathing that kept him going at the right pace.

"Most people who are poor are not on welfare and don't want welfare, because they work every day. They are the ones who served the meals today. They raise other people's children, and they cook other people's food, and they drive cabs.

"They are orderlies, they change the clothes of those who are feverishly sick and wash down their bodies in alcohol, and they empty their bedpans and clean out their commodes . . . and yet, when they get sick, they cannot afford a bed." He paused.

"People are dying in the admitting office [of hospitals] because they don't have a green or a yellow card to go up to a bed that sits empty waiting for those who have insurance to get sick. There are thirteen million Southerners without health insurance today," Jackson emphasized.

Then he began his attack on the Reagan administration in particular: "What does Reaganomics mean? It means 'reverse Robin Hood': take from the poor and give to the rich. Reagan thinks the poor have too much money and the rich have too little, so shift it."

He went on to describe industry under Reagan, feasting instead of reinvesting in America. He explained his point: "In Reagan's first term General Electric made $10 billion. That wasn't so bad, except wages and jobs did not correspond with profits. The number one exporter from Taiwan is not Taiwanese, it's General Electric, which owns RCA, which owns NBC, which advertises: 'Buy American.' They take jobs from America to Taiwan, not for better labor, but for cheaper labor, slave labor, to make maximum profit."

He then carefully brought in a local labor problem, at the nearby Canton paper mill of the Champion International Paper Company. He said: "Paper workers in this area are caught between jobs or environmental hazards. . . . We should have jobs and a clean environment."

And, as in most of his speeches, Jackson raised the issue of drugs in America: "We know drugs are killing our people, filling up our jails, destroying our children. Drugs represent the most inept dimension of our foreign policy and the most corrupt and sleazy because of the money involved."

He pointed out that while U.S. troops are based all around the world, "the number one threat on the streets today" was the drugs pouring into the United States. In Texas alone last year, he cited, "almost $2 billion in drugs came through 600 miles of border. We've got 300 patrolmen, one boat, one helicopter [fighting drugs at the border], and 350,000 troops in Europe."

Throughout the long speech, I was standing and kept drinking glass after glass of ice water in an attempt to quench my fever. I knew it must be high. As we were leaving the lunch, I decided to make the short ride across town to the school with my parents so we could have a brief visit and I could get some medicine for my fever. I quickly told Jesse I would meet him at the school, and it seemed okay. I didn't tell him I was sick, but my face was noticeably flushed and others saw I looked quite ill.

We rushed ahead of the motorcade, and I was walking with my mother and niece through the school parking lot when Jackson's black limousine pulled up. We three waved cheerfully at him. I knew how excited my niece and mother were, as was everyone else, at the opportunity to meet Jesse Jackson in person. But Jesse didn't wave. He simply gave one of his extremely cold, nasty glares that those closest to him were familiar with. The public seldom got a glimpse of that look, which my mother must have seen that afternoon. I didn't say anything, but I wondered to myself: What now? I couldn't imagine what the problem was after this very triumphant reception.

Jesse's car pulled up to the door of the gymnasium behind the school, and I immediately joined him. School administration officials and student leaders were there to greet us. I knew some of them, and they all thanked me profusely for arranging this wonderful occasion. We were then taken to a locker room behind the gym, which had been made into a temporary holding room where Jackson could catch his breath before going out to greet the students. The assistant principal and the student body president approached me and asked if I could arrange for Jackson first to meet and shake hands with the Student Council, of which I had been a member twenty-five years earlier. I was sure it would be okay, but I said I would ask him first.

As I walked over to him, I could again see him scowling angrily at me as the teachers and students stood eagerly waiting and watching. I couldn't imagine what was the matter. In spite of my unusually high fever and flu, I felt this was a wonderful moment in the campaign. But this most moving experience was marred by a public instance of Jacksonian abuse in the back of the gym that caught me completely by surprise and must have shocked the onlookers. When I made the request, Jackson viciously snarled, "No," and then he launched a barrage of criticism at me for riding with my parents instead of with the press, who were late because the bus driver got lost. I was stunned as I listened to his tirade. It had been becoming increasingly clear on the trip that he had to denigrate and criticize anyone who had just made a positive contribution to his campaign. He could never credit anyone with helping him. Staff were always to be put in their place, and publicly, if possible.

Then he strode angrily past me and the others toward the doorway leading to the gym. Flustered, I apologized to the teacher and students and said that he didn't have time to meet them, as we all rushed behind him. Out on the floor, Jesse Jackson was all smiles and beaming and waving his arms in greeting as the throng of students perched on the bleachers around the gym floor stood and went wild with cheering and applause. They had been waiting all day, and there he finally was, in their midst, seeming so happy to be there. I felt shell-shocked.

The president of the student body, Trent McDevitt, whom I knew, welcomed Jackson, and then he welcomed me as a distinguished graduate of Asheville High School. He proceeded to read a long list of details of my life, and I sat awkwardly awaiting the conclusion, knowing that Jesse was angrily smoldering, as he did when any time was being given to someone else. Finally, Trent concluded and then asked me to introduce my boss, the candidate Jesse Jackson.

Weak from both the fever and the shocking confrontation of a few minutes before, I stood to speak. Then I felt the pride I had come with as I looked around at all those white and black faces in my old alma mater. Speaking as briefly as possible in order to get to Jackson's speech, I said I was very proud to be a graduate of Asheville High School and proud of the distance we had all come in the twenty-five years since I'd graduated, and then I said I was especially proud to be able to come that day as the press secretary for this special and remarkable candidate for President of the United States of America, Jesse Jackson.

Jesse rose and said how happy he was that all of us could be here together that day. He then introduced both his mother and mine, and he explained that though they had come from different cultures in the South, they had both worked hard for the New South and in raising their children. Then he hailed the fact that in 1988 he and I could be working together. He said: "Working together, we represent the old barriers that have come down."

Even seasoned political reporters covering the Asheville visit later said they were moved by this special occasion. National Public Radio's senior political correspondent Linda Wertheimer described our visit there as one of the most moving events of the campaign and later admitted to me that she'd had to hold back tears during the scene at the school and Jackson's and my speeches about the importance of our being there together. Linda and I had been colleagues when I was at NPR, and I knew it was quite an admission for a reporter like her who had covered years of political events in America.

Southern Appalachia was again the location the next day—Thursday, February 25—for a moving campaign appearance by Jesse Jackson. Hazard, in southeastern Kentucky, was one of the last, neglected backwoods of America, and an infinitely more depressed area than western North Carolina. The printed-out "Daily Agenda for Rev. Jesse L. Jackson" described the purpose of the visit: to "highlight Appalachian poverty." After morning fund-raising and speaking in Louisville, the Jackson charter flew southeast to London, Kentucky, and then the entourage made its way by bus over the winding mountain roads to Hazard.

At Hazard High School a thousand men, women and children were waiting to welcome Jesse Jackson. In contrast to other areas in the South, most of this crowd was white—of farming and coal-mining families. The gymnasium was full of signs welcoming Jackson, and many of them were handwritten, misspelling his name as "Jessie."

Jesse launched full swing into his speech about poverty and economic justice for all, and here he looked out and felt that these poor white folks really knew what he was talking about. He again described the New South where there was a "new sense of social justice. No governors sitting in schoolhouse doors. No dogs biting children. We now have public accommodation, and that's progress.

We now have the right to vote, and that's progress. We now have open housing, and that's progress. But what does it matter if you have the right to jump into the pool and there's no water in the pool?"

The crowds were exuberant, and he paused only briefly for their thunderous applause before continuing: "What does it matter if you have the right to check into a motel and you don't have the money to check out? Civil rights must now have as its ally economic justice and economic rights. When profits go up, wages must go up, health care must go up, education must go up."

Then he explained his popular theory of Reaganomics, as he had the day before: "It's called 'reverse Robin Hood.' Taking from the poor and giving to the rich. GE made $10 billion in four years. It wouldn't have been so bad if workers' wages and jobs had also improved. They made $10 billion and paid zero taxes. Got a $100 million tax rebate while workers on unemployment had to pay taxes.

"Friends, that is not fair," Jackson boomed over the roar of the ecstatic crowd, many of whom themselves had been laid off from coal-mining and other jobs and were attempting to subsist on unemployment.

"We need Jackson action," he proclaimed as the throng leapt to their feet in raucous acclamation.

He put himself with these people as he encouraged them: "I grew up in poverty and deprivation. . . . If we the people maintain our self-respect, maintain our dignity, then no mountain is too high, no valley is too deep. Y'all be proud of yourselves. I'm proud of you. . . . Hold on just a little while longer. We the people are going to outlast Reagan."

And then looking directly ahead to Super Tuesday, he issued his rhetorical question: "Who you gonna vote for?" And en masse, the thousand mountaineers roared their response: "You."

Again, as with the day before in Asheville, even some of the toughest reporters admitted that they were dramatically touched by the scene in the gym. White farmers, many of them old men who'd originally opposed integration, reached out to shake this black candidate's hand and even hug him. The white mayor of Hazard presented Jackson with the keys to the town and said: "We want to put him in the Oval Office."

The next stop for Jackson and his entourage of media, staff, Secret Service and local officials was Bailey's, a little roadside diner just down the road from Hazard. The rally had invigorated Jesse, and he burst confidently into the little place and called out: "How're y'all? Vote for me."

Then, fully aware and very pleased that cameras were now following him everywhere, Jesse marched into the kitchen and began enthusiastically tasting the home-style cooking. The film crews and reporters crunched into the tiny room with him. He reminisced aloud about going home to South Carolina for his grandmother's food as he bit into a slice of corn bread and thrust a forkful of dumplings at one correspondent. Then he started mashing some potatoes, remarking: "These look like serious potatoes." And looking over at some other lunch fare, he joked with the cook: "Are these biscuits out of a can?" The owner of Bailey's adamantly defended his establishment's home cooking and exclaimed: "No, those are Lou's biscuits!"

Jesse got his adrenaline from events like these. And he felt especially moved by the crowds of white people who'd come out to welcome him in Appalachia, both in North Carolina and in Kentucky, over the past two days. He felt unusually reflective that afternoon as he rode on the bus with the press and his staff down the winding mountainous roads back to the airport. He felt like talking and unloading his thoughts for publication, and that day he had along the perfect outlet—*The Washington Post*'s Myra MacPherson, who wanted to conduct an in-depth interview that would be splashed across her newspaper's "Style" section on the morning of Super Tuesday. It was a great opportunity, so Jackson decided to talk about more than the usual issues that he discussed with reporters in group or one-on-one interviews.

He kept thinking about those crowds of white people who were now turning out for him across the country. Today, and for the past couple of months, almost everywhere he went Jackson would remind the whites in the audience: "And, my friends, when they fore-close on your farm (or take away your job at the plant) and turn the lights out, we all look amazingly alike in the dark."

On the bus, he turned to explain to MacPherson what he thought was going on, the phenomenon of his campaign. "It's a mutual growth process. What I call 'raising the comfort level.' But I must tell you I have never felt uncomfortable around whites."

The *Post* correspondent expressed some surprise at his claim. She thought this was "an astonishing Jacksonian rewrite of history," and she reminded him that during his 1984 campaign he often "talked movingly in 'we'–'they' terms of growing up black in the South." She recalled some Jackson quotes from that time: "[The chain gang's] white captain—never did have a black captain—was armed and sometimes had a dog. . . . Saturdays I'd sell peanuts and soft drinks at the stadium. Whites all around, drinking liquor. They'd say all kinds of vulgar things, call me nigger, try to short-change me. . . . Couldn't go to the front at the movies, couldn't use the bathrooms. It was *humiliating."*

That February afternoon in 1988, Jackson responded: "I'm not sure I had the anger that was projected. I recall in 1984 saying in my speech [at the Democratic convention] that in the face of racial challenges, people must become better and not bitter. I believed that for a long time." He attributed much to Dr. Martin Luther King, Jr., for teaching him to overcome his bitterness.

Jackson continued to explain what he was thinking after the lunch at the diner: "A black person has to be at least bicultural. You grew up on one side of town, but you worked on the other side, and you learned the manners and the ways of the majority culture. I've always had to live with white America, whether [we were] working as janitors or respecting whites as police and firemen or as the only public officials. So that I had a comfort level with whites. Like that Bailey's place? I was at home."

Then Jesse told MacPherson that he wanted to sleep a little while, implying that he might continue the interview later, and he stretched out his legs on the bus seat in front of him. But before dozing off, he repeated: "I was at home." And then he took one of his typical catnaps—his head bowed down on his chest while the rest of his body remained straight. It was his way of making up for the very little sleep he got at night.

Myra MacPherson thought about what he'd said and wondered whether deep down he really was a racist; and in the article she wrote about the interview, she recalled what one white friend of Jackson's had said: "I don't think Jackson has an ethnic or racist bone in his body, but I think he uses racism like a crucifix. He always holds it out—'You can't hit me because I got this thing here.' If you don't treat him like a mainstream politician, then he is being treated differently because he's black. If you treat him like everyone else and are tough on him, then you're being racist. All these candidates have some crucifix they flash at you all the time. I think Jesse's is more the ploy of a consummate politician, not symptomatic of an ethnic bias."

Later on during the trip, when Jackson woke from his nap, he continued to talk with MacPherson. He had a feeling this time that what he said might finally get published. "A lot has changed in four years. People who voted for Reagan then have subsequently been abandoned and deceived. They really voted for Reagan because they saw him as a fighter. But they missed the implication of Reaganomics. They see me as a fighter—a fighter they did not see themselves as likely being aligned with four years ago.

"Even with those who like the message but can't figure out if they can support me, the message is winning. Dealing with this burden of message and messenger is my own special kind of challenge," he explained. "But there is an outreach today from places that never reached out to what they thought to be the limited agenda of civil rights leadership. The agenda of Dr. King and others was always broader in its outreach than its appreciation was."

Jackson candidly admitted: "I do understand the process better now. In 1984 my basic challenge was to open up the party to be fair. And I put a lot of focus on the Voting Rights Act. That's how we [the Democratic Party] got the Senate back, that's how we beat Bork. I sit on the stage now and no one can challenge my Democratic Party credentials. In 1984 we were encountering so much hostility—from the party, from the media—we had to spend a lot more time fighting for honor, fighting for dignity."

He unabashedly described himself as "the conscience of the party" whose challenge was to become "the candidate of the party." He bragged that the other Democratic candidates now, in February 1988, borrowed his ideas and put them out as their own because they could operate "without the burden of the race factor."

Jackson pointed to the debates of the past few months and boasted: "They study my applause lines. That's a flattering way of conceding the relevance of the message. Dukakis picked up the idea of taking some of the excess in military spending and using it to invest in the infrastructure. Gephardt is beginning to use diversion for reinvestment. Just using [my] language lock, stock and barrel. You're beginning to hear them talk about South Africa more. Beginning to talk about the balance in the Middle East policy."

He explained, using gestures to emphasize his points: "I say Israel and the Palestinians are caught in a death grip. You and I fight in a bear hug. I got a knife and you got a knife. You rippin' out my back, I'm rippin' out your back." And he thrust an invisible knife between the shoulder blades of his listener. "I'm afraid to turn you loose. You're afraid to turn me loose. What you need is somebody to pry you loose."

He then pointed out that since the fighting in the occupied West Bank had escalated in the past three months, many others were also calling for negotiation between the Israelis and the Palestinians. He shrugged. "It's what I've been saying."

And he talked about how he would continue to carry on his campaign in the face of great opposition. "If you grew up as I grew up, you learn not to be afraid of people—or you capitulate. I did not capitulate."

MacPherson asked him what his response was to the charge that he would become a "spoiler" in the Democratic Party if he didn't win the nomination. He adamantly denied it, as he always did. "That's the old enigma-wrapped-in-mystery kind of sick talk. The reality is that when [Senator Edward] Kennedy lost to Carter in 1980, his people walked away, and he did very little. That didn't happen with me in 1984. I lost, and I traveled more between Labor Day and November than Mondale and Ferraro did. And people turned out. And in 1986 I worked and people turned out again. So there's no basis in my past actions. That," he emphasized, "is not my behavior pattern."

Later in the day, the correspondent doggedly pursued her interview and began to ask him about more personal subjects. What about all the current popular psychoanalysis of Jackson that was appearing in print, about his being driven by a "lust for legitimacy" because he was born illegitimate? She was referring primarily to Gail Sheehy's profile of Jackson that had recently appeared in the January issue of *Vanity Fair.* Jackson laughed at this. "I think it's silly. Mama dropped me when I was a baby. I got this soft spot right here." He pointed at his head, and then giggled and repeated: "I think it's silly. All this 'seizing the power and the glory.' Why couldn't the motivation be 'service' and 'justice'? A quest for human dignity or a desire to seek peace? Why must those who seek peace be driven by insanity? Be driven by some perverse motivation, otherwise 'given to sickness'?

"You have to let these opinions bounce off you," he concluded, "like a tackler who failed, and keep on running."

The correspondent forged ahead and asked the two questions he most disliked—about his behavior after Dr. King's assassination and about rumors of his "womanizing." Jackson became annoyed, as he always did when these issues were raised, and his patience with this interview began running out. To the first question, about allegations of his opportunism after King was killed, Jackson stated flatly: "I *never* respond to it. It has no useful or redeeming value. To whom does it matter, that continuous rehearsal of that?"

Then MacPherson decided to risk asking him about rumors of his extramarital affairs. She knew the history of this question with him, how he'd burst into a tirade the year before, just after the Gary Hart–Donna Rice scandal, when a correspondent from the Atlanta *Constitution,* Priscilla Painton, who'd long covered Jackson, asked him to respond to similar rumors about his philandering. Jackson had exploded then, in 1987: "Our marriage is private and it's stable, and I need not comment on the quality of it with you. I think you asking my wife and others about [specific] names . . . is very low journalism."

And nearly a year later Jackson was to be equally adamant about the subject. He decried the public scrutiny of the other candidate, Gary Hart, as "certainly a double standard from the historical standard. It's never been an issue before. You know, the second floor of the White House is off limits to the press. All kinds of things happen on the second floor, but that's your private domain. If it doesn't hurt national interest and national security, it is not a press issue." And with that, Jesse Jackson ended the conversation. And for the rest of the campaign, hardly anyone else dared broach this subject.

On Saturday, February 27, Jackson was in Atlanta for what was, in effect, the last major debate of the Democratic primary season. Up to that point, of the original seven candidates, only one, Bruce Babbitt, had dropped out. Over the succeeding two days, there would be two more debates, one in Houston and one at William and Mary College in Williamsburg, Virginia; but the Atlanta one would get the most coverage. By then there had already been so many debates that Jesse didn't feel he needed the full day of preparation he'd usually tried to get in before the previous ones. Jackson was also tired that morning because he'd arrived in Atlanta so late the night before that he didn't even get to the big Jefferson/Jackson Dinner until after many of the guests had left. But on Saturday morning he did manage to get in some briefing time while dressing, eating breakfast and talking with his two advisers on hand that day, Mark Steitz and Carol O'Cleireacain, who'd flown down from New York.

At 9 A.M., I managed to get him to break away to do two long, pretaped TV interviews, one for the Charles Kuralt show on CBS and the other with NBC's Tom Brokaw for a special. They were both important, and Jesse was eager to do them. They were slated to air a week later, just before Super Tuesday, when Jackson was also scheduled to appear on ABC's Sunday David Brinkley show. It was a coup for him to have all three major networks preparing Jesse Jackson specials.

At 10:30, we were off to attend a fund-raising rally for the Teamsters union. There, waiting for Jackson, was Billy Carter, the once controversial brother of former President Jimmy Carter. Georgia was the home state of the Carter family. Now Billy was quieter and dying of cancer, but he wanted to come out and throw in his hat for Jesse, and the candidate was pleased. For months, Jackson had phoned the former President and talked with him on various matters, asking his advice about running and about party politics. Jimmy Carter had told Jesse all along that he wouldn't endorse any candidate until one became the party's nominee. But he had also told Jesse, as the latter was fond of relating, that he was sure that had his mother, Lillian Carter, still been alive in 1988, she would have openly endorsed Jesse Jackson's candidacy early on. Ms. Lillian had endeared herself to many Americans during her son's years in the White House because of her warmth and energy. As a seventy-year-old woman, she had served in the Peace Corps in India. Her granddaughter Amy, who in 1988 was on leave from her studies at Brown University, where she had been known as an activist, had told the Jacksons she was behind him, but on that day in Atlanta the endorsement of the ailing Billy Carter (who died the next September, 1988) was the first public affirmation by the family.

After the rally Billy and his wife went with Jackson to his suite at the Hyatt Regency Hotel. Southern-style food had been ordered in. It was a quiet time as Jesse and Billy chatted warmly in low tones, and the rest of us devoured the tasty collard greens, corn bread and fried chicken.

Then it was time to go to the big downtown rally for the homeless that was being staged on the occasion of the Atlanta debates. (The Democrats would debate that afternoon, the Republicans the next day.) Billy Carter came along, too, despite his frail health. Gary Hart had called to ask if he could go along with Jesse. By that time he could see the handwriting on the wall and realized he would have to drop out of the race soon. In the meantime, he had decided to hold on through Super Tuesday, but everywhere he went he was usually confronted with boos. He figured he wouldn't be treated so badly if he went to such a rally in the company of Jesse Jackson. The latter knew it wouldn't hurt him to help Hart, especially because the two shared many political views and Jackson would be able to pick up some of his supporters—as he had already picked up some of Babbitt's and would later attract some of Simon's.

At the open-air rally, where thousands of demonstrators had come to publicize the plight of America's homeless—it was a demonstration that resembled those of the sixties—Jackson, Hart and Carter were welcomed by Atlanta's mayor, Andrew Young, and former mayor Maynard Jackson, both longtime black leaders. Neither had endorsed Jesse Jackson in 1984, and this time Andy Young had told him he wouldn't in 1988 because he wanted to remain neutral as the mayor of the site for the Democratic convention. But it was widely believed that Andy Young had never forgotten his annoyance at Jackson's behavior after King's assassination. Young himself had also been touted for years as the possible successor to King. But though he was the controversial United Nations ambassador under President Carter and later mayor of Atlanta, he never displayed the charisma that seemed to push Jackson into the national spotlight. Young and I had known each other when I was a correspondent overseas and he made several forays abroad, and he seemed surprised to see me as Jackson's press secretary. As always seemed to happen when any of us on the staff appeared to have outside connections, Jesse leveled an annoyed glance at me as Andy and I greeted each other as old friends.

From there, we had to rush to get to the new convention center in time for the 3 P.M. debate. Atlanta's debate was getting a lot of media coverage because it was being held at the site of the upcoming Democratic convention in July. Also, it was sponsored by the South's largest newspapers, the *Journal* and the *Constitution,* owned by the wealthy Cox family. Its relatively new editor, William Kovach, had been the Washington bureau chief of *The New York Times* and thus was considered to have influence with his former colleagues at both the *Times* and throughout the Washington news world, thereby attracting coverage of this major debate. Also, since the Democratic debate was being held on Saturday, it would be covered in all the nation's Sunday newspapers the next day.

Among the senior journalists who made a special point of covering the Atlanta debate was Kovach's former boss, A. M. Rosenthal, formerly the *Times*'s executive editor and now a senior columnist. And it was he who picked up on something that few had dared report before. He watched the Democrats that Saturday afternoon, and he said their debates were "intelligent but something was missing." The following week, Rosenthal wrote in a column on March 2: "The white candidates had been treating Mr. Jackson as if he were invisible and his supporters as if they did not exist. On the platform, they almost never talked to him, at him or about him. They never paid him the dignity of challenging anything he said. Nor did they give Southern blacks the courtesy of a straightforward appeal for their votes on primary day." Rosenthal acknowledged that "Mr. Jackson is by far the best speaker of the bunch, Democrat or Republican," but he said it was insulting to both Jackson and his supporters that his views and other qualifications were never questioned. Perhaps it was the effect of Jackson's "holding up the crucifix of racism," or perhaps the other candidates simply imagined that. At any rate, Jesse claimed to welcome Rosenthal's plea that he be treated equally.

After the debate, there were the standard news conferences in another large room in which each candidate, one by one, would step forward and answer reporters' questions about the specific points he had made during the debate. Jesse had left the stage after some of the other candidates and thus was down the line in order of appearance for the news conference. We were standing in the long corridor behind the large conference hall when Jesse ordered me to step inside and tell him who was already there. As I began walking in to check the scene to report back to him, I suddenly felt my breath being knocked out of me from behind. It was Jesse's fist smashing into my back. He was pushing me aside and snarling in my ear, "Get the fuck out of my way." I was stunned, and moved quickly out of his path. I soon realized that he had seen television cameras on other candidates and felt he had to push forward.

Jackson never mentioned his outburst, nor did I. From the news conference, we proceeded to another large ballroom where the *Journal* and the *Constitution* were hosting a lavish reception for the candidates and the special guests for the debate. It was a real mob scene, with elbows flying as people pushed to get to whomever they wanted to speak to and others picked at the hors d'oeuvres on the central tables. Then up came a great bear of a man, Bert Lance, all smiles under his dark tan. He clapped Jesse on the shoulders and told him he'd done a great job.

Bert Lance was Jesse Jackson's best white buddy inside the party. He was always at the other end of the telephone, early mornings and late nights, but he was behind the scenes. For this special weekend he'd driven down to Atlanta from his five-hundred-acre estate, Lancelot, seventy miles away in Calhoun, Georgia. Bert and I walked behind Jesse as the Secret Service guided him through the crowd. When I introduced myself, this fellow Southerner patted me on the back and exclaimed: "Well, I sure am glad to see you along working with Jesse. He needs people like you." I thanked him, and we chased on after Jesse.

The fifty-seven-year-old Lance was the Georgian banker who had been the controversial budget director for President Carter and then was forced to resign in 1977, after only nine months on the job, following a spate of later unproved charges that he was involved in bank fraud. Then, in 1984, Mondale brought him back out of the shadows at the Democratic convention, and Mondale's campaign manager, Bob Beckel, deputized him to work on Jackson, to persuade him not to spoil the party. Lance then befriended Jackson, and the two became pals. Lance was able to feed Jackson real party insider advice. He was always absolutely candid, sometimes brutally so, but Jackson could take it from Lance, and even liked it. Later, in 1988, Beckel, operating as a political consultant, described the Jackson-Lance connection as "one of the unique political marriages in the last couple of decades, and, for the Democratic Party, the most important relationship this year."

Late that night, after Jackson took in thousands of dollars for his campaign at the Knights, a black nightclub in Atlanta, we flew to

Tampa, Florida. The next morning, Sunday, February 28, at 7:30, Jackson would speak at another fund-raising breakfast before we headed over to the studio of the NBC affiliate for a live interview on the *Sunday Today* show. Before the interview, the program aired a special profile of the candidate put together by the show's host, Garrick Utley. We sat in a screening room and watched as the piece unfolded, and Jackson's face became stonier by the second as, once again, the whole story of his performance after the King assassination was retold. As we moved from that room back to the studio where the live cameras were ready to link him up in an interview with Utley in New York, Jackson glared icily at me, clearly blaming me for Utley's piece. Another aide, who knew his moods well, remarked that it was obvious from his look that I'd better stay out of his way for a while.

Monday night, February 29, we made a special trip to New York, for only one reason—to have breakfast the next morning with editors and correspondents of *Newsweek*. Again, this was the subject of a long, ongoing dispute within the Jackson camp about the value of such editorial board meetings. I had continued encouraging them because each time Jackson appeared at one, he performed better, and relations were being established that would ultimately be very useful. Austin and others kept discouraging these meetings, especially, Austin said, in the case of the weekly newsmagazines, *Newsweek, U.S. News* and *Time,* which had previously written so disparagingly of Jackson. I kept arguing that it could help Jackson tremendously if only he would establish collegial relations with the editors, the bosses, and not just rely on the reporting of the hardworking, but ultimately not so powerful, correspondents. It was at the editorial meetings each week—in New York for *Newsweek* and *Time* and in Washington for *U.S. News*—that the decisions were made about the cover and the other stories that would run the coming week. Correspondents could only send in story suggestions and ideas from the road; their bosses at the head offices made the decisions. Jackson agreed with me, but he usually let the argument run a while before final schedules were set—as always, at the last minute.

In the case of *Newsweek,* at the end of February I had learned that the magazine was considering a cover story on either Jackson or Gore, to run immediately after Super Tuesday. Thus, even though we were right in the middle of the Super Tuesday campaigning, it seemed well worth it to go to New York to meet the decision-makers. Jackson's picture on the cover of the national magazine was worth millions in advertising and would propel him from Super Tuesday into the next critical primaries elsewhere in the country. Jesse had said to go ahead and set it up.

For a change, we were actually early for the meeting. The editor-in-chief, Richard (Rick) M. Smith, came down to meet our limousine after he got a call from the Secret Service that we were on our way across town from the Milford Plaza Hotel, where the Jackson team had spent the previous night, to the *Newsweek* skyscraper at 444 Madison Avenue. Smith welcomed Jackson, joking about his amazement that Jackson was there on time, and then he hugged me in greeting. We'd become friends covering stories in the Indian Ocean years before, and later he'd been my boss at *Newsweek.* We were then whisked up the special side elevator to the "Top of the Week" corporate dining room. Jackson was gracious, even though he was a bit uncomfortable at having to correct the Executive Editor Stephen Smith, who seemed to think Jesse had grown up in Philadelphia. The next week, after the Super Tuesday vote, the *Newsweek* editors weighed a decision about whether to put Albert Gore or Jesse Jackson on their cover, and they chose the black Southerner over the white. Some of Jackson's staff would later complain about the content of the article, but Jesse knew that that cover picture was all that counted.

7

SUPER
TUESDAY

"**D**r. Martin Luther King, Jr.,
lies only a few miles from us tonight. Tonight he must feel good as
he looks down upon us," Jesse Jackson would say months later at
the Democrats' Atlanta convention in July.

But Jackson had used nearly the same words earlier in his campaign. On Sunday, March 6, two days before the critical Super
Tuesday election, Jackson spoke at King's former church in Atlanta, and he recalled King's famous "dream" speech twenty-five
years before. Jackson would refer to it then in March, and later in
July he would also say: "We sit here together, a rainbow coalition—
the sons and daughters of slaves sitting together around a common
table, to decide the direction of our party and our country. His
heart would be full tonight."

A quarter of a century earlier, Dr. King had led the history-
making civil rights March on Washington. There, on August 28,
1963, he stood at the Lincoln Memorial facing the Washington
Monument and the White House, and he had voiced the great
dream: "It is a dream deeply rooted in the American meaning of its

creed, 'We hold these truths to be self-evident, that all men are created equal.' I have a dream that one day on the red hills of Georgia, sons of former slaves and the sons of former slave owners will be able to sit down together at the table of brotherhood. I have a dream that one day even the state of Mississippi, a state sweltering with the heat of injustice, sweltering with the heat of oppression, will be transformed into an oasis of freedom and justice. I have a dream that my four little children will one day live in a nation where they will not be judged by the color of their skin, but the content of their character."

Jesse Jackson in 1988 was taking long strides to make King's dream come true. His very campaign was a tribute to the valiant groundwork King and others had laid. Jackson would say later at the Atlanta convention: "As a testament to the struggles of those who have gone before; as a legacy for those who will come after; as a tribute to the endurance, the patience, the courage of our forefathers and mothers; as an assurance that their prayers are being answered, their work has not been in vain, and hope is eternal, tomorrow night my name will go into nomination for the presidency of the United States of America."

That speech was made on July 19, 1988. Jesse Jackson had been laying the groundwork for it from the beginning of the election year. But for him, the most important period, the most critical elections were those primaries in the South, the New South, on March 8.

Jesse Jackson, born in the Old South of segregation, had come of age during the American civil rights movement and had worked with Dr. Martin Luther King, Jr., to begin to make his dream come true.

Jesse Jackson had always wanted to be the next great leader of his own people, African-Americans. He wanted to be legitimately recognized as the heir apparent to Martin Luther King. But he had never been accepted by King's family and close disciples, who were suspicious of him and his motives. There had been particularly bad blood between him and King's widow, Coretta Scott King. When Jackson had made his first run for the presidency in 1984, she had let it be known publicly that she refused to support him because she believed "Jesse hasn't changed" from the way he'd behaved with her husband before and on the day after he died. She would never forget, and until Jackson's second run for the presidency, she had, at least symbolically, held her husband's torch before the eyes of most black Americans.

Then Jackson ran again, in 1988. Blacks across America, and especially in the New South, were supporting him overwhelmingly. But still Jackson felt he needed a sign, even perhaps if it wasn't real, that Mrs. King was behind him. It was important for black America to see.

Thus, two days before the massive multi-state voting on Super Tuesday, Jackson decided that the most symbolic place for him to be on that Sunday, March 6, would be King's own church, the now historic Ebenezer Baptist Church in Atlanta. There the young King had begun preaching and spreading his dreams of the nonviolent civil rights movement. There his body had been buried after his tragic death in 1968, and the church had become a shrine for black America. There Jesse Jackson knew he should be on that important Sunday before the election which he hoped would finally drape King's mantle on his shoulders.

Jackson was taking a chance. He didn't know until the last minute whether King's widow would attend the church where he would be preaching. She had always gone there regularly whenever she was in Atlanta, but perhaps she would find an excuse not to be present that day. On the other hand, perhaps she was beginning to recognize that as Jesse Jackson became more and more powerful, she needed to be seen with him as much as he needed her approval. When he saw her out in the congregation that Sunday afternoon and welcomed her, he knew his opportunity had come. After the service, he invited her publicly to join him in laying a wreath on Dr. King's grave outside the church. She had no alternative.

Jackson finally got the picture he'd been wanting: Jesse Jackson and Coretta King together laying a wreath and saying prayers at the tomb of Martin Luther King. It didn't matter, he and his black aides said later, that she hadn't verbally endorsed him. What was important was that that photograph would go across America, and most blacks would believe that she was supporting him and that the two had finally buried the hatchet and were united. Jackson was right. Her widely publicized appearance side by side with Jackson at her husband's grave symbolized endorsement regardless of her continuing distrust and disapproval of the man. From that time forth, there was no more need to beg for or wait and hope for Mrs. King to give him her nod. Jackson had become the undisputed leader of black America, first in the South and later all across the country.

In the week leading up to Super Tuesday, Jackson used every opportunity to teach people about the history of the American civil rights movement. He pointed out the great changes over the past quarter century, and no one could deny them.

Jackson also knew something, as do most true Southerners, about the deep kinship the people of the South feel with one another, whether they are black or white, racists or not. He also knew, as again do most true Southerners, that they all, black and white, are proud of the New South and they can look back with a sense of accomplishment at the progress they have made.

This was something that the Northerner, Michael Dukakis, failed to understand months later, in August, when as presidential nominee he visited Philadelphia, Mississippi, and did not mention the tragedies of the civil rights movement that had taken place on the outskirts of that town. But if he'd been better informed, as Jackson pointed out, he would have appreciated the importance of the place for both whites and blacks. Three civil rights workers had been killed there in the sixties, and while the people of Philadelphia weren't proud of it, they recognized the enormous strides they had taken since then to end racial violence and to become integrated. Mississippi was a new place in 1988, and Mississippians were proud of it.

Alabamans, white and black, were also very proud of where they'd come since the sixties and before. On Wednesday, March 2, we flew to Selma, Alabama, the site of the historic "Bloody Sunday" march to win voter registration rights for blacks. The coming Sunday would be the twenty-third anniversary of that milestone in the civil rights movement. Although he wouldn't be there on the actual anniversary because he knew it was better strategy to preach that day in Dr. King's old church in Atlanta, it was important, Jesse believed, to go back to Selma close to that time.

Selma was also especially important for him because it was there that he had first become actively involved with King's Southern Christian Leadership Conference. When Jesse had heard and seen the news of the fighting between the civil rights marchers and the Alabama police—blacks being beaten, tear-gassed, clubbed with nightsticks and jabbed with electric cattle prods—he left his studies at the Chicago Theological Seminary and drove down South to join the movement. In a sense, that event had been a turning point for Jackson, a kind of conversion. Although he had been active in local civil rights efforts while a college student in North Carolina and then during his time in the seminary in Chicago, it was "Bloody Sunday" in Selma that jolted him out of his relatively quiet, scholarly life into the civil rights movement led by Dr. King.

Jackson liked to reminisce about that trip. He would recall the menacing car that appeared to follow him for miles as he traveled south. He described his feelings: "We had been driving all night, and they had been following us all the way to Montgomery—all night, a long, dark night. The fear made it darker."

At Montgomery, the state capital, Jackson and his fellow students headed west toward Selma, their destination less than a hundred miles away. Among those Chicago seminarians who had heeded the call with Jackson was a young white named Gary Massoni, who years later, in 1988, became Jackson's chief scheduler for his presidential campaign. They had missed the worst day of the bloody battles between the integrationists and segregationists, but the civil rights struggle was still going on when they arrived a couple of days later, and the enthusiastic and angry young Jesse Jackson threw himself into the center of the action.

One reporter, Betty Washington, then with the Chicago *Daily Defender,* a black newspaper, later described the scene outside

Brown's Chapel Church in Selma, where she had been surprised to see this unknown young man emerge. On the grounds all around the church, hundreds of marchers had camped and were listening to inspirational speeches by various SCLC members, including the battered black leader John Lewis, now a U.S. congressman from Georgia. Washington recalled: "Up popped Jesse. I thought it was strange that he would be making a speech, when he was not on the SCLC staff and had not been included in any of the strategy meetings. He just seemed to come from nowhere . . . but he spoke so well." Other SCLC members seemed to resent the "pushy" intrusion of this upstart, but Jesse ignored their resentment and from that moment on, he moved quickly ahead within Dr. King's organization.

On "Bloody Sunday" itself, the white mayor of Selma, Joe T. Smitherman, had stood vehemently with his police force to try to prevent the civil rights workers from reaching the Edmund Pettus Bridge, which crossed the Alabama River at Selma on the way to Montgomery. All across America, the young mayor's picture flashed on television screens, and he became a symbol of white racism, a stereotype of the South in the 1960s.

Twenty-three years later Smitherman was still the mayor of Selma, but in March 1988 he came out to welcome Jesse Jackson back. Together they walked through the dusty streets of a Selma housing development, and stood in front of a shack surrounded by poor blacks as the mayor said he needed federal assistance to help these, his people. He praised Jackson for doing more than any other national politician to bring attention to the social and economic problems of America today. He warmly thanked Jackson for coming that day and putting the spotlight again on his town, this time in a positive way. Jackson said that together they were all working to build the New South, where there would soon be economic as well as racial justice.

Together, the white mayor and the black presidential candidate walked onto the Edmund Pettus Bridge, and together they explained to reporters what had happened that horribly memorable day back in 1965. The mayor publicly acknowledged that he'd stood on the wrong side in the early sixties. Jackson, in turn, moved by the mayor's joining him and extending such goodwill, said it was time "to forgive each other, redeem each other, and move on."

A Pulitzer Prize-winning journalist, David Broder of *The Washington Post*, was among those traveling in the Jackson entourage that day in Selma. Later, in an article published on Super Tuesday, he reflected on Jackson's 1988 campaign: "To see and hear Jackson with a predominantly black crowd, in Greenville, Starkville or Selma, is to be reminded that politics is about energy and emotion, not just abstract ideas. It's a lesson Michael Dukakis and Albert Gore, Jr., and even Dick Gephardt, would pay Jackson to teach them."

That afternoon we made a special side trip from Selma to Austin, Texas, more than a thousand miles away. Texas's Commissioner for Agriculture, Jim Hightower, another populist like Jackson, had finally decided to give his full, public support to Jesse Jackson. For months, Jackson had been telephoning Hightower at every opportunity to talk politics, talk about how similar their views were and let him know how valuable his support would be. Hightower's endorsement was the first from a white elected official in the South.

On Wednesday afternoon, March 2, in the newly refurbished legislative chamber of the old Texas state capitol, Jim Hightower, whom many expected to run for the U.S. Senate in 1990, read aloud his "statement of conscience." Hightower, in his Texan nasal twang, gave his "whole hog" endorsement to the man he'd come to know over the past few years and whom he believed was the outstanding presidential candidate that year.

Some Texans maintained that Hightower's stance was political suicide. Others praised his act. Hightower later told us that his father, a George Wallace supporter in 1972, had telephoned him immediately after his televised announcement. "Daddy's never been a diehard fighter for civil rights . . . but he said he'd been watching Jesse Jackson on TV and was impressed that nobody could trip him up. He said the important thing was that I took the stand, I stood up for my convictions."

Another call Hightower got that day, he later recalled, was from one of his predecessors on the Texas Agriculture Commission, John C. White, also a former chairman of the Democratic Party. He quoted White as congratulating him: "There are only two or three times in your career when you get a chance to stand up and do something that you will remember. You've just done one of yours."

Jesse Jackson was ecstatic with Hightower's decision. The Texan was giving him the big break he'd been hoping for—elected white support. Within months, Hightower became a permanent fixture on the Jackson campaign trail and was soon known for ridiculing "Democrats who are afraid to talk like Democrats" and for his oft-repeated line: "There's nothing in the middle of the road but yellow stripes and dead armadillos." Always, no matter whether he was dressed in a suit or in jeans and cowboy shirt, this short, wiry Texan wore his boots and hat. For the campaign, he seemed the perfect person, white, down-home, country, to introduce the more serious black politician, Jesse Jackson.

Jesse Jackson and Jim Hightower had hit it off well the first time they'd met back in 1986 at a Rainbow Coalition conference on family farms. They were almost the same age, Jackson only one year older. Not only did they share political viewpoints, but they also were both great speakers. Jackson, who considered himself with some justification to be America's greatest living orator, was impressed with Hightower's talent for public speaking. Jesse remarked that day on the "little white guy who could talk that talk." Hightower was also particularly noted for the sense of humor he displayed in his speeches. He was one person who could make Jackson laugh and say: "Wish I'd said that." Jesse soon began to recognize that this populist had power among the whites, blacks, rednecks and Hispanics of the great state of Texas, and he knew he could use Hightower's support. By the next year, in 1987, Jackson had bestowed on him the honor (which its recipients sometimes called "questionable") of putting him on his early-morning telephone list. From then on, Hightower said, "if it was after midnight or before six [in the morning], it was going to be Jackson."

Like Georgia's Bert Lance, Jim Hightower was the other white man who would become a constant companion and adviser to Jesse Jackson during the 1988 campaign. With such men, Jackson never showed his mean streak. Instead, he deferred to them and valued their advice. They were treated as equals and buddies, and Hightower was more and more impressed the closer they became. He once remarked: "As I watched him up close, my feelings strengthened, from interest in and appreciation for what he was saying, to respect for his intellect and passionate commitment to the issues. I became convinced that this isn't just a guy who has hit upon a good scam and is taking it for a ride."

In spite of the euphoria the Jackson team felt that day about finally capturing Hightower's endorsement, there was some growing friction within the traveling group that had not existed before. Jackson's longtime aides, those who'd been traveling the longest with him, attributed the new tension to the presence on the road of Bob Borosage. Borosage had taken a leave of absence from his post at the Institute for Policy Studies in Washington and had officially come on board with us the day before, on March 1, when Jackson had passed through the nation's capital. He was to be Jackson's chief policy adviser and he planned to travel much of the time with Jackson. The other traveling issues adviser, Mark Steitz, had left the group that day to take a few days off at home in Washington. Both were white men in whom Jackson presumed expertise, and they got on well with him and seemed to have a calming effect on him. As with Steitz when he was around, Jackson wanted Borosage at his side at all times, constantly calling "Bob, Bob, get Bob here," as he had previously called "Steitz, Steitz, where's Steitz? I want Steitz." Mark, with his good humor, worked well with the rest of the traveling team.

But when Borosage showed up, he immediately wanted to take control and even appeared to think he was the traveling campaign manager, since Gerry Austin didn't travel with Jackson all the time and wasn't along the first four days that Borosage joined up as a permanent adviser. Borosage had originally—in mid-1987—been offered Austin's post and had turned it down, but now Jackson seemed to have given him authority over the other staff members.

Austin never acted in an authoritarian manner, and the traveling staff began bristling at Borosage's imperious commands. When I snapped back at him the day after he'd started traveling with us and said he was interfering in my business and I didn't appreciate it, he spluttered that I was "overly sensitive." But after that he didn't bother me very much as I tried to do my job, and we managed to get on well. Kgosie Matthews and Bill Morton muttered incessantly against him but seldom told him off directly. Sometimes they would retort, however, that he had no right telling them what to do. The candidate, usually within earshot, acted as if he were unaware of the problems Borosage was creating.

By the time the real campaign manager, Gerry Austin, rejoined us on Friday, March 4, tales of Borosage's attempted usurpation of his role had reached him, and he was on the alert and prepared to put a stop to what was creating unnecessary tension within a group that had previously managed to get along well together, despite Jackson's own mercurial moods. After two days, Gerry finally reached his limit and decided to put Borosage in his place as soon as possible.

An unexpected opportunity came on Sunday night, March 6, on the last flight of the day, from Louisiana to Texas. Three traveling reporters invited Austin to join them for dinner that night in Dallas, along with Bob Borosage, whom they'd already invited. Austin told them bluntly that if they wanted him to come, then it would have to be him alone, without Borosage. He stated flatly that he, Austin, the campaign manager, was the one to discuss strategy and organization with them; Borosage's domain was policy, and Austin didn't interfere with his job. The reporters wanted to talk more with Austin then, so one of them walked to the front of the plane, where Borosage was sitting behind Jackson, and informed him that they couldn't go for dinner with him after all. Bob looked puzzled and then shrugged his shoulders and leaned over to whisper what had happened to his friend Barbara Shaler, who had joined the group two days earlier. She was a labor relations expert who had advised Jackson in the past. He then leaned back in his seat as if sloughing off the blatant slight.

By the time Super Tuesday came around, however, Gerry Austin ordered Borosage to start keeping a lower profile and not to travel with Jackson except on special occasions. The week after Super Tuesday, traveling without Borosage made life on the road go a lot more smoothly. But the smaller corps was also concerned that Jackson would learn that one of those reporters wrote in *The Washington Post* about the friction that had visibly erupted within the Jackson camp between his campaign manager and his chief policy adviser, without naming the latter. Of course, Jackson learned about it but, for the time being, he simply stored the knowledge of the bad blood between the two men in his mind for later use.

That last week before Super Tuesday, Jackson became increasingly tense about his and the campaign's relations with the traveling media. He simply didn't like anyone on his staff talking with them. Even Borosage, whom he consulted constantly when no reporters were around, was chastised for interjecting comments when Jackson was talking with reporters. Bob then held his tongue. The rest of us knew to keep our mouths shut when he was talking. Usually, as I'd been instructed, I would sit near Jackson and the reporter and record the interview, and advisers, such as Steitz, would sit quietly nearby, listening in case they later needed to correct Jackson privately or to advise him on some point that was raised.

Several times that week, when I was in the back of the plane talking with reporters quite innocuously or even arranging the very interviews that he so wanted to give to as many reporters as I could line up for him, Jesse suddenly got up from his seat and marched past me, glaring angrily. There were several occasions, during the many flights that week, when he stomped past me in the aisle, and even though I moved out of the way to give him room, he stepped squarely on my feet, and it hurt. The first time it happened, I was so shocked that I figured it must have been an accident, but several more times convinced me, sadly, that he'd done it on purpose, to signal me to quit talking. Incredible as that seemed, I realized this action was not dissimilar to his socking me in the back the Saturday before at the Atlanta debate.

Reporters could not help but notice the angry glares Jackson would level at any of us talking with them, and a few of them remarked openly that they could see that this candidate had his staff so terrified and intimidated that most were afraid to speak to the press, even to answer basic questions. One morning that week, Friday, March 4, in San Antonio, during a "block walk" in a Hispanic neighborhood, correspondent Jay Levine, of the ABC-TV affiliate station in Chicago, was asking me simple questions about how the campaign was going. My answers were positive, of course, but in no way revealing of any inside strategy or secret. Jay kept looking nervously over my shoulder to where Jackson was standing behind me. Afterward, Jay, who had been traveling with us from the beginning of the campaign and knew Jackson well, said apologetically to me: "Perhaps we shouldn't have done this interview. Jesse was sure glaring nastily at you the whole time." When we went to Chicago the next week, the Reverend Willie Barrow, who was then heading PUSH for Jackson, exclaimed immediately when she saw me: "You sure gave a good interview the other night. That kind of thing will really help the campaign." I thanked her, but I thought how Jesse still wouldn't have liked my speaking at all on television. I had early decided it wasn't worth it and tried to avoid such interviews.

From the start Gerry Austin, as campaign manager, would give interviews, but Jackson always got miffed when he did. Often, though, Gerry was not on the road and would give them from Chicago, and Jackson would only learn about them later and would sometimes flatly voice his disapproval, not of what Gerry said but of the fact that he'd spoken publicly. In those early months, however, Austin would stand up to Jackson and tell him there was nothing wrong with certain aides, such as himself, talking with the media about his campaign.

Gerry later told how, during that week before Super Tuesday when he was traveling with Jackson again and was giving an interview to a top reporter on the campaign plane, Jackson marched back, glared at him and ordered him to get up at once and come up front to talk with him. Gerry recalled that he then went forward and told Jackson in no uncertain terms: "Look, Jesse, you can't go and try to humiliate me in front of reporters. You've got to learn to accept that others can speak for you, and you shouldn't always try to stop it." Jesse left him alone, by and large, for a while, Gerry said.

Jackson himself loved to project the image that he was the reporters' friend, in contrast to his staff, which he said was anti-press. Thus, as he had done earlier that week on a bus between Baltimore and Washington, D.C., he would publicly lambast me if there was no food provided for the traveling press corps, even though he knew it wasn't my job to buy the food and bring it on board. Also, the campaign travel coordinators were under orders to save money. By the end of that last week before Super Tuesday, the food situation, indeed the actual lack of provision of food on some flights, had become so bad that it was even mentioned in some news stories about the campaign. Finally, the traveling media presented a petition to Jackson demanding that they be fed. He then signed the petition himself with a great flourish, as if he had had nothing to do with there being no food.

Jesse Jackson always carried on this kind of love-hate relationship with the media. He said the campaign had to cater to the press. "We are here for them," he would say. "We have to take care of their needs." Yet his contempt for the media and his desire to lord it over them was often reflected in his showing up late for live broadcast interviews and editorial board meetings. Often, as I would be the only one pushing Jackson to get to an interview on time, he would snap at me: "Calm down. It's only TV." Then he would saunter in, sometimes a few minutes late, but all smiles, as if he were above the laws of precision required by modern technology.

That last week before the Southern primaries Jackson was thrown briefly off balance by a surprise question from one journalist. On the afternoon of March 4, as we were flying from Odessa, in the far west of Texas, to Miami, Florida, a *Washington Post* correspondent, David Maraniss, asked him to "assume the role of President Jackson and describe what you would do in the first days of your administration." Maraniss reported that "Jackson first treated the question as a joke, pulling his hat over his eyes before giving it serious consideration."

Jackson did seem unusually taken aback, I realized as I saw him look anxiously across the aisle toward Bob Borosage, as if asking for help, though he'd only the day before warned him not to interrupt his interviews. I knew that Jackson was wary of this reporter in the first place, because Maraniss had written earlier articles he viewed as critical. But I saw that Jackson was surprised that finally a reporter was treating him as he'd been demanding, as a serious, viable candidate seeking the presidency of the United States. It was a kind of breakthrough, all of us listening realized, and then Jesse projected himself into the imaginary role. It was the first real chance to spell out his agenda.

The content of Jackson's response was published the following Monday, March 7. The headline for the article in the *Post* that day before Super Tuesday was: "Jackson's Agenda Rooted in World View of Villains and Victims." Maraniss faithfully reported: Jackson "said his first step would be to convene a bipartisan domestic summit conference at Camp David focusing on the federal deficit. Mayors, governors and investment bankers would be invited along with members of Congress. Among the proposals President Jackson would present at the summit: raise the taxes of the richest percentile of Americans; restore many of the corporate taxes cut in 1981; demand that Europe and Japan pay more for their defense; borrow against public pension funds to rebuild America with affordable housing and energy-efficient transit.

"His second domestic priority would be to stem the flow of drugs into the United States. He said he would appoint a drug czar, 'similar to President Carter's energy czar,' to deal with what he considers 'the no. 1 threat to the character of this country.' To combat drugs, Jackson would increase funding for the Coast Guard and Border Patrol, provide countries dependent on drug crops with incentives to grow alternative crops, increase rehabilitation programs for drug users and beef up drug education programs.

"The foreign policy of a Jackson administration, he said, would be based on the principles of self-determination, international law and human rights. He would end all U.S. support of the contras in Nicaragua and promote a nonaggression pact among Central American countries. He never would have allowed the invasion of Grenada. The Central Intelligence Agency's mission would be to gather intelligence. He would eliminate all funding of the Strategic Defense Initiative.

"But the essence of Jackson's foreign policy rests with his confidence in his skill as a negotiator—the talent he displayed in 1984 by getting Navy pilot Lt. Robert Goodman released in Syria and political prisoners set free from Castro's Cuba. His approach to the tensions in the Middle East would be highly personal.

"Jackson believes that the only way to end the hostilities in the Middle East is by 'ridding Israel of the burden of occupation.' He would do that by helping create a Palestinian state—unarmed, he says—while at the same time guaranteeing Israel's security. The deal would be struck at a Camp David-type meeting among the leaders of the United States, Israel and the Palestinians. 'Major-league negotiations,' he said. 'No emissaries.'

"When asked how he would persuade the Israelis to sit down at the negotiating table with PLO leader Yasir Arafat, Jackson expressed confidence that he would find a way. He noted that Reagan began his administration by calling the Soviet Union an evil empire and is ending it by negotiating missile reductions with the Soviets, implying that past rhetoric does not always dictate future decisions.

"'Why is Arafat alive today?' Jackson asked. He answered the question by saying Arafat is alive only because 'America and Israel agreed he was more valuable alive than dead.' "

Then Maraniss raised questions about whether Jackson had the management skills to be President. The reporter repeated the charge that many leveled regarding the fact that Jackson had never held elected office and during his years at PUSH he gained a reputation as a "good idea man with weak follow-through." Jackson looked annoyed but listened as Maraniss proceeded. He asked what his response was to the suggestion, often made by his critics in the Democratic Party, that he would resemble Reagan too much in not paying attention to daily details. The irony of that criticism was that others, especially his staff, who were constantly frustrated by Jackson's refusal to delegate and his preoccupation at times with details of his schedule, believed that he would also resemble Jimmy Carter in his overattention to minutiae.

Jackson responded that afternoon on the plane by saying the comparison with President Reagan was unfair and disclaiming any similarity, pointing in particular to the recent Iran-Contra scandal of the Reagan administration. He said: "Reagan is not faulted for operating above the minutiae, but for immorality. People found his management style refreshing. The management style was not the problem. The problem was the direction they took, the contempt for other branches of government, the sleaze factor of trading arms for hostages."

So often Jackson had repeated the same ideas, the same lines, but they were seldom reported. Now, finally, he had been given a framework in which many of them could be presented, and correspondents like Maraniss and news organizations like the *Post* were beginning to report his answers. Jackson and the rest of us on staff were delighted.

That last week running up to Super Tuesday, from Wednesday, March 2, through Tuesday, March 8, Jesse Jackson and his traveling team flew back and forth across the South. Touching down in an average of five cities per day, we visited eleven of the fourteen Southern states which had Super Tuesday primaries or caucuses. The remarkable orator, Jesse Jackson, gave at least one and usually several speeches in Alabama, Texas, Mississippi, Arkansas, Oklahoma, Florida, Louisiana, North Carolina, Maryland and Georgia.

Even in Tennessee, where Jackson had no scheduled speaking engagement that last week, he talked to the local television when we spent the night in Memphis on our way across the Mississippi River for a rally in West Memphis, Arkansas. The campaign had decided to ignore Tennessee that last week of campaigning because Albert Gore was its "favorite son" and was predicted to come in first in his home state. Jackson had often been to that state earlier, and his strategists expected he would keep his solid corps of black support to place second. Virginia and Kentucky were the only Southern states holding Super Tuesday primaries which Jackson didn't visit that week. He'd gone to Kentucky's Appalachia the week before, and the campaign staff had no reasonable hope of winning the rest of the state. As for Virginia, he'd already visited there a number of times earlier, and he knew he had a solid support group there which would give him a first place in the election.

South Carolina and West Virginia were the two Southern states holding their caucus and primary, respectively, at later dates. As for the non-Southern states, like Washington, Hawaii, Idaho and Nevada, also holding primaries on Super Tuesday, the campaign decided there simply wasn't enough time to make side trips to visit them. The South was Jackson's critical region, and all our energy had to go there at that time.

In the last weeks before the big day, there had been a lot of discussion between Jackson and his traveling team on the one side and Austin and scheduler Massoni back in Chicago on the other about where he should be, physically, on the night of Super Tuesday. There was initially the view that he should be in Atlanta, the city regarded as the capital of the New South and also the site of the Democrats' summer convention. Then there was some thought given to going on to Chicago that night and being there to signal Jackson's moving on to Illinois, the next primary after Super Tuesday. But the strongest feeling from the beginning was that Jackson should be in Texas at the end of the Southern swing and should hold his "victory party" in the state's largest city, Houston.

Texas was the largest state in both size and population of all those voting on Super Tuesday, and it was the most important state in terms of delegate numbers. Most polls were predicting that the Democratic winner in the Texas caucus would be Michael Dukakis, who had millions of dollars to spend on television advertising and organization and who also happened to speak fluent Spanish, which won him great popularity with the large Hispanic minority of Texas. The predictions had Jackson placing second, close to Gore, but there was still a chance, according to the Jackson campaign strategists, that he could win. Texas also presented a special problem in that its caucus system required that the voters go twice to the polling place—first in the morning to cast their ballots and then again in the evening to stand up and be counted for their preference. Most observers didn't find the system very democratic, but it was what still existed that year and candidates had to work with it. Jackson was especially skilled in encouraging his supporters to go out and vote. In this case, he had to remind them to go twice. Thus, his presence in "the great state of Texas" was perhaps crucial in those last two days.

Jackson was wound even more tightly than usual those last forty-eight hours. Tuesday was the big day he'd been working toward for years. For the first time since the campaign began, we began picking up more important supporters who joined the bandwagon and flew along on the plane to be part of Jesse's entourage. The liberal white Tennessee Democrat John Jay Hooker, who had worked with the Kennedys in the sixties and later made an unsuccessful gubernatorial run in his state, had flown to Little Rock the week before to announce his endorsement of Jackson, and he then rejoined the traveling campaign in Texas on Monday, March 7. But the mood was tense and Jackson acted angry anytime the staff and press spoke with each other. Jackson had always cast an angry glare at me whenever the gregarious John Jay told him how our families had been longtime friends in Nashville, and this day was no exception. Another endorsement had just come on March 7—from a white Democrat and noted feminist, Sissy Farenthold, who had years before made an unsuccessful gubernatorial bid in Texas and had been suggested as Jimmy Carter's running mate in 1976. Jim Hightower and Jackson's old buddy the Hispanic former governor Toney Anaya of New Mexico, who had supported him in 1984, came on board, too, as well as California's celebrity disc jockey Casey Kasem and his modishly dressed wife, a blond version of the black singer Grace Jones. Jackson seemed annoyed whenever the press wanted to interview any of these newcomers, and rather than understanding that those interviews with Hightower, Farenthold, Hooker, Anaya or Kasem enhanced his own story, he kept glaring and frowning anytime one of them went to the back of the plane to talk with the reporters.

In Houston that night at a rally, another longtime friend and supporter, Marion Barry, the controversial black mayor of Washington, D.C., arrived to join the team for the last twenty-four hours. Barry had been one of few major black politicians who had endorsed Jackson in 1984. Barry and I hadn't seen each other in twenty-three years, since the time we had had breakfast in Manhattan to discuss work with the Student Nonviolent Coordinating Committee (SNCC). Jackson just grunted when Marion and I told him about it, and it once more became clear that Jackson simply did not want anyone who worked with him in any way to have any important connections that weren't directly through and with him. That night, however, after leaving Texas and flying to Alabama, Jesse felt very much the center of attention when he was cheered by almost ten thousand people who had come to hear him speak during an Al Green concert in the Birmingham Civic Center. It was a roaring send-off for Jesse Jackson on the eve of Super Tuesday.

The next night, back in Houston, Jesse Jackson was nervous as he began to get the polling results. He was clearly a victor in five states and came in second in all the rest. Gore also won five states, but Dukakis took seven. Neither took as many seconds. Jackson placed second overall in the number of delegates won. Even the old Texas politician John Connally, the former Democrat turned Republican, stopped by backstage in one of the improvised network television studios to greet and congratulate Jackson.

It was Jesse's night, but inevitably scheduling caused confusion. The "victory speech" had been planned for one time that turned out not to meet the networks' demands. Rather than asking that Gerry Austin come talk with him about it, Jackson, in his usual way, simply asked me for the facts and then asked Bob Borosage, who was always at his elbow, to help him make a decision. It turned out to be a mistake in that it caused confusion and gave evidence of disorganization. Then Jackson became furious and began blaming me for the mix-up, but Gerry Austin showed up and told him it wasn't my fault, that it was his for asking Borosage to make a determination which was clearly something Austin himself should have been called in to handle. Jackson and the rest of us were upset by the appearance of disorganization and last-minute changes. Mark Steitz, who was there too, was annoyed because he had been constantly advising Jackson to leave the scheduling to the schedulers. And Gerry Austin was frustrated because, once again, Jackson behaved as he customarily did, by asking whoever was standing nearest to help him make major tactical decisions. Austin became adamant that Borosage should stick only to policy advice and get out of campaign management. Sadly, for all of us, on the night we should have been so pleased with the good results of the long-awaited day, we were all left with annoyance at the unjustified criticism and chaos left by Jackson as he walked out into the crowds of cheering well-wishers at his "victory party."

One thing I felt pleased about, however, was that that evening I had received a telephone call from NBC anchorwoman Connie Chung making a first request for a special interview with Jesse Jackson—for the summer convention in Atlanta. Certainly, I told her. It was a step in the right direction. That night all the networks interviewed Jackson, and again the next morning starting at 6 A.M. Jackson didn't say so, but he seemed proud of the distance he'd come with the media since Iowa a month earlier.

8

THE SOUTH CAROLINA CAUCUS: THE ILLINOIS PRIMARY

"Why can I challenge you in this way? 'Jesse Jackson, you don't understand my situation. You've been on television. You don't understand. I see you with the big people. You don't understand my situation.' I understand. You see me on TV, but you don't really know what makes me me. They wonder, 'Why does Jesse run?' Because they see me running for the White House, they don't see the house I'm running from.

"Writers were not always outside my door. When I was born late one afternoon, October 8, in Greenville, South Carolina, no writers asked my mother her name. Nobody chose to write down our address. My mama was not supposed to make it, and I was not supposed to make it. You see, I was born of a teenage mother, who was born of a teenage mother. I understand. I know abandonment, and people being mean to you, and saying you're nothing and nobody and can never be anything. I understand.

"Jesse Jackson is my third name. I'm adopted. When I had

no name, my grandmother gave me her name. My name was Jesse Burns, and I was twelve. So I wouldn't have a blank space, she gave me a name, to hold me over. I understand when nobody knows your name. I understand when you have no name. I understand. I wasn't born in the hospital. Mama didn't have insurance. I was born in the bed, in a house. I really do understand. I lived in a three-room house, bathroom in the back yard, slop jar by the bed, no hot and cold running water. I understand. Wallpaper used for decoration? No. For a windbreaker. I understand. I'm a working person's person. It doesn't matter whether you're black or white. I understand work. I wasn't born with a silver spoon in my mouth. I had a shovel programmed for my hand."

Jesse Jackson, when he ran for President in 1988 at the age of forty-six, had two hometowns, "two houses" he was running from for the White House. They were in different states, two totally different worlds of the United States. One was Greenville, South Carolina, where he'd been born in 1941, been educated through high school and made his home until after he got married and moved North after graduation from college in 1963. Greenville, of course, would always be home, as the place where one grows up in the South usually remains for most Southerners. Then, as a married adult, Jackson and his young wife moved to Chicago, Illinois, where in 1963 he enrolled at the Chicago Theological Seminary, and settled down for a quarter of a century. Chicago became Jackson's adopted hometown, and like many Southerners, black and white, in the late twentieth century, he was at home in both worlds—the slow, small Southern town and the fast, big city.

Coincidentally, in the 1988 election year, the South Carolina caucus, on March 12, and the Illinois primary, on March 15, were to be held in the same week, both immediately after the critical Super Tuesday voting. While Jackson's focus for months had been on Super Tuesday, he knew that he couldn't relax until after the elections in his two home states.

Jesse was invigorated the morning after Super Tuesday, and despite some advisers' suggestions that he rest after the superhuman pace he'd kept up during the past weeks, he had no intention of letting up. Instead, he wanted to concentrate on Illinois and make a couple of swings down to South Carolina, where he felt more confident that his grass-roots support would come out for him in force.

At 5:20 A.M. on March 9, I was at Jesse's door to take him to the Houston Convention Center for a series of TV and radio interviews. Everyone wanted him on their program that morning. We had originally been planning to hold an early-morning press conference, at 7:30, in order to get on schedule for the the rest of the day. But when Jesse was reminded of this, he became furious, demanding what in the world was I thinking to have such an early news conference; it was too early. I was flabbergasted. It was on the schedule and it had been approved. For some reason, Jackson was attacking me again. Mark Steitz, who'd come along with us that morning, just shook his head and commented that it appeared I really had become Jackson's scapegoat and that it seemed he was looking for almost anything to attack and criticize.

However, Jackson's energy and ideas still seemed boundless. In typical style, when he arrived at Chicago's Midway Airport on Wednesday morning after flying from Texas, Jesse decided to hit the city's media immediately. He wanted the voters to see him, so he suggested a "point of action." Along the route home, he knew of a perfect site to visit, a symbol to those people for whom he was carrying his message of "economic justice." And so at midday, Jackson's car drew up at the gate of the General Electric plant in Cicero. The workers there had been closed out without notice, and Jackson wanted to give them his support. That media event would be featured on the six o'clock news shows; then later that evening he would make a major homecoming appearance for the late news.

The PUSH headquarters on Chicago's old North Side was the scene for his Illinois homecoming, and several thousand of his staunchest black supporters turned out that cold March night to hear their leader once again. The crowd was overwhelmingly black, for Chicago is a racially divided city, a contrast from the beautifully mixed crowds who had cheered Jackson on in the South. There were tears of joy as their triumphant favorite son returned "home."

He had started his political career there with these people back in 1971, when he had founded PUSH and thus proceeded on a different path from that taken by the other civil rights leaders. As a national leader running for President of the United States, he was proud to return, and he let them know how much he appreciated their loyal support over the years. It hardly mattered to these people that Jackson was now accused by outside observers of not being the best manager of that remarkable organization. He had done well by them, most believed, and now he was carrying their concerns and their hopes right to the top.

The very next morning, Thursday, March 10, we headed west by bus to Chicago's lily-white suburban areas. Naperville was a town in the heart of Republican country—there were hardly any blacks or Democrats for miles around. And Jesse Jackson wanted to be right in the midst of those people's children, the offspring of white middle-class Republicans. Regardless of what their parents said about him at home, Jesse Jackson knew he could excite teenagers and children if he could speak to them face to face.

The gymnasium of North High School was packed. The students, who seemed more color-blind than their parents, had been waiting for Jackson, who, as usual, was running late. We'd already been more than an hour late for the morning's first event at the religious Wheaton College because he'd been held up by his doctor's visit to the house to give him a routine physical and to check on his gout condition. It was lunchtime, but the cafeteria was closed in order that everyone, including the school workers, could be present in the gym for Jackson's visit.

At the last minute, in the limousine en route to the school, Jackson decided that he would launch his latest plan to combat drug abuse in front of the offspring of this privileged Republican stronghold. He hoped it would get the media's attention on the issue again and also show him among the white students of Illinois. As we pulled up at the school, Mark Steitz, the traveling issues director, was rushing to finish typing out the drug plan on his portable computer. Then I hurried to get help from the school's administrative assistants to copy and staple the papers together and have them ready for distribution to the press. Jackson used the telephone in the principal's office for a few minutes and then strode into the cheering gym.

Time and again, Jackson would point to drugs as "the biggest threat to our national security." He believed it when he said, "No issue is more important." For months, he had been raising the issue, and finally that day in Naperville he produced specific solutions. After years of being the one consistent voice crying out against drugs in America, Jesse Jackson finally, in 1988, put the drugs issue on the front burner for many American politicians, and he was determined to stay in the lead on the subject.

At North High School, he laid out his plan:

1. Cut drugs off at the source by raising the importance of the issue in foreign policy;
2. Secure U.S. borders by beefing up Customs and the Coast Guard and appointing a "drug czar";
3. Battle drug dealers by increasing law enforcement funding;
4. Provide drug rehabilitation treatment to all who want it;
5. Expand drug education and prevention;
6. Make the necessary financial commitment in each of these areas.

Every time Jackson had visited schools across the country, he had talked about drugs and used all his powers of persuasion to coax young people away from them. That day, Jackson asked his standard questions:

"How many of you have ever taken drugs? Please stand." As usual, almost the entire student body stood up.

"How many of you have friends who died from drugs?" About half stood.

"How many of you have known someone who has contemplated suicide?" Again almost the entire audience got to their feet.

Then: "How many of you plan now to stay away from drugs?" Most of the students stood and cheered.

Jackson told them: "We can't stop the supply of drugs if you keep giving up hope and stepping up the demand for drugs."

Jackson then began his standard chants, and the students followed with unabashed enthusiasm. "I am somebody . . . Down with dope . . . Up with hope . . . I am somebody . . . Respect me . . . My mind is a pearl . . . I can learn anything . . . in the world . . . I am somebody . . . Down with dope . . . Up with hope . . ." They were basically the same refrains he had led students in chanting across America for years as he had led PUSH and later run for President in 1984. Now, in 1988, there were just a lot more students who were getting swept up in the energy exuded by this superstar. Only now he was also addressing the children of America's affluent.

That afternoon the principal and teachers of North High School expressed their appreciation to Jackson. Probably even the conservative parents were mostly grateful to Jesse Jackson for including North High School on his schedule and encouraging their children to stay away from drugs. "Nothing," the principal said, "has ever excited these students so much. You, Jesse Jackson, have inspired them as none of us has ever been able." All over the United States, it was the same. It was the same conclusion most teachers and principals had reached when Jackson had visited their schools.

And as usual, Jesse himself was energized by his meeting with the students. They were the hope of America. They were also his personal hope for eventual election to the highest office in the land.

Jackson's campaigning in South Carolina was limited during the brief time between Super Tuesday and his native state's separate caucus only four days later. He and his strategists were fairly confident he could win it because a caucus on a Saturday would most likely attract more black than white voters.

Most of the daytime hours on Friday, March 11, were devoted to a final swing through South Carolina. It was really a pro forma effort, with a rally in the morning at the University of South Carolina in Columbia, the capital, then on to another, mostly black rally in Charleston at the Longshoremen's Hall, and then a final rally with a sparse, but mixed audience at Francis Marion College in Florence.

On one of the flights that day a *New York Times* reporter was on board. As customary, I went to the back of the plane and talked with the reporters to see who would like an interview with Jackson. At first the *Times* reporter wasn't interested, but finally, after some coaxing, he agreed. The interview appeared on the front page of the *Times* the next day, and Jackson was pleased. But then he turned on me and said: "You shouldn't just react to interview requests. You should be out getting them to come." I was, as often by then, amazed. He had no idea of the time that was spent then encouraging interviews.

That morning it had been announced that Gary Hart had dropped out of the race, and Jesse had immediately taken time to phone him while we were at the South Carolina ETV station to tape an interview for CNN. At the same time, Jackson telephoned Jimmy Carter to discuss the new Democratic configuration of only five remaining presidential candidates—Jackson, Dukakis, Simon, Gore and Gephardt. Jesse was feeling confident in his home state and was looking forward to returning the next afternoon for his "victory party" in Greenville. That night, however, we first had to fly back to Chicago for a major fund-raising reception with thousands of affluent guests at the Chicago Hilton.

Saturday, March 12, was caucus day in South Carolina, but before returning there we flew to East Lansing, Michigan, for Jackson to deliver the commencement address and receive an honorary doctorate at Michigan State University. It was a moving event. The vast hockey stadium had been converted for the day into the university's graduation arena. Tens of thousands of students, graduates receiving doctoral, master's and baccalaureate degrees, their parents, family, friends, as well as faculty and media, were packed under the huge, long dome. All present were inspired by both the grandeur of the occasion and the power of the speaker, and it must have been many of the people in the audience that day who, two weeks later, voted to give Jackson his miracle in Michigan.

But Jackson's mind didn't linger on Michigan, for he was eager to get back to South Carolina that evening to eat his mother's delicious home-cooked food and to savor the taste of the victory he expected. Later that night we were scheduled to fly back to Chicago to be ready early Sunday morning for another grueling day of campaigning.

Going home to Greenville was always nostalgic for Jesse. It was nestled in the foothills of the Blue Ridge Mountains and had once been the textile capital of the world, but by the time Jesse was growing up there, it had declined and the 15 percent black population of the small city was just a poorer version of the poor whites.

As we flew in and as he walked around there, Jesse was often preoccupied and spoke of his memories. He liked to talk about all the mixed blood he'd inherited—from ancestors who were black slaves, white slave owners and Cherokee Indians—all American. His birth and growing up had taken on a mythical quality for him and also for analysts trying to explain what drove this remarkable man. The core issue, not only for the armchair analysts but for Jackson himself, was his being born out of wedlock—an illegitimate child, a bastard.

In 1941, Helen Burns, Jackson's mother, was a pretty high school student, living at home with her mother, Matilda Burns. Helen had grown up, like many blacks, as an "outside child," never knowing a father. His grandmother was illiterate and worked as a maid for a white family and spent the little money she earned on her daughter, who had a beautiful singing voice. Then, as Jackson would say, "the cycle of pain" was repeated, and his sixteen-year-old mother got pregnant by a married man, their next-door neighbor, Noah Robinson, a relatively wealthy black man.

Jesse's mother had to give up her singing ambitions and the scholarships to music colleges she'd just won. She first went to work as a maid, like her mother, and later went to beauty school and became a hairdresser. With her mother's help and later with the man she married, Charles Jackson, a janitor, she raised little Jesse, who was born in October 1941. Years later, in 1987, Jesse dedicated a collection of his speeches and writings, entitled *Straight from the Heart,* to his stepfather, whom he always called "Charlie Henry." Jackson wrote of his late stepfather that he "adopted me and gave me his name, his love, his encouragement, discipline and a high sense of self-respect."

But Jesse's birth was always remembered as a scandal in their church and their neighborhood, and for years people would remember and taunt young Jesse. In the neighborhood play area, Happy Hearts Park, the little boys would tease Jesse with "Your daddy ain't none of your daddy. You ain't nothing but a nobody, nothing but a nobody." Years later the preacher-politician would cite his illegitimacy in his inspirational speeches to young blacks and then to America in general: "You are God's child. When I was in my mother's belly, I had no father to give me a name. . . . They called me a bastard and rejected me. You are somebody! You are God's child!"

But it was his real father whose attention Jesse always seemed to want to win. Jackson's early biographer, Barbara Reynolds, in her 1975 book, described a poignant and oft-repeated scene from Jackson's childhood—the young illegitimate son standing for hours in the back yard of his blood father and looking in the window until Noah Robinson would appear, at which point Jesse would flee back home. The father, for his part, used to watch his illegitimate son play in the schoolyard, and he would sometimes give him little presents, but his wife never tolerated the development of a relationship between the father and his son or between her own boys and her husband's illegitimate son, little Jesse.

There was always a contrast in wealth between Jackson's family and the Robinsons, and as a child he was envious of his stepbrothers' advantages. One of them, Noah Robinson, Jr., seemed to have everything, including much lighter skin and enrollment in a private school. Years later, when it was Jesse who had the power as head of Operation Breadbasket, he tried to help his stepbrother, but Noah's business shenanigans always brought some embarrassment to Jesse. However, when the media tried to tie them together by implication, they never succeeded, and Jesse's response was often: "This guilt by association business isn't fair. Nobody gives Jimmy Carter or Billy the burden of each other's brotherhood. That's not fair."

Jesse always talked about how he had never spent the night in the house of his real father. But when he was older, he would phone Robinson on Father's Day. And in 1987, when CBS's Mike Wallace was doing a special about Jackson for *60 Minutes,* Jackson included a visit with Robinson as part of the guided tour of his hometown that he gave the TV crew.

Noah Robinson, Sr., has recalled how little Jesse, at the age of five, boasted that he already knew what his calling was to be. He quoted Jesse as saying to him: "Didi, one of these days I'm going to preach." Robinson then said: "You talking about preaching, you don't even know your ABCs." But Jesse insisted: "My granddaddy Jesse's a preacher, ain't he?" Robinson's father and several ancestors had all been preachers.

"Just you watch, I'm going to be more than you think I can be." Then, as a teenager, he began to talk about his dream that he would lead his people across a river, and he boasted confidently: "I'm a born leader."

On March 12, 1988, that young man was a candidate for President of the United States, and he was flying back home to savor victory in his native state. It was getting toward dusk when we landed in Greenville. At the airport, Jesse told the welcoming party of local campaign officials to drop whatever other plans they'd had, because he wanted to go straight to his old home community for the benefit of the reporters and television cameras before it got dark. He wanted America to see where he'd come from, and maybe then they would see why he was running for the White House. Certainly, they would marvel that a black man from a slum could get so far. It was more striking than Lincoln's log cabin.

The city directories of the 1950s called the area Fieldcrest Village, "a housing project for colored located at the end of Greenacre Road." Jesse's mother and stepfather had managed to obtain a place in the village in the 1950s when Jesse was entering adolescence. It was a step up for them. Jesse would say: "Federally funded housing gave me the chance to have a proper house and helped me get where I am today."

Every time Jackson went back to Greenville during his 1988 campaign, he would return to this place, where he would see again the poor, bare yards and the plain, box-shaped two-story brick buildings, the clusters of row houses with no artistic grace. The poor still lived there, and each time Jesse returned, they would come out to greet their "favorite son."

That night, as the sun was setting and the caucuses were about to close across South Carolina, Jesse gathered the band of local and national newsmen to listen to his story. He spoke nostalgically of the community feeling of the place; it wasn't an anonymous neighborhood. He would always tell the same story: "We didn't have a neighborhood, we had a community. There's a difference between a bunch of neighbors and a community that's made up of common unity where there's a foundation."

He would explain: "There were two or three people in the neighborhood who just kept big pots of vegetable soup on. When folks didn't have any food, they couldn't go to the Salvation Army because they were black. They couldn't get social security; they couldn't get welfare. But folks had a tradition of being kind to one another, because that was our roots."

It was starting to rain, and Jesse ordered umbrellas brought for his mother and grandmother, who had met us at the airport and had come back to visit their old Fieldcrest Village. We all walked along the streets—reporters, staff, friends and supporters—to the very house where Jackson had grown up. It was one of several in a row block. There was a small living room and kitchen downstairs and two bedrooms and a bath upstairs.

Jesse then talked about his early childhood and told the story of using the wallpaper as a windbreaker. Then he told about his grandmother collecting the patches to sew the quilts to keep them warm. And he pulled his grandmother, Matilda Burns, to him and put his arm around her frail shoulders. In 1988, she was eighty, and her daughter, Helen Burns Jackson, standing next to her, was in her late sixties.

Jackson spoke fondly, as he always did, about his maternal grandmother: "My grandmother doesn't have any education. She can't read or write, but she's never lost. She knows the worth of prayer."

He looked down warmly at her under his arm. "To the world she has no name, and she has no face, but she feels like she has cosmic importance because there's a God she communicates with in the heavens who is eternal. And so she knows that every boss is temporary, that every rainy day is temporary, that every hardship is temporary. She used to tell me: 'Son, every goodbye ain't gone. Just hold on; there's joy coming in the morning.' "

When listeners heard Jesse tell this, they felt a sudden sense of recognition. Jesse was fond of using that line in his speeches: "There's joy coming in the morning," which he had first heard from his grandmother. She had taught him to have hope. And Jesse acknowledged then, as always, that despite his roots in poverty, he was raised with hope. Despite the pain, he would say, he rose above it and grew and expanded and now he was running for President of the United States of America.

That night the Jackson campaign celebrated its South Carolina victory in a little auditorium at Greenville Technical College. He'd won the caucus with an overwhelming majority, more than 50 percent. Jesse's real father didn't attend, but his beaming mother and grandmother were there along with his daughter Jackie. Jesse needlessly reminded the relatively small crowd of well-wishers once more of his origins in Greenville poverty and exhorted them: "Just because you're born in the slum doesn't mean the slum's born in you."

Most of the national and local media were in Columbia, where the other candidates were. They didn't seem to notice that the winner of the South Carolina caucus was elsewhere, but their editors had sent them to be with the pack in the capital. Still no one was taking Jackson very seriously. It didn't matter then to the media that a black man had won by a landslide in his Southern home state. In looking ahead to the next primary in Illinois, the news molders were interested only in the white Democrats, whom they considered the more serious candidates. Jackson's plans were irrelevant to them. Most pundits and editors had granted Jackson his day in the sun on Super Tuesday, but after that he was to be considered written off.

The next two days, March 13 and 14, were a whirlwind of campaigning up and down Illinois—first on Sunday in Chicago, then leaving at 8 P.M. for East St. Louis and Collinsville, and from there early Monday morning to Alton, to Carbondale, to a rally in the Capitol Rotunda in Springfield, to Bloomington, and finally back that night to Chicago in time for live interviews at 10 and 10:30 at the ABC and NBC affiliates, respectively.

In the NBC interview, Jackson gave a quick negative response to a question about whether he would consider having a female running mate if he were the nominee. It happened that Geraldine Ferraro, the first woman to have run for Vice President, was participating by a televised hookup in the special program, and her unveiled grimace at his statement was clearly seen by those of us watching the screen. Jesse seemed oblivious. Later, when Bob Borosage and I commented on his remark, Jesse bristled, saying there was no way that he, a black man, should say he would have a woman running with him. It would, no doubt, be a dead loss, he insisted. He didn't care what Ms. Ferraro thought—there was no love lost between them anyway.

Early the next morning, I returned a call to CBS anchorman Dan Rather at his home because he'd been trying to reach Jesse's residence in Chicago but the Jackson phone was busy nonstop. Rather wanted to get word quickly to Jackson before he read a newspaper report that Rather had ridiculed Jackson in a mock interview at CBS. Rather wanted Jackson to know that he was denying the allegation.

I was trying to reach Jesse by phone anyway because I needed to talk to him about some other matters. A free-lance crew doing a PBS documentary about the Jackson campaign had been traveling with us for the past couple of weeks and had become frustrated because Jackson never let them film any of the behind-the-scenes action they wanted. Originally, they'd been given permission to do this, but they just showed up one day on the road before we had any notification from our Chicago headquarters. Jesse had resented not being informed in advance because he always insisted on giving approval for any such media coverage. Thus, for days they had been pestering me to do behind-the-scenes shooting. Jesse kept listening to the requests but saying nothing. Finally, the night before the Illinois primary, the crew told me they were fed up and, whether I got them the permission or not, they were going to drive over to Jackson's house to get some family pictures the next morning. I told them I would keep trying to contact Jackson, and said that, if they did go, they should wait outside in their car until my assistant, Delmarie Cobb, who would be at the house that morning, got them the permission. I never got through on the telephone to the Jackson house despite countless attempts.

What happened then was that the crew arrived in their car and then one of the Jackson sons, who saw them and felt sorry for them sitting out in the cold, invited them inside. The crew thought this was the permission, and they went with Jonathan into the Jackson kitchen with their camera. Just then Mrs. Jackson came downstairs, still in her dressing gown, and went into a rage about there being a film crew in her house. She ordered them out and screamed at Delmarie for bringing them inside. She then went to tell Jesse how irate she was at this invasion of their privacy.

The problem was that I wasn't there and didn't know anything about what had happened. I had stayed behind that morning in order to be sure the press bus arrived earlier than Jackson did at his polling place at Bryn Mawr Church on Chicago's South Side. After he voted, he stopped to eat in a nearby diner. The PBS crew mentioned to me there had been a mix-up at the house, but they didn't give me the details then and I proceeded to get permission for TV crews to enter the diner to film Jesse eating with his sons and some staff. As he rose to leave, he marched angrily up to me, facing the camera behind me, and started hurling abuse at me for "violating" his house and privacy. Even his other aides were shocked that he had lambasted me, once again, so viciously, but this time fully aware that a television camera was rolling away.

Later I went back to the Hyatt Regency Hotel and telephoned Mrs. Jackson to apologize. At first she said she didn't recognize my name and said she thought I was "that black girl (Delmarie Cobb) at the house," but then I explained who I was and said I was sorry about the crew's entering without her permission. She was then very pleasant and said it was all right and she was sure Jesse had vented his anger at me because she had been so angry with him in the morning.

That evening Jesse stayed at home so late that he missed many of the television and radio interviews that had been scheduled. He finally arrived at the Hyatt Regency at 8:45 and gave a number of interviews before his victory speech that was scheduled for ten o'clock. As we walked along the back corridor from the interview rooms to the ballroom where his victory party was in full swing, he halted outside the door. He said he wouldn't go in until his wife, Jackie, showed up. "Where is she?" he asked in general. "Why isn't she here now?" She finally arrived, and he first fussed at her and then, relieved, he and his family walked in to greet his old Chicago friends cheering his victory. He'd come in second, and the winner, Senator Simon, wasn't expected to last much beyond Illinois in the presidential primary season. So, once again, Jesse found victory even in second place. He was going the long distance.

Jesse Jackson had claimed to run as a "favorite son" in both South Carolina and Illinois. Yet in neither was he claimed as a "favorite son" in the traditional sense of that political term. In South Carolina, he was not a resident, but a "native son" who had grown up black during segregation. But times had changed in South Carolina, and when he won the caucus with 55 percent of the votes, the state's newspapers would begin to claim him as their own even though he'd left their state years before. And in Illinois, where he again called himself a "favorite son" candidate, another "favorite son," Senator Paul Simon, was also running and won the state. But Jesse came in second in the state, and he took the majority of the votes in his adopted hometown, Chicago. Then he could relax. At the midway point of the season, the three major contests were out of the way, and he could proceed with confidence and hope.

9

THE
MICHIGAN
CAUCUS

"We find common ground at the plant gate that closes on workers without notice. We find common ground at the farm auction where a good farmer loses his or her land to bad loans or diminishing markets. Common ground at the school yard where teachers cannot get adequate pay, and students cannot get a scholarship, and can't make a loan. Common ground at the hospital admitting room, where somebody tonight is dying because they cannot afford to go upstairs to a bed that's empty waiting for someone with insurance to get sick. We are a better nation than that. We must do better than that."

The Michigan caucus, on Saturday, March 26, was next in line, but on Wednesday, March 16, the morning after the Illinois primary, still in Chicago, Jesse was thinking of his victory in his adopted state and looking further ahead to bigger primaries in April and June. He had placed second, which meant Jackson had emerged triumphant over the other remaining Democratic presidential candidates. But he still had major primaries ahead of him, first in New York a month away and then in California, nearly three months off. We were halfway down the stretch.

That morning I went to Jesse's room at 5:50 and he was ready to go. Off we walked down the long corridor of the vast Hyatt Regency Hotel to the other side, where the television networks were set up. NBC's *Today* show was first. Jesse always felt comfortable talking with Bryant Gumbel on the *Today* show; he was fond of citing him as an example of how far blacks had come. Jesse would say: "Remember when NBC announced Gumbel would host the show, and people wondered how they could bear to get up every morning and see a black face on their television screens. And now he's the number one morning-show host." And then Jackson would usually roll off a list of other black firsts in 1988: "Now the number one sitcom artist in America is Bill Cosby, the star quarterback in the Super Bowl was Doug Williams, the chairman of the House Budget Committee is Bill Gray, the President's National Security Adviser is also a black, Colin Powell, and I'm out front in the Democratic primaries. The world around us has changed. Who would have thought this twenty-five years ago—not even four years ago?"

After NBC, we walked next door to where CBS was set up, and he went live on their morning show as well. This was a far cry from Iowa, only two months earlier, when no morning show requested Jackson's presence the day after the voting. When he had finished the CBS interview, I placed a call to Mutual Radio and put him on the line to their Crystal City headquarters in Virginia across the Potomac from Washington. After completing that he started dialing numbers himself and calling for people's reaction to the Illinois vote. The only staff with him that morning were myself and Bob Borosage, who had rejoined us in Chicago for the Illinois primary, and we both stood aside while he dialed memorized numbers to friends around the country. After he made several calls on the CBS phone, I told him we had to leave because the television producer needed to pull his lines and close down the room.

That morning we had scheduled a press conference for 7:30, just before we were to take off from Chicago for Washington, so we had an hour to kill. Jesse seemed more relaxed than he had for a month, since before Super Tuesday. Getting past Illinois appeared to have been an important psychological hurdle for him.

As we walked past the lobby, Jesse decided not to go back to his suite and instead stopped for breakfast right there in the open restaurant. John Conyers was coming down for breakfast then and joined us. The longtime black member of Congress from Michigan tried to get Jackson to talk about his plans for the upcoming caucus in his state, but Jesse still wasn't interested in focusing much on it. As he ate his cereal and fruit, he talked in general about how his message was getting across. It was clear Jackson was a newly confident man that morning.

Later that day, when we arrived at Washington's National Airport, Jackson was informed that Senator Albert Gore, Jr., was just leaving the Butler Aviation Terminal. Jesse sent word that he wanted to meet with him privately for a few minutes. When they came out of the meeting and faced the press, it was Jackson who was the most in command this time. Previously Jackson acted uptight and nervous around Gore, but not anymore. Now it was Gore who was trying to keep up and he seemed slightly nervous. As I was standing behind the two men, while they were taking questions from the press, I observed Gore virtually shaking as he kept trying to balance on his toes. The young senator from Tennessee stood in that difficult, and obviously uncomfortable, position the whole time he was next to Jackson. Gore presumably didn't want to look shorter than Jackson in the photographs. He had not done well in Illinois and knew he was facing an uphill battle in his race for the Democratic presidential nomination.

I had suggested we come to Washington because the family and journalist friends of the American hostage Terry Anderson had arranged to hold a special commemoration service that day, urging help for his release. On March 16 three years earlier, Anderson, the AP bureau chief in Lebanon, had been taken hostage in Beirut as he was coming home from playing tennis. There were now many more

American hostages in Lebanon, but he had been held captive the longest at that time.

Jackson had spoken at the first service held for the hostage two years earlier, and I had reminded Jesse that Anderson had been one of the reporters who had covered him in Damascus and then flown home with him and Goodman. Jackson was interested in being at the service, but he had warned me the weekend before when I was trying to make arrangements for his attendance: "Sure, I'm interested, but I can't be a fly on the wall. I have to have a role in it. I *am* a presidential candidate."

The problem was that the organizers were adamant that Jesse not have a role in the service itself. The newsman in charge, David Aikman of *Time,* said they were all quite happy for Jackson to attend, but they insisted that he couldn't make a speech during the service. They didn't want to turn this special vigil into a political platform for one politician. Jackson would be allowed to participate in a news conference in the parish hall after the service. I informed Jackson of this arrangement, and he agreed. The hostage crisis was one of Jackson's issues, and he realized it would be useful to be seen as continuing to support efforts to resolve it.

Because of the unscheduled meeting with Gore at the airport, we were a little late in arriving at Holy Trinity Catholic Church in Georgetown. But the service was held up and began after Jackson arrived and got seated.

A couple of weeks later, *Time* magazine printed a photograph of Jackson at the service. It was captioned: "Jackson in action: at a service in Washington commemorating Hostage Terry Anderson." The picture showed Jackson looking solemn as he held a candle. To his right were his policy adviser, Bob Borosage, and myself. Anyone who knew Jackson well or had sat through that service with him would have known that that look on his face actually reflected annoyance and seething inner anger.

The two hours inside that church were among the most agonizing I'd ever spent. I could feel how uncomfortable and annoyed Jesse was at having to sit that long without talking and running the show. Perhaps the most uncomfortable moment came when Jeremy Levin, a former hostage and CNN bureau chief in Lebanon, introduced the important guests at the service. He never mentioned Jesse Jackson at all. I quickly scrawled out a note and passed it back a couple of pews to David Aikman; the note said that I thought they owed Jackson the courtesy of welcoming him. Aikman signaled my message to the front of the church, and some minutes later it was announced that Jackson was among the guests. (The irony was that a couple of months later a book about Oliver North, written by Ben Bradlee, Jr., cited Jackson as being very instrumental in bringing about the release of Jeremy Levin from his captivity in 1986. Perhaps it was an oversight, but it was Levin who ignored Jackson's presence that day at the commemoration service.)

Finally, the seemingly interminable service was over, and we were allowed to adjourn to the parish hall for the news conference with Terry Anderson's sister. I introduced Jackson to a number of my journalist friends, including Charles Glass, the former hostage and ABC correspondent. I could sense a kind of unease in Jackson, which was becoming commonplace when he was in the midst of a group that one of his staff knew better than he did.

That afternoon he would find an opportunity to put me down, put me in my place, I thought. Later, at the Howard Inn in Washington, after an interview with *Washington Post* columnist Carl Rowan, the two men discussed how Rowan would write some positive columns about Jackson's campaign. After Rowan had left, I was standing around with Borosage talking with Jackson. Instead of attempting to include me, he barked a typical order: "Liz, go get me a Coke."

I spent the remainder of that afternoon arranging a breakfast meeting for the next morning with top editors and correspondents at *Time.* As always, it was difficult because most of the staff still opposed the idea of Jackson's going to such editorial boards. Jackson was inclined to do it, but then neither he nor his scheduler was willing to make a final decision until late in the day. In the meantime, my contact at *Time,* Washington bureau chief Strobe Talbott, needed to know in time to make plans and to arrange for top editors, including the powerful assistant managing editor John Stacks,.

to fly down that night from New York in order to attend an early-morning breakfast.

If Jackson canceled out after agreeing or was typically late, then I knew the *Time* people would pounce all over it as proof of what they had been thinking all along about Jackson. Most people in the establishment media were convinced that he could never be taken seriously as a candidate because they viewed him as irresponsible, disorganized, always late, uncontrollable, dangerously egotistical. These meetings with editors were an attempt to change that image among the media.

At 7 A.M. sharp that Thursday, March 17, we arrived on time at *Time*'s modern office on 1050 Connecticut Avenue. Strobe Talbott met us at the side door and remarked upon this unusual punctuality. Then he began to apologize that the food wasn't ready. Something had happened with the caterer, and I could sense Jackson thinking: this time the punctual ones weren't ready for him.

Upstairs we were milling around, waiting for food to arrive. Jackson had been introduced to the *Time* contingent there to meet him, but I couldn't help catching the angry glares Jackson was giving me, yet again, as I talked collegially and comfortably with Strobe and various other editors and reporters I'd known from my past. I couldn't understand why Jackson never seemed to realize that my coming from their ranks and then going to work for him added to his credibility.

Instead, he decided it was again time to put me down. He walked back to the kitchen off the small conference room where we were meeting and summoned me to follow him. The *Time* people and his advisers, Borosage and Carol O'Cleireacain, remained outside, while the caterers inside were scurrying around.

Then in stage-whispered angry tones, he started attacking me: "You violated me yesterday." Jesse was fond of accusing people of "violating" him. "You should never have allowed those L.A. *Times* reporters on the plane to come sit next to me while I was sleeping. I then had to wake up to face them, and I wasn't ready. That was wrong. You violated me."

I was aghast. Why berate me like this in public? Well, I was getting used to it. The incident had happened twenty-four hours before. Why hadn't Jackson brought it to my attention earlier? I figured it was because he'd forgotten it or because he hadn't had such a perfect public opportunity the day before to lambast me in front of my former colleagues. Perhaps it had been a mistake to let those L.A. *Times* reporters, Doug Jehl and Tom Rosenstiel, sit next to him while he was sleeping. But he had told me to bring them up from the back of the plane so he could give them an interview. By the time we'd reached the front of the plane, he had gone to sleep. Then the plane was about to land, and the passengers were told to take their seats immediately. So I figured the reporters might as well take the empty seats next to Jackson since they were already up front, and they could catch a few words with him after we'd landed and he'd woken up. It didn't seem to bother him at the time as he spoke with them. There had also been plenty of other times he'd taken similar catnaps in front of reporters. He only seemed to become angry about it a day later when he noticed my old ties with people like the *Time* bureau chief.

Once we were out of the kitchen, Jackson put on his best face and the meeting at *Time* went well. Jesse was becoming much more relaxed in talking with these members of editorial boards and I could see his self-confidence growing among them. The two advisers with us that morning, Borosage and O'Cleireacain, were very pleased with his performance. He seemed comfortable handling all of *Time*'s questions, even though the day before, when I'd pressed him to meet with *The Wall Street Journal* at their Washington bureau, he'd flatly declined, saying he wasn't ready for them yet.

This was the first real lull in the campaign, and several traveling staff members were dropping off at that point to get a few days' rest. I was also staying behind for a few days to see my doctor and to move into the house I'd recently bought but hadn't yet had the free time even to sleep one night in. Out on the street, Jesse and I gave each other a quick hug goodbye. From inside the limousine, he flashed me his usual thumbs-up sign. I thought it meant he had been pleased with his meeting with *Time*. With him was a former chairman of the Democratic National Committee, John C. White, who had been at the *Time* meeting and had been invited by Jesse to ride with him to the airport.

Before heading home, I thought I would touch base with several news organizations to beat the drum for Jackson. I went back up to Strobe Talbott's office and talked with him about the morning session and about the possibility of having both Jesse and Jackie Jackson attend an off-the-record dinner with *Time*'s political reporters. I also talked with friends at the Washington bureau of *The Wall Street Journal* to assure them that Jackson would meet with them at some point, and I went by the *New York Times* bureau. The people I talked to were always fairly skeptical about the candidate, and by then I had to admit to myself that I, too, was skeptical about the man's private character.

I felt fairly discouraged that morning about my thankless task. I always had known it would be difficult to work with Jackson. Yet I had assumed if anyone could handle it, I could. But over the past months of constant and intimate contact with him, I had come in for a myriad of surprises, many of them admittedly exciting but many others basically disillusioning.

Serving as Jesse Jackson's press secretary was a contradiction in terms. He couldn't abide having any intermediary between him and the media. He also harbored intense jealousy about other people's personal contacts within the establishment. Rather than appreciate what I could offer, he loathed me for having it to offer. It had become an often unpleasant, and always thankless job. His constant unwarranted abuse and mostly unjustified criticism were beginning to wear me down.

I knew that Jackson had had a long history of treating certain people this way. One former colleague of Jackson's from the early days at SCLC, Jonathan Power, wrote about Jackson: ". . . as the roar of the crowd seemed to go to his head, our friendship became strained, as did his relationship with Andrew Young and other close associates of Dr. King. Onstage flamboyance is one thing; imperious treatment of associates is another. Most of us pulled back." Power recalled that in 1988. I had been forewarned by many, but I had believed in his message and the historic importance of his campaign, and I wanted to try to hang on, preferably if I could rearrange my job so that I was not always in the position of scapegoat for Jackson. Other members of the staff often remarked that I had become Jackson's scapegoat for everything that went wrong, either because of my personality or because of the tension inevitably caused by the nature of my position—being in the middle between him and the media he both loved and hated.

Jackson himself, and the aides closest to him who liked to imitate him, were fond of the expression "use and abuse." It reflected the harsh realities of politics, they said. Thus, it seemed only natural to describe Jackson's behavior that way—he abused me and most other staff members in countless ways. Unlike some of the others, though, I would often try to talk back and defend myself when I felt the criticism was unjustified. But some, like Kgosie Matthews and Bill Morton, said they learned that the only way to deal with his incessant criticism was never to answer back. They would say: "Once the Reverend has an idea about something, or has decided to attack you, then there's no changing his mind." Their advice was just to learn to take it and never try to argue with him, even when it was patently evident that the criticism was completely unjustified.

The many memories of recent humiliating and unpleasant incidents on the road with Jackson were what I was mulling over that early morning on St. Patrick's Day as I walked away from *Time*'s Washington bureau, heading across Connecticut Avenue and Farragut Square to the Army-Navy Club Building, where *The New York Times* had recently moved its Washington bureau. I was going to talk with some friends there and try to persuade them to do more stories about Jackson, but, in fact, I was reaching my own limit in working with the man.

It was almost an ominous coincidence, then, when one of the editors at the *Times* remarked to me: "Well, Liz, tell me how it really is to work with Jesse." I just stared, and the editor coaxed: "Come on. We hear he's really not a nice person at all, but we can't print the nasty things we know about him."

I didn't comment but just mumbled: "Oh, it's fine. The work is completely around the clock, though, even more full-time than being a reporter."

The reality for me was that it was very unpleasant to be around someone who was incessantly critical and totally egocentric to the extent that no one else mattered at all. It was also frightening. I knew it would become very difficult for me to defend my position as this man's press secretary. At first I had believed in him. I still believed in most of his issues, but I could no longer throw my heart behind the man as I had at the beginning.

I also could sense that my personality got on Jackson's nerves. While he liked strong women, he couldn't bear to have them around him much of the time. His wife, for example, never traveled much with him—they would drive each other crazy—nor did Ann Lewis, who worked as his adviser. It wouldn't have worked. And in my position as press secretary, or rather doing the job as I believed it should be done, I was constantly at odds with the candidate—pushing him to be on time, pressing him to make decisions about schedules, introducing him to my important connections, trying to get him to cut short his press conferences, requesting interviews all the time. And on top of it, I had come from the media.

I continued to mull over this terrible ambivalence I now felt about working for Jackson. Fortunately, the next day, March 18, Kgosie Matthews telephoned me from the road to say that there were very few reporters traveling on the campaign plane and so I could use the time to get things in order at home. Also, he said that most of the other staff who had stayed behind in Washington would also wait till next week rather than spend campaign money to fly on commercial flights to catch up with the charter in California over the weekend.

A few days later, on Wednesday, March 23, I talked to Gerry Austin, who said that my being in Michigan wasn't as important as what I could be doing building up our contacts with the Washington media chiefs. He also suggested that I get all my personal affairs wrapped up since this might be the last break for a while. He told me to plan to meet the Jackson team soon after the weekend of the Michigan caucus, probably in Connecticut that Monday. I was extremely relieved to have a break, not from the frenetic pace but from the incessant criticism and moodiness of Jackson. Although I pursued the contacts, I found myself constantly thinking about how I might gracefully get out of this unpleasant job.

Jesse Jackson didn't go into Michigan with any great expectations. In fact, if the truth be told, his thoughts were never solidly on Michigan: mentally he went from the high spots of Super Tuesday and Illinois to New York and California, where he hoped he would be able to take the real prizes.

Also, Jackson had suffered an initial disappointment in Michigan. Coleman Young, the black mayor of Detroit, Michigan's largest city, had refused to endorse him. On a Saturday morning, March 12, even before the Illinois primary, Mayor Young made a point of appearing in Detroit with another candidate, Governor Michael Dukakis, just as Jesse Jackson was flying in to East Lansing to receive an honorary doctorate at Michigan State University.

Jesse learned the news as we arrived in Michigan that Saturday morning (the day of the South Carolina caucus), and he couldn't hide his annoyance. Mayor Young had been among the many black politicians who, in 1984, had refused to back Jackson and instead went with Walter Mondale. But this election year, 1988, most black politicians were coming out for Jackson. Whether they were happy with him personally or not, most didn't have the courage to endorse a white candidate over this now phenomenal black one. Ninety-five percent of black America was aligning solidly behind Jesse Jackson. In spite of Jackson's declarations that race should not be an issue, he firmly, and humanly, believed that, as the nation's leading black politician, he was due the allegiance of every black in America. Coleman Young was a rare renegade.

Publicly, Jackson seemed undaunted by the news of what he considered to be Mayor Young's betrayal. Privately, he was furious and was apprehensive that Young's position might be taken as a signal for defection by other Michigan blacks and as a sign to Michigan whites that even their state's leading black wouldn't sign on to the

Jackson campaign. In a way, once Young had defected, Jackson seemed subconsciously to write off Michigan. He would do his usual frenetic stumping through the state, but he did not harbor any hopes for a major victory there.

But Jackson's other black advisers in Michigan, chiefly his campaign chairman, Joel Ferguson, and Representative John Conyers, were optimistic. Both were longtime friends of Jackson's and both had solid support throughout their state. Ferguson, a burly, handsome businessman with offices in Lansing and Detroit, knew everyone in Michigan. Starting out poor, he had become a contractor, building low-income housing, and now he was a millionaire. He had the same kind of grass-roots network of contacts in Michigan that Jackson had all over America. And early on, before the Michigan caucus, he had told Jackson not to worry.

It was important for Jackson's success that the state held a caucus and not a primary. The caucus is a system that Jackson had often decried as undemocratic, because the voters had to stand up at the caucus and announce their vote publicly. However, he also knew it could work to his advantage, because in a caucus usually only the hard-core, most dedicated voters turned out to participate. And in the Democratic Party that could be a majority in support of Jackson. Other, more conservative voters, who would cast their votes privately in a primary, would often not care to commit themselves publicly in a caucus. In almost every caucus Jackson did better than in a primary in a state with an equivalent racial and socioeconomic profile.

Also, Jackson's message to the threatened autoworkers in Michigan made a difference. It wouldn't matter whether he was black or white. Their jobs and thus their livelihood, family life, and homes were imperiled. If a black man could save their jobs, his color was irrelevant. Across Michigan, the angry and frightened autoworkers and other blue-collar workers picked up on the Jackson message.

Across Michigan, Jesse Jackson had trumpeted his "Workers' Bill of Rights." At rally after rally, he had enumerated his proposals to help the workers of America:

Number one—*Workers have a right to a job*. People need jobs and there are jobs which need to be done. We can build the housing, roads and bridges that we need as well as provide care for this nation's people. We can end plant closings without notice and unemployment without hope.

Number two—*Workers have a right to a democratic union*. All workers, including public employees, should be able to organize themselves into democratic unions, have those unions recognized and work under a collective bargaining agreement.

Number three—*Workers have a right to a living wage*. People who work full-time should be able to rise out of poverty on their pay. American families need family wages. Young workers, our youth, need opportunity.

Number four—*Workers have a right to a healthy life and a safe workplace*. Workers need affordable and accessible health care, a right to know the dangers at work and good faith enforcement by skilled experts of the laws meant to protect their lives.

Number five—*Workers have a right to both work and family*. No one should be forced to choose between a paycheck and a sick child, or between keeping their job and giving birth.

Number six—*Workers have a right to pension security*. A pension belongs to the worker, not to the company. Every worker is entitled to one as secure as FICA. Workers should have a voice in ensuring that their pension funds be used in their own interest, not against them.

Number seven—*Workers have a right to fair competition*. International trade needs a level playing field. Recognition of the basic democratic rights of workers at home and abroad to organize, to bargain collectively and to have enforced workplace standards is needed. Free labor cannot "compete" with slave labor.

Number eight—*Workers have a right to freedom from discrimination*. There also needs to be a level playing field at home —affirmative action for those locked out of better-paying jobs and pay equity for those locked into low-wage jobs.

Number nine—*Workers have a right to education that works.* Workers need basic education for basic skills, vocational education for current jobs and lifelong education for a changing economy.

Number ten—*Workers have a right to respect.* The contributions of workers, past and present, deserve a prominent place in the education of future workers. Those who give a life of labor deserve to have the companies for whom they work reinvest in their industry, in their community and in their country.

The workers of Michigan recognized that someone finally was talking to them about their problems. No matter that Jesse Jackson had been trying to publicize his "Workers' Bill of Rights" long before he got to Michigan. It was there that for the first time the majority of the voters took what he was saying deeply to heart and welcomed the messenger with their endorsement.

Michigan was a miracle on a candidate's campaign trail. On Saturday, March 26, the Michigan voters in the Democratic caucus surprised not only America and the world but also Jesse Jackson himself when they cast the majority of their votes for him. Jackson resoundingly won the Michigan caucus with 55 percent of the vote. His closest opponent, Michael Dukakis, took only 28 percent.

Jesse had long believed that there was fertile ground across America for his message of hope, of economic and social reform. He had known that the workers and students, white liberals and urban poor, the groups who made up his Rainbow Coalition, were in Michigan. But he was privately as surprised as everyone else that it was in Michigan that his campaign took off.

Jesse Jackson had finally won a large non-Southern industrial state. And he had done it by taking 40 percent of the white vote. At last the media and the establishment had to take this man seriously and try to interpret what had happened in Michigan. It was no longer possible to deny that the Jackson message was not only being heard but also being accepted by Americans outside Jackson's traditional poor and black constituencies.

Jackson's Michigan campaign chairman, Joel Ferguson, had kept his word: he delivered his state. And in Mayor Coleman Young's hometown, Jackson got the last word: "Governor Dukakis got the mayor's endorsement. I got the votes." After Michigan, no American black Democratic politician would make Young's mistake. From then on, they felt compelled by Jackson's wave of popularity, whether they personally liked him or not, to get on the bandwagon if they valued political survival. Jesse Jackson was aware of this and took full advantage of his increased leverage as he rode on toward the summer and the July convention.

10

THE WISCONSIN PRIMARY

"Common ground. Easier said than done. But you find common ground at 'the point of challenge.' This campaign has shown that politics need not be marketed by politicians, packaged by pollsters and pundits. Politics can be a moral arena where people come together to find common ground."

"The point of challenge" had been a pet idea for Jackson since he began his campaign. It was the point where he and the people could meet together and challenge what was wrong with their country, where he could lead the people to see new directions and new possibilities. Jesse Jackson's quest for the presidency was itself a "point of challenge."

The ten days following his miracle in Michigan were a "point of challenge" for him, his campaign and America. The next big test was the Wisconsin primary on April 5. In between were the Connecticut primary on March 29 and the Colorado caucus on April 4. They were all opportunities for Jesse Jackson and America to prove a number of important points. Did his race matter? Did his personality matter? Could Jesse Jackson survive success?

The news of his victory in Michigan had come out too late on Saturday night, March 26, for the major newsmagazines to change their covers for their Sunday publication. But the following week, both *Time* and *Newsweek* put Jesse Jackson's face on their covers. It was victory for Jesse, and his confidence skyrocketed.

Those "ten days that shook the campaign," as a *New York Times* editorial later described them, raised questions about the candidate, his opponents, the voters, the power brokers and the media in ways that no other point in the campaign did. It was truly a point of challenge for everyone. The problem was that no one could agree on the answers. The victory in Michigan necessitated a reexamination of Jackson's stature and potential as a candidate. If the voters and the political establishment did not want Jesse Jackson as the Democratic nominee, their reasons were not necessarily what Jackson automatically assumed they were. He believed the basis of any rejection could only be his color. Many voters, however, would say there were other things, not his color or even his positions, that frightened them away. Many feared that he would behave impulsively, even dangerously, in the White House. Before Michigan, he responded that they simply feared having a black there.

But what Jackson himself needed to demonstrate was whether he could remain as self-controlled as he had appeared throughout most of the preceding three months. After the Michigan victory, however, the people around him and the traveling media began to recognize the Jesse Jackson of the 1984 campaign, as he turned his program back into the freewheeling chaos that had always reigned in the past.

Journalists covering Jackson and even his aides said that the guiding line within the campaign after Michigan became resignedly "Let Jesse be Jesse. There's no stopping him now." Now Jesse could do whatever he wanted: change his schedule more frequently than ever, break out from the Secret Service's protective circle, insult the powers that be, even those who tried to be friendly, put excessive pressure on his staff and usurp whatever remaining power his campaign manager might have had in the past.

Time magazine reported that Jackson's inclination to change his schedule at the last minute became almost the norm rather than the exception, and an article the week after Michigan told of Jackson's suddenly rushing off in the middle of the day to see Stevie Wonder. But an inside observer described the meeting as even stranger than the *Time* reporter had suspected. It was early afternoon, Tuesday, March 29, in the midst of a busy campaign schedule in Manhattan. Suddenly Jesse made a detour to stop by Bill Cosby's apartment in the East Sixties. The comedian had also invited an Asian-American actress friend, Jody Long, to attend. She said she never understood why she was invited for that particular occasion. She was put at a table with Jackson, and then in rushed Stevie Wonder. The singer had had an idea for a new commercial: a number of blind people all proclaiming their support for Jesse Jackson, sight unseen. During the discussions that ensued, Jesse hit the actress's leg with his knee under the table. Then he reached over and touched her arm and began repeatedly to apologize. She later admitted that it was then she began to understand the "magnetism" she'd heard so much about, but she couldn't understand why he kept apologizing. An aide who knew about the bizarre meeting remarked on the contrast between Jackson's profusely apologizing to a perfect stranger and his never apologizing for anything to those close to him. Finally, Jackson left Cosby's apartment, after encouraging Wonder to go ahead with his plan, and proceeded, very late, to his next appointments.

For the first time in the campaign, too, Jackson discarded his previous decision for 1988 to stay away from interfering in foreign affairs. That week after Michigan, he became so cocky that he leapt into the U.S.-Panamanian drug fray by sending an open letter to Panama's President, Manuel Noriega, urging him to step down. Later, when his flamboyant interference began to get negative press, Jackson backed away and blamed his communications office in Chicago for having discussed his letter with the press. Bert Lance, who had advised him from the start to downplay his inclination toward foreign adventures and focus on domestic issues, was not consulted about this latest Panama venture. Lance later told *The Washington Post:* "He never asked me about that one, but if he had, I would have told him, 'There's an old saying in politics, "There aren't any voting precincts in Panama." ' "

Some inside the campaign followed Jackson's lead and went wild with overconfidence. Other, more thoughtful ones were worried. They feared that after nearly reaching the goal, Jesse was losing stability. Though he could keep up the frenzied pace as before, he couldn't seem to "maintain steadiness," as he had long urged on himself and others around him.

At first there was elation among Jackson's outside advisers. Then some became worried. Even at a distance, they could sense that Jackson's euphoria was bringing a return to the wild, disorganized campaign style he'd displayed in 1984. One such concerned adviser was quoted in *Time* that week as remarking of the inner circle: "They think they've won. They've declared victory. They may just rest on their laurels and blow this thing."

But others, such as Texas Agriculture Commissioner Jim Hightower, believed that Jackson had been moved positively by the way white crowds had responded to him. He explained that his conversations with Jackson that week, as the throngs went wild with enthusiasm, took on a much more philosophical tone than previously when he'd traveled with Jackson and they'd mostly talked tactics. Hightower later told reporters, "[Jackson] kept saying, 'What is this phenomenon? What are we tapping into here?' "

Hightower answered Jackson: "You are touching people in a nonpolitical way." And then Hightower said of Jackson: "He recognized it, too, and he was trying to figure out what it meant politically. They were more than responding to a political message. Political analysts consistently underestimate the incredible rage that people feel about the unfairness of life's situations."

Soon after Michigan the media began a campaign of "scrutiny," but their examination of Jesse was still not the same as it would have been for another such successful candidate. The new "scrutiny" was more publicized and talked about than real. The media's spotlight on Jackson seemed to elevate him still more instead of raising the questions that needed to be addressed.

The country now seriously recognized that Jesse Jackson could be elected. Those who had refused to consider the possibility before had to admit that such an outcome was conceivable. The Jackson campaign had begged the media and the establishment to see him as a viable candidate, but now that that was happening, there was a paradox. Jesse didn't want to be taken so seriously that he would be criticized as freely as any white candidate might be. Seriously, yes, but if scrutinized as other candidates were, he would take it as racism. The media naturally claimed impartiality in their coverage of Jackson. They might have been stronger had another, milder-styled black been running, but Jesse Jackson could be a very intimidating individual. The reality was that only such a hard-driving man, the unique Jesse Jackson, could have pushed America into a position of considering his electability in 1988.

A few pundits, such as Charles Krauthammer, Mary McGrory, George Will and William Safire, dared raise the issue of whether Jesse Jackson himself, the person, was qualified to be President of the United States of America. Most in the media allowed Jackson to have it his way, to make it a simple issue of whether Jackson as a black person could be elected to the presidency. Unfortunately, reporters feared that any criticism of Jackson would be construed as racism. For most, there seemed to be no solution, no way out. Even those traveling with Jackson, who knew more about his mercurial personality, would not dare write about it. And the more powerful he became, the more they realized that they would have to temper any criticism if they were to be allowed to continue following him, not only in this campaign but in the future.

Jackson declared publicly that he wanted the scrutiny. He just wanted it to be "fair and not racist."

One network correspondent put the dilemma well: "I know I'm not a racist, but I also know that it would be very easy to do and say things now vis-à-vis Jesse that could easily be interpreted as racism. I'm willing to do tough pieces on Jesse, but you can be sure that we'll look at every damn syllable. It's absolutely clear to me that if Jesse were a white man, he'd probably be getting . . . kicked around rather royally by the press."

The other front-runner, Michael Dukakis, also seemed hesitant to criticize his opponent, or even to call himself the better candidate. The day after his loss in Michigan to Jackson, Dukakis refused to say what made him more qualified than Jackson. Dukakis simply stated: "I'm not going to answer that question."

Then, in Wisconsin, after the Michigan caucus, Senator Albert Gore, Jr., attacked Dukakis for his cowardice in dealing with Jackson. Gore accused Dukakis of being "absurdly timid" and "just scared to death of saying a single word" against Jackson. He went on to suggest that Dukakis had given Jackson complete immunity from any criticism. Gore argued that Jackson "should be treated equally."

Another candidate still in the race after Michigan, Senator Paul Simon, was embarrassed during the Wisconsin campaigning when his wife, Jeanne Simon, made the mistake of comparing Jackson to Hitler. The senator from Illinois had to issue an apology for her statement, in which she had said: "All [Jackson] can do is talk. Adolf Hitler made some good speeches, too."

Jesse publicly ignored these remarks. Privately, though, he was rather shocked by Mrs. Simon's. They were from the same state, and she and her husband had always acted particularly friendly to Jesse.

As for Gore, Jackson had always found him irritating and believed him to be a closet racist from Tennessee. Jackson liked to boast that he was a "real" Southerner who had gone to high school and college in the South. But Gore sometimes got back at Jackson for that by pointing out that the private school, St. Alban's, where Gore had gone was the same place in Washington, D.C., where Jackson sent his sons. Gore himself had always acted uneasy around Jesse, often, presumably unconsciously, making condescending remarks. Jesse and those of us who had been with him in Washington on January 17 wouldn't forget how Gore had talked down to his fellow candidate while they were together preparing to appear on ABC News's Sunday morning show *This Week with David Brinkley*. Gore was trying to be jovial, but it came out wrong when he told Jesse to straighten his tie and then added: "You know, I just can't take you out anywhere in public." It was taken as an inadvertent racist slur.

At the same time that he was bursting with confidence, Jesse Jackson was also being torn by paranoia and anger toward the establishment. He felt that his victory had instantly set off a "Stop Jesse Jackson" campaign. Jackson called on Texas congressman Mickey Leland, his campaign manager for Texas, to get to work to offset any anti-Jesse movement in Congress. Leland held a press conference, and without naming names he let the country know that anyone trying to stop Jackson now would be considered a racist. Other black leaders around the country also began making similar charges. Sadly, Jackson always resorted to this tactic—of charging "racism"—if anyone spoke against him.

Spurred now by his fears of a "Stop Jesse" movement, Jackson felt he should meet with some of the white political establishment in the Democratic Party who had been ignoring him. He wanted them to show him the respect he now deserved. He asked Ann Lewis, his adviser in Washington, to organize something. He also called for help from other party insiders, Bert Lance and John C. White, who followed through immediately. It was characteristic of Jesse to ask several people to carry out the same assignment: that way, he figured, it would eventually get done. That was part of his management style.

Lewis, the savvy fifty-year-old former executive director of Americans for Democratic Action, a woman with many connections through the Democratic National Committee and her work with President Carter, had been hoping all along that she would be able to organize a rapprochement between the party and Jackson. She'd been working on this for months, but she had not yet been able to get any of the crusty party elders to meet with Jackson, much less give him their blessing.

The year before, the DNC had excluded Jackson from a special dinner it held in honor of every past and potential presidential candidate. Ann Lewis had been especially chagrined because of the humiliation she knew Jesse felt. But she told him then: "They are not the party, we are. The reason there's a Democratic Senate is not six guys in a room in Washington in bow ties. If you give them the power to shut you out, you're giving them a power they don't have." Yet she knew, as did Jesse, that he needed them, sometimes more than others did. And he needed an event symbolizing that he'd been accepted as at least a serious candidate by the party elite.

On March 30, the Wednesday after Michigan, a few but by no means all of the elders of the Democratic Party gathered for breakfast at Washington's elegant Jefferson Hotel. They had come to meet with this "phenomenon," Jesse Jackson, and to hear what he had to say. The venerable eighty-one-year-old Clark Clifford, the former Defense Secretary, who had advised eight Presidents, served as moderator. The official host was Bernard Rappaport, a liberal Democratic funder from Waco, Texas. Bert Lance had flown up from Georgia and brought his wife, La Belle.

The "power breakfast" couldn't have been a more perfect symbol, except that the reality didn't quite fit. Most of the guests appeared to be somewhat ill at ease, and while Jesse certainly was happy at last to be invited to mix with these Democratic power brokers, he, too, was uneasy. Everyone knew that the guests had come as an acknowledgment that this was now a force to be recognized within the Democratic Party, but they had decidedly not come to give Jackson their endorsement. The mood was later described as "respectful."

Former Democratic National Committee chairman John C. White, whom Jackson had been wooing ever since the middle of March when he attended Jackson's breakfast at *Time,* noted that the guest list was "heavy with chieftains" from defeated campaigns: Frank Mankiewicz (McGovern, 1972), Berl Bernhard (Muskie, 1972), Richard Moe (Gephardt, 1988) and Robert Neuman (Representative Morris K. Udall and Governor Bruce Babbitt). Jackson's own campaign chairman, Willie Brown, Speaker of the California Assembly, flew across the country for the event. There were also others, like the economists John Kenneth Galbraith and Elliot Janeway, who had advised previous Democratic administrations. But there were a number of leading Democrats who didn't attend, including Robert Strauss, another former DNC chairman and a leading power broker in Washington.

Clark Clifford, with his white hair and bushy eyebrows, opened the breakfast. In his gentle, persuasive voice, he assured the guest of honor that no one in that room would ever be party to any effort to stop Jackson's campaign. He declared that a Jesse Jackson presidency would bring to Washington "the best brains the party and the country have to offer." Over the past few months, Clifford had often been listed by Jackson as one of his advisers because Jackson had phoned him a few times. After this breakfast, Jackson frequently told reporters that Clark Clifford was among his "top policy advisers." There were the pictures of them hobnobbing and sitting next to each other early that morning in a Jefferson Hotel dining room to prove it.

Then Jackson delivered his "standard campaign pitch." He was quieter and spoke more precisely than usual. He enunciated his words carefully instead of falling into the more slurry style that he often lapsed into in speeches. The fact that the night before Jackson had lost the Connecticut primary was easily dismissed by his pointing out that it was in Massachusetts governor Dukakis's backyard. He announced that John White had agreed to help him in Atlanta if any brokering was needed at the convention. Jackson chose his words carefully as he addressed this special group and remarked: "John White on the inside is worth more than a crowd demonstrating on the outside."

Then the floor was opened to questions, but there were only three. One was about his association with the Nation of Islam leader Louis Farrakhan, which Jackson dismissed as settled, maintaining that he had dissociated himself from his former ally and that he believed in "redemption, not punishment." To the second question—whether he'd prepared himself enough to deal with the scrutiny to which he would now be subjected—he acknowledged that as yet his preparation was "not enough." To the third question, about defense spending, Jackson gave a concise answer: "We cannot ex-change the short-term pleasure for long-term pain." That referred to his belief that the military should get less and social programs more in the national budget. That notion jangled the nerves of some of the defense-oriented guests.

Jackson had earlier described the breakfast meeting to the press as an example of old wineskins "expanding to make room for new wine." Then inside the meeting, when several guests offered their assistance to Jackson, he appeared to rebuff them with what he thought was a joke: "Sometimes you can make energy out of trash." He meant that perhaps he could find a way to use them even if they had been thrown out. Everyone laughed politely. Conservative crit-ics later commented that it was typical of liberals to take such verbal abuse with smiles as if they deserved it or were afraid of being called racist if they took umbrage at the remark.

The breakfast lasted less than an hour, but Jackson was pleased. It looked good, he told aides, even though he had not come away with any new endorsement. More than a hundred reporters were waiting outside the room, and bedlam ensued in the hotel's nor-mally quiet and discreet lobby when the guests emerged. The first to speak was Clark Clifford. He described the preceding hour as "an extraordinary event" and went on to say: "The meeting has been devoted to listening to Jesse Jackson tell us about his contact with the American people." He concluded his remarks with: "The Dem-ocratic Party has always been the party of innovation. It's possible that Jesse Jackson may be the one to bring innovation to our party."

Senator Tom Harkin, Democrat of Iowa, came out to deny re-ports of panic about Jackson in the Senate. But Mickey Leland was also there, and he continued spreading rumors among the hungry press that a dangerously widespread "Stop Jesse" movement was being organized in Congress.

Reporters then turned to another guest, Bernard Rappaport of Texas, and asked him whether he, as a Jew, had any problems with Jackson. Although at the time Rappaport was still a supporter of Senator Simon, he said: "I don't think he's anti-Semitic or anti-Israel. The whole thing can be solved by people like me in the

Jewish community. We have to say what he just said." He also said that he didn't predict there would be a problem for Jackson with the Jewish vote in New York.

Jackson's campaign chairman, Willie Brown, displayed edginess when a reporter asked him: "You came here to get acceptance?" Brown sharply retorted: "What are you talking about? We came here to close this thing out and get votes. Dukakis was here Monday, and did you ask him if he came here to get acceptance? We didn't solicit anybody's support. We didn't pass the plate."

Later Gerry Austin commented: "The meeting was nothing, just bullshit. The purpose was only to get a lot of those kinds of people all in a room together with Jesse." The meeting succeeded in getting the well-publicized, symbolic pictures the campaign had long been seeking.

Jackson knew the meeting didn't mean "acceptance," but it represented a step a lot further down that road than he'd ever been before, and he was riding high. He knew there were really only one or two other Democratic candidates to consider besides himself—Dukakis and Gore. Gephardt was preparing to drop out of the race the next week, and Simon was expected to pull out after Wisconsin.

In fact, later that day, Jackson felt powerful enough to cancel a tête-à-tête tentatively scheduled for that afternoon with Senator Albert Gore, Jr. That morning in New York, Gore had attacked Jackson by saying that the country is "not choosing a preacher, but a President" and that the "presidency is not a pulpit." Later, when Gore arrived at National Airport just as Jackson was flying out, Gore said: "My attacks are not personal and there is no reason why anyone should think that Jesse Jackson ought to be treated differently from any candidate in this race."

Jesse didn't care what Gore or any other candidate said at that point. The world was chasing after him, and he was on his way to Wisconsin to win a major primary, and then on to New York, and beyond. He knew he had ignited a great fire of hope among blacks and whites across America. His message was winning. And he also believed that his charismatic personality would carry him forward to victory if the voters would just take the leap of faith and deem him "electable."

Wisconsin was a state like Michigan that could prove fertile ground for Jackson's message. Although blacks made up only 6 percent of the population, Wisconsin had a long liberal tradition, and liberal whites were attracted to Jackson's left-wing positions. On campuses like Madison, Jackson was already popular among the new generation of anti-establishment students. The state had also been suffering economically, and conditions had become progressively worse in the last years of Reagan's presidency. Wisconsin's imperiled farmers and industrial workers looked to Jesse Jackson as a ray of hope. Wisconsin was also very important in the election process because it held a primary rather than a caucus. That meant there would be more voters, and the voting would be more representative because it would be by secret ballot. Also, Wisconsin had a strong tradition of voters turning out the vote. Of Wisconsin's 4.8 million population, almost half voted in 1984.

The Wisconsin primary was also important because the state required no party registration. Thus a voter could wait until he got inside the privacy of the voting booth to decide which party to vote for that time. The Republicans had threatened to cross over and vote Democratic to give their vote to Jackson in order to throw the Democrats into turmoil. The Republican governor, Tommy Thompson, had denied that he was encouraging crossovers, but many Republicans said they been given the signal. While Jackson publicly would decry this practice, he knew that such Republican shenanigans would only help him muster more votes. Members of the Democratic establishment who were privately engaged in efforts to halt Jackson's success were seriously concerned that crossovers would give him many more votes than the other candidates.

Jesse Jackson had over the past few years identified himself with the struggles of Wisconsin's farmers and unemployed industrial workers. In 1987, only the year before, Jackson had come and marched with the striking meat-packers at the Patrick Cudahy meat-packing plant. The town of Cudahy was an overwhelmingly white industrial suburb south of Milwaukee. Before the fifteen-month-long meat-packers' strike shook the suburb to its foundation, few of the residents would have imagined considering a black as President. But Jesse Jackson's solidarity with them and the national publicity he gave to their problem changed that view, and Jackson now expected many to support him in Wisconsin. As one meat-packer, who was quoted in the press, said: "Jesse Jackson was the only one who came down and marched with us last year. You remember that."

Kenosha, Wisconsin, was another place that Jesse Jackson had turned into a symbol of the nation's economic woes under the Reagan Administration. Kenosha had started during the Iowa campaign and it was a classic example of how Jesse would get the idea of helping in a crisis somewhere and then put his ideas into action.

On January 28 Chrysler announced that it planned to cut out five thousand jobs at its Kenosha plant. The Kenosha work force was then 6,500, of which 80 percent were whites; by September there would be only one thousand workers. We were in Austin, Texas, at the time and Jesse was preparing for a press conference in the state capitol. The beeper from Chicago headquarters told me to call them. Pam Smith, the communications coordinator there, said that Frank Watkins wanted me to "tell the Reverend" as soon as possible about Chrysler's action.

I told Jesse about Kenosha as we were striding down the corridors of the capitol building. He asked me for some details and then put everything in his mental computer. Later that afternoon, addressing the state's AFL-CIO convention, Jackson referred to the Kenosha shutdown and already had coined a line that he would use time and again: "If the United States government can bail out Chrysler and Mr. Lee Iacocca, then it can bail out the town of Kenosha."

Four days later Jesse was preparing to go to Kenosha as soon as possible. He'd had the brainstorm overnight, just after we'd arrived back in Iowa from the weekend in Chicago. It was Monday morning, February 1, and we were in Dubuque, Iowa. Mark Steitz and I had gone to Jesse's room in the Dubuque Inn at 8 A.M. to begin preparing for our coming week in Iowa and one day in New Hampshire. Jesse said we would have to change our schedule, but it was important. "It's a point of challenge," he said. "We should pin our 'Workers' Bill of Rights' on the Chrysler plant gate. That's a point of challenge."

Jesse directed me to get hold of the mayor of Kenosha. "We need to get an invitation," he instructed. "We have to go as their official guests. We'll have the UAW invite us, too." I finally reached Mayor Eugene Dorff at his Kenosha office and then the UAW local president, Ed Steagall. When Jesse explained what he wanted to do, they extended the invitation he needed.

Then he told me to get hold of Lee Iacocca, chairman of Chrysler Motors in Detroit, but he was unavailable. It wasn't till the next morning, as we were leaving little Niederhauser Airport in Waterloo, Iowa, to fly to Racine, Wisconsin, the nearest airport to Kenosha, that I finally got through to Iacocca's chief aide, Mike Glusac. Jesse got on the phone and informed him of his plans. We were on our way to Kenosha at that moment, and Jackson intended to give national publicity to the plight of Mr. Iacocca's plant.

It was freezing when we landed in Wisconsin, near the shore of Lake Michigan. The windchill that damp day reached twenty-two below zero. Both the mayor and the UAW local president met Jackson at the Racine airport and took us first to the union hall for private meetings with the union leaders.

Late in the morning there was the town rally that had been organized overnight when the town learned of Jackson's impending visit. It was held at the Fifty-second Street Chrysler Overpass. More than five thousand people turned out in the bitter-cold open air to listen to Jesse Jackson. Just beforehand, the Secret Service got word that several threatening phone calls had been made, so Jesse donned his bulletproof vest. He didn't wear it all the time. He believed that God was protecting him.

Afterward, over lunch back at the union hall, Jesse persuaded both Mayor Dorff and Ed Steagall to fly back with us to Iowa. They could tell the people of Iowa how Jesse Jackson had come to help their people. Steagall later recalled: "Jackson offered his people to help us. Everywhere he went [after that day in Kenosha]—Iowa, Texas, Florida—he talked about the injustice the Chrysler Corporation was doing the people of Kenosha."

Easter 1988 came a week after Jackson's victory in Michigan, the day before the Colorado caucus, and two days before the Wisconsin primary. It also fell one day before the twentieth anniversary of the assassination of Dr. Martin Luther King, Jr., April 4, 1968.

Jesse Jackson celebrated his Easter, April 3, in Denver, Colorado, where he delivered two sermons in two different churches—at the First Baptist Church, where two congregations came together (one predominantly black African Methodists and the other predominantly white Baptists), and at a largely Hispanic Roman Catholic church. In both sermons he used old and new stories from his repertoire to draw comparisons among his own 1988 campaign, King's civil rights movement and the resurrection of Jesus Christ.

"In the case of Dr. King and Jesus, we cannot separate them from the politics of their day," he said. And he repeated the story of the birth of Christ, as he had in many other speeches—telling how Jesus was born to homeless parents, to an unwed mother, to people who were being taxed without representation.

Then he said that his campaign had generated new hope in America. He maintained that the crowds coming to him were signs that "hope has been unleashed."

"That Easter is going on suggests that we have survived the long midnight," Jackson said. "We cannot stop the government from crucifying righteous people, but then government cannot stop righteous people from being renewed—in the next election."

Throughout the weekend in Colorado, he tied the anniversary of King's death directly to the Colorado election: "April 4 is the day in 1968 when Dr. King was assassinated. April 4 is the day to revisit the agenda and finish the unfinished business of the dreamer." By now, Jackson was pointing to his own achievements as much as to King's and the civil rights movement of a quarter century ago in invoking a new black messiah.

The week after the Michigan vote, Jackson's TV network coverage jumped from 3.3 minutes from the previous week to a record 21.7 minutes. He was ecstatic. With the media hotly pursuing him everywhere now, Jesse was convinced then that all he needed on the road was a "press secretary" who would "babysit the press."

The day after Michigan I was still at home preparing to rejoin the team, but I was also still struggling with how I could gracefully bow out. After a week away, I knew I found Jackson's behavior and treatment of me unbearable, and I was trying to figure out what and how to tell him. I had left a telephone message for Gerry Austin to phone me before my departure later the next day. On Monday morning, March 28, Gerry called and said that for the past twenty-four hours he and Jesse had been taking a look at the new direction of the campaign and what changes they needed to make. When Austin said that Jesse had decided he didn't need or want me on the road all the time, I admitted my own dissatisfaction with the job. Although I felt some disappointment, I was also extremely relieved.

Essentially, Austin said, what they were thinking about was having me work part of the time on the road and part out of the Washington office, which would be within commuting distance from my house. Austin told me: "There is some sort of a tension between you and Reverend Jackson. It seems to be a personal thing, and it's probably him. He probably doesn't like strong women working around him too close. There's no denying Jesse's a sexist."

Jackson himself never felt he had to give anyone any explanations. Also, he never liked to deal personally with staffing problems. And in this case, as Gerry suggested, Jackson wouldn't want to admit the truth, the real causes for his discomfort, because they were perhaps diametrically at variance with his rhetoric.

Austin went on to relay what Jackson himself had been saying about the job: "All he really wants, as he says, is someone to babysit the press on the road. Your asset is who you talk to, and you can do that from almost anywhere, even from your home telephone. Anyway, let's all think about it and figure out how we can work out your job on the campaign."

On April 4, Austin phoned again, and we were able to work out a deal. I left the post of press secretary but agreed to stay with the campaign for a while to work as a "media consultant," at least until June 15, after the California primary. In the meantime, Austin said, I would be free to write about the campaign as well as discuss it with national journalists. I still believed in the issues, the Jackson political message and the historic significance of Jesse Jackson's campaign for the presidency. But it was with an extraordinary sense of relief that I knew I did not have to go back to that work on the road with Jackson. I felt as if my prayers had been answered.

Jackson was careening along by then anyway, and he didn't think he needed any help, particularly since the Michigan caucus the previous week. The media were eating out of his hand, and Jesse Jackson didn't want anyone between him and them. On June 13, I telephoned Jesse at his house in Chicago to tell him I would be leaving to write a book about his campaign. He mumbled: "I'll need to know more about it, but I'm too busy now." I said I would call later, and he said: "Okay, dear, we'll be in touch." But he didn't return my calls after that.

On April 5, Jesse Jackson lost in both Colorado and Wisconsin. The front-runner in both states was Governor Michael Dukakis. In the more important Wisconsin primary, Jackson won only 28 percent of the vote to Dukakis's 48 percent. Dukakis even beat Jackson two to one in Kenosha, where Jackson believed he had given his soul.

Jesse was downcast. Publicly, he acknowledged that it was a slow, but incremental process he was engaged in, persuading the American people that it would be possible to elect a black President. After his showing in Wisconsin, he pointed out: "The large crowds that came in Wisconsin with many whites, the more they come and the more I have access to them, the more their fears are relieved and the more we find that we're all one and we have a lot in common." But now there was this double defeat. He confided in some aides that he was sure it was the result of a racist "Stop Jesse Jackson" campaign.

Pundits called Michigan "a fluke." To have thought that a small turnout in Michigan's caucus meant that Jesse Jackson was the nation's front-runner for the Democrats was "a misreading of the tea leaves," one said. Most agreed that Jackson had hurt himself later in Wisconsin and Colorado by overraised expectations.

After Wisconsin, many news organizations' editors and executives were asking themselves whether they had overplayed Jackson's Michigan victory and had perhaps overestimated his strength after underestimating him for so long before.

At ABC News, political director Hal Bruno said that Michigan "was a small thing in terms of the number of people involved, and it was a caucus, not a primary. It was probably, therefore, played for more than it was worth. But you cannot take away the fact that it was a major event for Jesse."

Both major newsmagazines, *Time* and *Newsweek,* did some soul-searching about their previous week's cover stories on Jesse Jackson. *Time*'s senior editor for national news, Walter Isaacson, explained their rationale: "The reason we did a Jesse Jackson cover was not to talk about that week's situation in the Democratic campaign. It was to talk about something that is of major historic importance in a nation where blacks have been unable to achieve true political power for two hundred years."

Newsweek's executive editor, Stephen Smith, said that their reporters and photographers had been impressed with the crowds of white faces following Jackson in Wisconsin, but they later realized that crowds are not necessarily going to vote for him. He said: "I think we've seen that it's part his charisma and part the celebrity of the candidate. And I suppose that even though he ran in 1984, there is an element of curiosity about a black man making history. I think the crowds show a large measure of enthusiasm, but I think maybe the press got a little overenthusiastic about his Michigan result."

Many Wisconsin Democrats later said that in the early days after Michigan, they had been swept away by the excitement of Jackson's campaign. They were carried away by the charismatic leader's moving speeches, and were tantalized by the notion of making history by electing a black to the office of President. But then, they said, they weighed his qualifications as potential nominee and President, and they decided to vote for the seemingly steadier, more centrist Dukakis.

Most believed that in the final moment before their votes were cast, race was not the issue. As *New York Times* political correspondent E. J. Dionne, Jr., later wrote in an analytical article entitled "Jesse Jackson Made History While Losing Wisconsin": "Let it be recorded that for at least one week in American history, in a middle-sized Midwestern state, a broad range of white voters took the Presidential candidacy of a black man with the utmost seriousness."

11

THE NEW YORK PRIMARY

"Common ground. When people come together, flowers always flourish—the air is rich with the aroma of a new spring. . . .

Take New York, the dynamic metropolis. What makes New York so special? . . . It's the invitation of the Statue of Liberty—give me your tired, your poor, your huddled masses who yearn to breathe free. Not restricted to English only. Many people, many cultures, many languages—with one thing in common, the yearning to breathe free. Common ground."

New York to Jesse Jackson was the microcosm of America, the great nation where human diversity could meet and find common ground. That was his dream, but his union with a large segment of New York's population seemed elusive.

New York City was Jackson's kind of place: fast, electrifying, dynamic, media-oriented, constantly moving, powerful, compassionate yet often cruel. A place where Jesse could operate, a place that hardly took note of celebrities because there were so many, New York City would welcome Jesse Jackson as a celebrity. And he couldn't stand *not* being noticed.

New York, the city and the state, both attracted and frightened Jackson. He had been looking forward to the New York primary, set for April 19, since the beginning of the campaign. Early in the season, polls had shown Jackson leading in New York, and he knew it would be his watershed. Its size and the diversity of its population gave it its power. A candidate who could win there could become the party's nominee. In 1984, 87 percent of New York's eligible black voters had turned out to vote for him. He had won 25.6 percent of the state total and placed third in the delegate count. He believed he could now win many more whites because his message had begun appealing to the white constituency of his Rainbow Coalition, all represented in New York—blue-collar workers, liberals, homosexuals, students, environmentalists, peace activists.

New York had 255 delegates at stake, but in 1988 the primary was more critical than usual because of its timing. It came midway in the primary voting season. By its date, April 19, over half of the nation's primaries and caucuses had already been held. Thus the field was narrowed, but still for the Democrats there was no clear winner, no definite front-runner, as the Republicans already had in Vice President George Bush. Dukakis at that point had the lead in terms of national convention delegates, but Jackson had a chance for an upset victory. He could even endanger Dukakis's tenuous lead by placing a close second in New York. The only other remaining Democratic candidate was Senator Gore, and Jackson hoped that Gore would take away some of Dukakis's votes. Jackson was pleased there were three candidates left, not just himself and Dukakis.

But despite the fact that it was springtime in New York, there was the smell of bitterness and hatred emanating from the tension between the Jews and the blacks, a tension that had been exacerbated years ago by Jesse Jackson himself. How to deal with the Jews was a major problem. He hired a Jewish campaign manager and several Jewish advisers and asked them to prepare background papers on the subject.

In 1984 Jackson had called New York City "Hymietown." He had called Jews "Hymies." He had publicly associated with an avowed anti-Semite, Louis Farrakhan, the black leader of the Nation of Islam in America, a man who had said that Hitler was right to have tried to annihilate the Jews. In New York City lived the largest population of Jews in America. Most of them had not forgiven Jackson his slurs. They mistrusted him enormously and feared him intensely. Jackson knew enough to sense that, but he never seemed to understand why or what he could do about it.

Now he had to face America's mainstream Jews head-on because of their power and population. In a place where there should have been so many important issues to discuss, a place where Jackson's broad message of hope could appeal to so many disenfranchised, the New York campaign devolved into a single issue—the Jewish issue. What was Jackson's relationship with the Jewish community? What about his position on the Middle East? Was he anti-Semitic? Why wouldn't he renounce the outspoken Louis Farrakhan?

Even to some of his closest associates, it seemed that Jackson himself never understood the depth of the problem. Yes, he had mistakenly referred to New York as "Hymietown" and Jews as "Hymies" in 1984, but he believed he had apologized. Of course, he insisted he wasn't anti-Jewish. Yes, he had dissociated himself from Farrakhan in 1984 and again this year in 1988, but he refused to cut him off completely and denounce him. Yes, he had embraced Yasir Arafat in 1979 and had called for a Palestinian homeland, but now the U.S. government under President Reagan was coming around to his views on Israel and the Palestinians.

Many believed the problem was that Jesse Jackson, in spite of his bold rhetoric denouncing racism, was deeply racist. They said his racism was not, as one friend had described it, used only as a crucifix by a consummate politician. From childhood, when he had been treated as a second-class citizen by the law, by whites in general and by some Jews in particular, he had become bitter and angry toward nonblacks, and he set them apart from himself and his people. He had spent much of his adult life trying to overcome his negative racist feelings, and by and large he had done a good job, certainly in terms of his public rhetoric and beliefs.

In 1984, he had used the derogatory terms in an off-the-record conversation with a black reporter. Often when he met other blacks he would say: "Let's talk nigra talk" or "Let's talk black." He would do it even in front of the whites with him, and it seemed to be his way of cutting them off. That day in 1984 he had done it with the veteran black *Washington Post* reporter Milton Coleman. At National Airport, Jackson was waiting for a plane when he saw Coleman. Then he said his typical "Let's talk black talk." Jackson was furious when his words were printed, because he said he thought they were off the record.

Then, in 1987, when Jackson hired Gerald Austin, who was Jewish, to be his national campaign manager, he and Gerry talked about his Jewish problem. Gerry overcame his personal objections about the "Hymietown" remarks after he confronted Jackson on the matter: "I said it was doubly offensive to me—I'm Jewish and a New Yorker. Jackson said it was a stupid thing to say and that he apologized. I also told him: 'I'm for a Palestinian homeland just as long as it isn't Israel,' and he said so was he. [But] we realize there is a segment that will never forgive." Gerry felt that Jesse had done enough, had apologized enough. He would just have to carry on, spreading the message that he believed in, and Gerry thought that mainstream Jews would eventually respond. But Gerry came from the most liberal Jewish tradition. He didn't buy the conservative Zionist line.

On one radio call-in show after another in New York, after his appointment as Jackson's campaign manager, Austin in his tough, blunt voice retorted: "How many times does the man have to go to the temple to atone for his sins? He's done it. He shouldn't be forced to atone again." That was Austin's bottom line on the Jewish issue all the way through the New York primary campaign.

Some other members of the staff and some Jewish advisers felt Jackson had to do more, especially about Farrakhan. But Jackson refused. As one Jewish *New York Times* editor told me: "Until Jackson publicly breaks with Farrakhan and finally resolves that issue, he'll never be accepted by the Jews." Jackson, however, felt satisfied with the advice he got from his Jewish campaign manager. That was sufficient, he insisted.

Early in the campaign, months before the New York primary erupted with all its ethnic tension between Jews and blacks, a top Jackson aide distributed an anonymous background paper containing talking points on "Jackson and his relationship to the Jewish community." It was to remain the Bible for Jackson's and his staff's dealing with the issue. It had six topic headings: on his relationship until 1979; on "Hymie" and "Hymietown" (1984); since 1984; on Soviet Jewry; on Farrakhan; on the Middle East. Nowhere did it suggest that Jackson himself might have to do more to change the situation. The points were all defensive.

Under the heading "his relationship until 1979," there were two points. Before 1979, it said, Jesse Jackson was perceived as a good friend of the Jewish community, noting that he had spoken out against the American Nazi Party's march in Skokie, Illinois. Then, in 1979, it said, he came under significant criticism when he visited the Middle East and met with many Arab leaders, including PLO chairman Yasir Arafat. The paper pointed out that it was wrong to characterize that meeting as anti-Jewish on his part, because he had gone to urge Arafat to call for mutual recognition between the PLO and Israel.

On the subject of "Hymie" and "Hymietown," the Jackson campaign background paper first explicitly accused the black reporter of behaving unethically and unprofessionally by breaching a private confidence. It then implied that *The Washington Post* turned it into a big story because powerful interests were concerned because Jackson was then running at 16 percent in the New Hampshire polls. The matter should be considered closed now because, as the paper pointed out, Jackson had spoken to the issue both in the synagogue in New Hampshire and at the Democratic National Convention.

The paper then listed a number of steps Jackson had taken since 1984 "intended to reduce fears and build bridges of understanding between himself and the Jewish community, as well as improve black-Jewish relations in general." The list included private meetings with Jewish leaders across the country, speeches to national Christian-Jewish conferences, participation in black-Jewish events and dialogues, speaking to the Reform rabbis' organization, the Union of American Hebrew Congregations, in Washington, D.C., and visiting a Nazi concentration camp and speaking against the Holocaust and anti-Semitism.

The paper pointed out, also, how Jesse Jackson had spoken directly with Soviet leader Mikhail Gorbachev about the issue of Soviet Jewry when he attended the Geneva summit in 1985. Jesse himself often reminded his audiences that he alone had raised this issue at that time and, as the paper put it, "before the cameras of the world." Even though Jackson frequently pointed to that gesture as important in demonstrating his sincerity in helping and working with Jews, no one seemed to have taken much notice.

On the Middle East, the paper maintained that Jackson in 1988 was the only candidate with a viable peace plan for the region. It would "provide true security for Israel by providing justice for the Palestinians—two sides of the same coin." How many times would Jesse himself say this? And toward the end of the campaign, many American Jews, Israelis and the Reagan administration were urging such a solution—negotiation between Israelis and Palestinians.

On the subject of Louis Farrakhan, the campaign background paper stated Jackson's final position: "(1) He is not a part of the 1988 campaign. (2) In 1984, [Jackson] disassociated himself from Farrakhan's objectionable remarks. But this didn't satisfy some who wanted him to repudiate the personhood of Farrakhan."

The paper then elaborated on Jackson's position vis-à-vis Farrakhan. It stated emphatically that Jackson would never "repudiate the personhood of Farrakhan": "This he refused to do! Rev. Jackson is a minister who believes in separating the sin from the sinner. One should condemn the sin, not the sinner. Black civil rights activists like Rev. Jackson repudiated the rhetoric and behavior of Bull Connor, Orval Faubus and George Wallace in the 1960's but did not repudiate their personhood. When Rev. Jackson debated with KKK head David Duke on television, he repudiated Duke's statements, his philosophy and his behavior—but not his personhood. In the non-violent tradition, this is perceived as strength (not as a weakness) in the civil rights movement."

Perhaps Jackson's philosophy of separating the sin from the sinner was simply in diametrical conflict with the wishes of his Jewish detractors. Jesse's belief in such a philosophy was real. He was always making public gestures of forgiveness and understanding to demonstrate this conviction. He seemed incapable of understanding, for example, why Jews would insist on hunting down and punishing the remaining Nazi leaders. Once he was discussing that subject with a small group of staff on his campaign plane. Finally, Gerry Austin could stand it no more and told Jackson bluntly that it was obvious he didn't comprehend the Jewish feelings about the Holocaust. Jackson then started saying that he didn't want to punish the descendants of slave owners, but Austin interrupted to say that was different because those descendants had not been the criminals. In the case of the Holocaust, in contrast to American slavery, the perpetrators themselves were still living.

Louis Farrakhan was anathema to Jews and to many other sensitive whites and even some blacks who recognized the dangers he posed. They pointed out how his inflammatory words had fueled tensions between blacks and Jews. In 1984 he had praised Hitler as "a great man," and he'd labeled Judaism "a dirty religion." He had publicly threatened Jews with retaliation if their criticisms hurt Jesse Jackson. For some reason, Jackson refused to acknowledge the dangers Farrakhan posed to his future, to his political aspirations. As one white aide in 1988 said: "Can't he see that Farrakhan could reappear any day and wreck his campaign? He should renounce him once and for all."

In the case of Farrakhan, however, there was another factor that weighed more importantly for Jackson than his nonviolent philosophy. That was Jackson's fear that in renouncing Farrakhan he would alienate a significant number of blacks by giving in to the Jews' demand. Many black friends and advisers had told Jackson this. They defended his position. For four years they had urged him

not to give in to the Jews, not to forswear his old ally Louis Farrakhan.

Probably, by 1988, with his popularity so great among blacks,
such an action would have alienated very few black supporters at
all. Jesse most likely knew that, but by the time of the New York
primary in April, his steadfast refusal to repudiate Farrakhan had
become a matter of principle for him. The more the Jews pushed,
the more entrenched he became in his determination to stand his
ground. In April he insisted that he wanted to get on with other
things, spreading his message of hope.

But New York was not going to let him have his way. He might
want to bypass the Jewish issue, but others controlled what happened in New York. It became the single dominant issue of the
whole statewide campaign. Beginning with New York City's Jewish
mayor, Edward I. Koch, enthusiastically followed by the media
packs, Jackson's relations with Jews became the central theme of
the New York campaign. New York City would never let Jesse
Jackson forget that he'd called it "Hymietown."

And New York's Mayor Koch wouldn't let Jackson forget he'd
referred to him and other Jews as "Hymies." Even before the candidates came to town, while they were still out campaigning in the
Wisconsin primary and Colorado caucus, Koch fired the opening
and most memorable salvo. On ABC's *Nightline* show on Friday
night, April 1, the weekend before the Wisconsin vote, the fiery
mayor of New York City said Jews have "got to be crazy" to vote
for Jesse Jackson. The next morning his words were on the front
page of Saturday's *New York Post* and dominated weekend television and radio news. Koch had launched the New York campaign
almost a week before the candidates could even get there.

Jackson was incensed. He had been sincerely trying to be conciliatory and had harnessed his tongue for the most part throughout
the campaign. Not only had he hired Jews; he had given his Jewish
advisers high visibility. That Monday, for example, in the April 11
issue of *Time,* which appeared on the newsstands on April 4, there
was a box inset showing the faces of four of his key advisers, and
three of them were Jewish—Gerry Austin, Carol O'Cleireacain and

Ann Lewis. That kind of coverage didn't help him with his traditional black supporters, but he hoped it would help him in New York. But, Jesse confided to his close aides, nothing seemed ever to appease the Jews. They were simply against him, he said, most likely because of his advanced positions on the Middle East. They would never forget that photograph of Arafat hugging him in 1979. But he still wouldn't acknowledge the other problem: Farrakhan's omnipresent shadow behind him.

Jesse decided to try to keep the campaign focused on policy issues, not ethnic conflict. After Wisconsin, he went to Arizona to campaign briefly in advance of its April 19 primary and then to Indianapolis on April 6 before flying the next day to New York. On the plane he talked with his aides, mostly Austin and Steitz, and planned how they would concentrate, not on the Jewish issue, but on his budget and tax proposals, his foreign and defense policies, his education and health-care plans. He said he would keep pushing his war on drugs, his focus on economic violence, his support of gays and lesbians and his call for an end to AIDS, and he would emphasize his concern for women and the elderly.

As for the Jewish issue, he said they should ignore Koch's remark. Bert Lance had advised Jackson to turn the other cheek and make peace with the Jews. But Jackson really was naïve, it seemed in retrospect, to think that the New York and national media, or even Koch for that matter, would let the subject die. But aides and reporters remarked that Jackson was so overconfident by then about his control over the media that he couldn't imagine the issue getting out of hand. Thus, on his way to New York, when he made the statements: "People forgive and move on. It's the only way you can really function," and "I did what no one else has ever done. I expressed my feelings in July 1984 to four hundred million people," he thought that was sufficient. He tried to underscore a need for harmony by speaking of his talks with Gorbachev about Soviet Jewry and his marching with the Jews in Skokie to protest the planned neo-Nazi march. His words and claims fell on mostly deaf ears.

Jesse Jackson's will was not as powerful as he might have

thought; there were forces greater than his own during the New York primary. Indeed, he kept trying to publicize his message and produce details of his various social and economic programs, but the media would not hear them. They were, to be fair, noted in the newspaper of record, *The New York Times,* but most of the rest of the media were interested in only one thing—the battle between Jesse and the Jews, led by Mayor Koch. In the end, both men were hurt by the conflict.

On April 7, Jackson's first day in New York since the campaign for that primary began, he began to realize that his previous statements about the Jewish issue had not at all put it to rest. He didn't know it then, but it would get worse and worse. Each day, when he would be trying to talk "message," to broadcast some substance, he would be hit again by Koch, other politicians or the media with more and more questions about his relationship with the Jewish community.

Jackson was welcomed in New York on Thursday, April 7, by the New York Democratic Party chairman, Laurence J. Kirwan, who said his state's primary would be "the hardball capital of the world." On that first day, he attended a midday candidates' forum at the *New York Daily News.* The editorial-page editor predicted: "It's going to be nasty. The big battle is going to be containing the propensity for it to turn into a bloodbath." And no prospect could be more appealing to the New York tabloid press.

Everywhere Jackson went that first day, he was barraged with questions about the Jewish issue. Jackson kept trying to change the subject back to his message: "Let us keep this campaign above any form of racial or religious bigotry or anything that incites such a reaction. We deserve an open, free, fair and clean election. I'm determined to keep this campaign at that high plane. So I would hope that no responsible leader would scream 'fire' in a theater and incite people's fears." Jesse tried to be conciliatory and to keep his cool, but even he was flustered by the end of the first day.

His campaign manager, Gerry Austin, had become visibly angry with the incessant questions about Jackson's position on the Jewish issue. Gerry kept shouting at reporters to stop putting Jesse on trial again. "Look," he said, "[Jackson] said things he shouldn't have said and he's apologized. There's no reason for putting him on trial. We don't accept this as a one-issue campaign, and the people who are angry at him and listen to Mayor Koch are not going to vote for him anyway."

Another Jewish supporter of Jackson got even angrier. Barry Feinstein, president of Local 237 of the International Brotherhood of Teamsters, who had just endorsed Jackson's candidacy, blasted out with his opinion as he stood next to the black candidate. He said in angry tones: "The mayor's rhetoric is inappropriate. It is divisive. It is wrong. The issue is not whether Ed Koch speaks for the Jews of this city. He does not. He doesn't speak for me, and I am as Jewish as any Jew who ever lived."

A lot of other Jews felt the same way, and some would say so. Others were afraid. Many more basically agreed with the mayor, but by the end of the campaign the consensus was that the mayor had overstepped the bounds of propriety, and he had also hurt himself in a city with such a large nonwhite population. He'd even hurt himself with many Jews who felt he had ultimately embarrassed them by acting so vicious and downright racist. They believed he'd stirred up racial tension in a city that hadn't needed any more. Some began to sympathize with Jackson and said they believed that overall he handled himself well in the midst of endless attacks.

That first day in New York, Jackson conferred constantly with Austin about what tack to take. Austin advised him not to accept a number of invitations from prominent Jewish organizations. This, actually, wasn't a new policy, since for the most part over the months Jackson had turned down invitations to speak before Jewish groups. He and Austin and Watkins thought such appearances would do him more harm than good. They believed that it would take only a few attackers in such a group to destroy whatever positive impact Jackson might have had on the rest of the group. They knew that anything negative coming from such a meeting would be broadcast all over the media. A few other advisers disagreed with this decision. They felt, as I had about the importance of Jesse's sitting down and meeting with major editorial boards, that Jackson would gain more by meeting and talking with these Jewish groups than by avoiding them. Jackson refused that advice.

The very next morning, Friday, April 8, *The New York Times* published a column by its former executive editor, Abe Rosenthal, in which he urged Jackson to "seize the moment." Rosenthal wrote that Jackson "has it in his power in New York to dispel once and for all the fear among so many American Jews that by what he has said or not said, he has shown anti-Semitism, or at least distaste for Jews. This would be a healing balm for all American society."

Rosenthal acknowledged that Jackson considered the whole problem unfair and wished it would just go away, but the fact of the matter was that it existed. Rosenthal said: "The job of a national leader, which Mr. Jackson has become, is to confront an unpleasant reality, grapple with it and change it."

He concluded: "Like him or fight him, what counts about Jesse Jackson is that he is more inspiring to American blacks than any candidate in history. It lies within his power in New York to be not only a politician but a healer, thus inspiring to all Americans, including those who do not vote for him."

Jackson saw the Op-Ed page column first thing that morning. He expressed frustration. What else could he do? he asked rhetorically of his aides. What he did was incorporate some of Rosenthal's words and suggestions into his speeches in the coming hours. At the very first meeting of the day, a labor breakfast at Sardi's restaurant, Jackson proclaimed that he was making every effort to "build" and "heal" relationships with the Jewish community. But as with many of Jackson's plans, he failed to furnish details.

The truth was that Jackson always paid special attention to what Abe Rosenthal wrote about him. After Iowa, when Rosenthal had suggested that Jackson could be offered a newly created post of "drug czar," Jackson picked up on the idea and capitalized on it. Just before Super Tuesday, Rosenthal alerted the media that Jackson should not be taken for granted any longer. Now he was advising Jackson to mend his relations with Jews. Jackson was impressed with the power of *The New York Times* and such a personage as

Rosenthal. But it irked Jackson, too, that these people were so powerful. He never knew how to deal with them, and he would often try to demonstrate his own superiority with counterproductive tactics. A few days after Rosenthal's piece, Jesse Jackson arrived two hours late for a meeting with the *Times*'s editorial board. Everyone was riled, saying Jackson never changed, and at least two of the editors left before he finally showed up as a protest against his rudeness. Jesse thought he had won, but those editors declared they would never forget "his childish behavior."

But in New York, Jesse Jackson was still a celebrity, as well as the "main event" for New York Democrats. He was a media star, and everybody wanted to see a star, whether they would vote for him or not. In some white neighborhoods, reporters described the onlookers as watching with fear in their eyes as the black candidate strode along as if he were oblivious to their inner feelings. The campaign was really all about Jesse, and he knew it and relished it in spite of the abuse he continued to get on the irritating Jewish issue.

Jesse Jackson kissed babies and ecstatic ladies, black and white and brown and yellow, all over the state, as he had all across America. Jackson successfully courted all his white constituencies in New York—the gays and lesbians, the liberals, the students, the labor unionists. Liberal publications such as *The Nation* and *The Village Voice* endorsed his candidacy. And he was pleased.

But Jesse Jackson was happiest in New York City, he would say, when he was out with his own people, "our crowd"—the blacks of Harlem and Queens and Brooklyn. They were his original constituency, and they loved him. The more abuse the Jewish mayor and his friends heaped upon him, the more they supported and protected him. He was theirs, and they his. Gerry Austin succinctly described the Jackson strategy for New York: "Campaign strategy is real simple. It's like duck hunting. We go where the ducks are."

"Jesse! Jesse! Jesse!" they would shout at every stop Jackson made in the poorer sections of the city. In Harlem, people hung out windows trying to get a glimpse as he walked along Adam Clayton

Powell Boulevard. Voices squealed: "Jesse's here," as he made his way through the crowds, around the garbage cans, past the boarded-up shops. They chased his entourage along the streets, as women cried and old men held back tears. Teenage girls grabbed at him. Parents held their infants up to him to kiss. Boys and young men reached out to shake his hand and look at him with awe. He would stretch out his arms and say: "Hey, fella!" He would wave his arms to the adoring crowds and shout: "You're all beautiful. I love you very much." Jesse was elated. At the same time, he regretted that there weren't white faces in the crowd, as he'd become accustomed to in both the South and the Midwest.

Jesse Jackson had brought them hope, the last time around in 1984 and now even more so in 1988. For the first time these African-Americans, upper-class, middle-class and poor, all felt like more equal citizens of the United States because of what he had done for them. He had given them a new self-image and a new national image. They were thrilled by the possibility, which he had created through the sheer force of his charismatic personality, that a black person could run for and conceivably win the highest office in the land.

Jackson lost the New York primary to Michael Dukakis by a five-to-four margin. It was a campaign that left bitterness in everyone's mouth. Racial and religious tension had marred the event. Jackson won 94 percent of the black vote, but only 17 percent of the white. Both figures were up from 1984, but the racial divisions in New York were obviously much more hardened than in some states where Jackson had recently fared much better. According to *New York Times*/CBS exit polls, only 8 percent of the Jewish voters cast their ballots for Jackson, compared with an overwhelming 77 percent for Dukakis. The Jews' fears had not been allayed by Jesse Jackson in 1988. The Jewish issue had not been laid to rest. Jesse Jackson left New York with a worse sense of defeat than he'd felt anywhere else so far.

12

THE RUST BELT
PRIMARIES

"**L**eadership must meet the moral challenge of its day. What's the moral challenge of our day?" All across America Jesse Jackson put the question before the people, and he would give his answer: "Economic violence." Then he would explain why this was America's current moral challenge: "We have public accommodations. We have the right to vote. We have open housing. What's the fundamental challenge of our day? It is to end economic violence. Plant closings without notice. Even the greedy do not profit long from greed. Economic violence."

Then he would launch into a stirring soliloquy on the plight of the poor, all afflicted by economic violence, in the great land of plenty. He would begin: "Most poor people are not lazy. They're not black. They're not brown." Jackson, the great orator, would pause as the audience waited expectantly. Then the surprise statistical answer: "They're mostly white and female and young. But whether white, black or brown, a hungry baby's belly turned inside out is the same color."

He would continue as the crowd was caught by every new, unexpected phrase and turn of language: "Most poor people are not on welfare. Some of them are illiterate and can't read the Want Ad section, and when they can, they can't find a job that matches the address. They work hard every day. I know, I live amongst them . . . I'm one of them. I know they work. I'm a witness.

"They catch the early bus. They work every day. They raise other people's children. They work every day," Jesse's cadence would begin to accelerate as he rolled out the list of the poor's activities.

At this point in the speech, many in the audience, especially blacks accustomed to gospel-church tradition, would be chanting: "Yes, Jesse, yes" and "Right on" and "Uh-huh."

He would proceed, lyrically: "They clean the streets. They work every day . . . They drive the cabs. They changed the beds you slept in in hotels last night. They can't get a union contract. They work every day."

Wherever he gave this speech over the months of the 1988 campaign, the crowds would be electrified with the power of recognition. Jackson would pause a moment for applause, and then continue: "No, no, they're not lazy. Someone must defend them because it's right and they cannot speak for themselves . . .

"They work in hospitals. I know they do. They wipe the bodies of those who are sick with fever and pain. They empty their bedpans. They clean out their commode . . ." By now Jackson was at the peak of his oratorical rhythm. The crowds were hypnotized. "No job is beneath them, and yet when they get sick, they cannot lie in the bed they made up every day."

Jesse Jackson would pause briefly again, to let his words sink in. Then he issued the challenge: "America, that is not right. We are a better nation than that. We are a better nation than that."

Jesse Jackson's "Ode to the Poor," as journalists began to call this great modern American soliloquy, was one of his finest oratorical gems during the 1988 campaign. He recited it several times a week during the campaign season. And then, for the millions who had still never heard it, he delivered his poem again at the Democratic National Convention. Rich or poor, no one who heard was left unmoved.

"Ending economic violence" was his theme, and economic violence was found everywhere in America. Jackson could point to evidence of it wherever he went, regardless of the state and its economic profile. But he knew that it was especially abundant in the so-called Rust Belt in 1988, the last year of the Reagan administration. The Rust Belt included those older industrial states where antiquated industries were declining. Workers had been laid off by Reaganomics, which supported multinationals and failed to provide incentives for reorienting and retraining American labor.

The Rust Belt was where Jackson was headed immediately after the New York primary. He would have preferred to go straight to California to campaign where he knew there were a lot of supporters for his Rainbow Coalition. Instead, for the next three weeks, he would have to concentrate on the Rust Belt primaries—the first big one in Pennsylvania on April 26, then Ohio and Indiana on May 3 and finally West Virginia on May 10.

The problem in all those states was that racial divisions seemed much more rigid, more a fact of life, similar to what he'd found in New York. The pundits had already written him off as a probable loser in those states, and Jesse privately was less than optimistic. Fortunately, that three-week schedule also included the primary in the District of Columbia, where he felt confident of a victory.

The twenty-four hours after the New York primary were a tough time for both Jesse Jackson and his staff. Some described it as the roughest point in the whole campaign. Open recriminations and dissension divided the staff much more than usual. Jesse, who usually managed to confine his angry glares to the privacy of the airplane or holding rooms, could hardly contain them all that day. He was angry and hurt. Less than a month earlier, he had been savoring the sweet taste of his Michigan victory and the wild adulation that had followed. Now he'd just endured his major defeat of the season. He knew he would be able to bounce back, as he always did, but this time he wanted a chance to ponder and regroup.

Immediately after New York, the media and the Democratic political establishment proclaimed total victory for Michael Dukakis.

Jesse Jackson was being treated as a burnt-out star, and he went into a temporary slump. He privately blamed even the Jews on his staff. And many of his black staff and friends blamed them, too. Pressure was mounting for him to begin removing them from influential positions in his campaign. Most had outlived their basic usefulness, to demonstrate to New York Jews that he had Jews in his inner circle. There was real dissension in the ranks. Black-Jewish conflict was beginning to be revealed throughout his Rainbow Coalition campaign. In Pennsylvania, where the next primary would take place, Jackson's state campaign chairman, Philadelphia councilman Lucien Blackwell, openly complained about having "a Jewish lesbian" working on the state campaign. That particular woman had for months performed organizing miracles for Jackson across the country, but Jesse needed a new scapegoat for his failure. The Jews had ruined him, he believed, as he pulled out of New York. Publicly, of course, Jackson displayed his usual energetic hopefulness.

Because of his despondency, it took Jackson almost two days to get rolling again. At first, his campaign appeared more disorganized than was generally the case. His speeches rambled and wandered much more than usual, and his schedule was in unprecedented chaos.

On top of it all, Jackson's principal aides, campaign chairman Willie Brown and campaign manager Gerry Austin, suggested that he should now be considered a good vice presidential candidate. Jesse was furious when he learned what they had been saying publicly, and he let them know with repeated chastisings.

Within a couple of days, however, Jackson had pulled himself together. Senator Gore had pulled out of the race after New York. Now there were only two, Jackson and Dukakis. Jackson was his former buoyant self when he addressed a group of black Pennsylvania leaders on Thursday night, April 21, in Philadelphia. He urged them: "Hold your heads high. Renew your faith. Expand your hope. Let the children feel it. When the sun comes out in the spring, flowers blossom, eggs crack, chickens start talking chicken talk, and hope is alive. Everything in the universe moves when there is hope in the air.

"We're too poor to be pessimistic," he continued. "Got too much experience to be cynical. We know that joy cometh in the morning. We are winning, and we will keep on winning."

By Friday, April 22, he was telling a rally at West Chester University that "the race is neck and neck. Dukakis has thirty percent [of the cumulative popular vote in the primaries so far], I have twenty-nine percent . . . I am a long-distance runner, and I have a smooth stride." Jesse was indeed back in stride.

But he was also running late, as usual, and that same night he arrived several minutes after his first live, one-on-one televised debate with Michael Dukakis had already started. Yet his tardiness gave him a chance to make a *deus ex machina* kind of grand entrance onto the television screen, as he rushed through the curtains onto the stage at the University of Pennsylvania in Philadelphia. Later, he maintained to reporters that he didn't think his habitual tardiness should be viewed as a potential problem if he were President. He explained that when one is President, one doesn't have to go to the people, because they come to the President.

He spent the next five days taking his message of hope across the state of Pennsylvania. From the slums in the racially divided city of Philadelphia to the abandoned steel mills along the Susquehanna and Monongahela rivers, he proclaimed his plans to end economic violence. On that Friday, April 22, the Jackson campaign released a position paper proposing that billions of dollars be put into day care. He called for national health care and reinvestment in America. He denounced plant closings and the export of American jobs abroad.

The next morning, Saturday, April 23, Jackson addressed a crowd of striking factory workers in Columbia, Pennsylvania. By the end of his speech, the enthusiastic strikers were shouting his chants with him: "Change the course, change the course." In McKeesport, he encouraged more striking workers with the words: "I want you to have your jobs back, and I want a new job. I knew I could not run with the rabbits and then hunt with the hounds. I stood with you."

No recent presidential candidate had promised such a commitment to organized labor as Jesse Jackson had, but not all the white blue-collar workers in America's Rust Belt were buying his lines. Although he had boasted in the past that his support was among working-class whites, exit polls in all the previous primaries had revealed that his white support came primarily from well-educated liberals—a fact he never liked to acknowledge or discuss. He was glad, of course, that they were voting for him, but he didn't have a way to categorize them for his ideal coalition of the disenfranchised. The liberals never liked to acknowledge that Jackson pretended they didn't really matter for him.

But in Pennsylvania, on April 26, Michael Dukakis won by a landslide, nearly 80 percent to Jackson's 15 percent. And it was made worse for Jackson by the fact that Pennsylvania was a winner-take-all state in terms of convention delegates. Thus, all the state's 178 delegates were handed over to Dukakis. Despair seized the Jackson campaign again.

Many inside the campaign blamed Gerry Austin for implying immediately after New York that Jackson was throwing in the towel for the presidential nomination. Jesse allowed that view to prevail. Gerry himself was fed up. He described the Pennsylvania primary as botched and mismanaged and privately blamed Jackson's free-wheeling, disorganized style. Now he knew why so many others before him had turned down the job of Jackson's campaign manager. He had become Jackson's latest scapegoat, and there was no one in charge, other than Jackson himself. And to a professional manager like Austin, that spelled disaster.

Jackson's black campaign chairman for the state, Lucien Blackwell, who had at the beginning of the campaign week blamed Jews for the New York loss, now blamed Jackson's concentration on poor whites as the reason for his failure in Pennsylvania. He said it was the national schedulers' fault that the candidate wasted his time stumping in western Pennsylvania "trying to drum up blue-collar votes that did not materialize. I believe we should have concen-

trated on Philadelphia." Blackwell knew that no scheduling decision was ever made without Jackson's spending hours deliberating
on and finally approving it. But also, for both Pennsylvania and
New York, the national schedulers maintained that they had lost
control of the schedule to the local officials, like Blackwell. But it
was Jesse Jackson who ultimately approved his schedule.

Over the course of the campaign season, Jackson had usually
stayed over in a state on election night. No matter whether he had
come in first or second, or even fourth as in the Iowa caucus and the
New Hampshire primary, he had held a "victory party" to celebrate, whatever the outcome. The night of Dukakis's landslide in
Pennsylvania, Jesse Jackson was in Ohio, and there was no party.

The next major primaries were in Ohio and Indiana, both Rust
Belt states; both elections would be held on May 3. Jesse had to
look ahead. That night, instead of listening to the returns of defeat
in Pennsylvania, he was cheered by a mass reception at a Toledo,
Ohio, union rally. The crowds there represented the true Rainbow
Coalition and lifted Jackson's spirits again.

Campaign insiders called that night of defeat on April 26 and the
next morning the nadir of Jackson's primary campaign. Yet Jackson's spirits were higher than they had been after New York. In the
latter, the defeat had seemed more personal and thus more bitter.
His trouncing in Pennsylvania could be blamed on other factors—
the socioeconomic makeup of the state and also, conveniently, the
dissension and mismanagement within the Jackson organization.
And for that, Jackson blamed others, including Austin, whom he
would give one last chance. In the meantime, Jackson would privately prepare to replace him.

That morning of April 27 in Cincinnati, Jackson didn't feel like
dealing with his staff. He was in a reflective mood and wanted to
talk with a journalist whom he could count on to record his words.
He chose David Broder, the veteran pundit and Pulitzer Prize-winning reporter from *The Washington Post.*

Jackson strode into the hotel coffee shop and pulled up a chair
across from the distinguished, white-haired Broder. The candidate

ordered his usual dish of fruit, cereal and water. Jackson actually would have preferred to have eggs and bacon and grits and sausage, but he knew they weren't good for him. He had been steadily gaining weight over the past months because he had stopped exercising. Gerry Austin's frequent reference to him as "Baby Doc," after the fat black Haitian dictator, had been getting on his nerves along with everything else about Austin.

Jesse Jackson felt like talking and thinking out loud about his campaign with David Broder, who had covered more than three decades of national politics. He spoke slowly, reflectively, between bites.

He didn't talk much about Pennsylvania or New York; they were in the past now. He wanted to think about all the positive signs he'd received over the past months when white Americans had come out to support him and thus to change the American political landscape. He recalled his meeting with the former Ku Klux Klansman in Beaumont, Texas, back in February—the man wanted to have his picture taken with Jackson to show that this time he wasn't on the wrong side of history.

Jackson then talked about the people at his Toledo rally the night before: "White families, mothers, fathers, children sitting there. I watched them, and I thought what a distance they had come to be there, listening to me. Whatever their age, they had probably never heard Martin Luther King. The culture of the times, the environment they lived in, prevented it. Even if they heard him, they couldn't really hear him, grasp what he was saying. He was pure threat."

Jackson continued, musing out loud, as David Broder listened. Jesse said of himself: "I come as therapy. I'm probably the first black man they've really been able to hear. They've come so far, these people, and this country's come so far. Racism is not irredeemable. It's not genetic. It's the product of the environment, and the environment is changing."

Jesse Jackson gained great energy from speaking, whether quietly to a listener like Broder or over the telephone to friends and contacts in the middle of the night and early in the morning or to mass rallies or to schoolchildren across America. Speaking, in whatever forum, was Jackson's adrenaline. The rapt listener, whether an individual or a crowd, administered the dosage.

That morning, while the campaign staff reeled from the weeks of defeat, Jesse Jackson was oblivious to the gloom overwhelming his aides. After talking with Broder and knowing his words would be printed, Jackson then caught the early bus with all the reporters to go and speak where he was perhaps happiest—at a school.

At Withrow High School in Cincinnati, Jesse Jackson, the hero, told his captivated audience of teenagers, blacks and whites: "Excellence is doing your best against the odds. As I run for President every day, I run against the odds and yet I defy the odds."

Then he led the rapt student body in his special chant, as if reminding himself once again: "I am somebody."

Pundits wrote that day that his odds of winning were lengthening, but he ignored their predictions. Throughout the day, he spoke enthusiastically of his chances: "We're going to run hard all day and much of the night. There's a lot of faith and hope in this campaign."

Jesse was right. And a lot of that faith and hope was in the hearts and minds of young Americans. They were too young to vote that year, but he knew they could vote by the next election or the one after that, and he had every intention of running again.

The day after Jackson's visit to the Cincinnati high school, fifteen students participated in a discussion about his visit, while several reporters listened to their revelatory comments.

A white football player, Robert Reinhardt, was one of the students sitting on the stage behind Jackson. He described his view: "Sitting up there behind him, I saw something that I had never seen before at the school. First of all, I figured many of the black students would be excited. But I saw a lot of white students who are never enthused about anything, who don't even like to come to class, who usually, when they get in the auditorium, talk and are rude, I saw them get up and applaud. It made me feel pretty good because everybody was joining in. It made me think, hey, maybe somebody really does care about us. In fact, I went to work that night saying to myself over and over again: 'I am somebody!' "

A black senior, Caroline Clark, whose ambition was to be elected to Congress, said that Jackson inspired her. "When you think of politics, what do you think of? White people. They have the business world. They have politics. History. You look at history, you don't find very much about black people when you study history. Jesse Jackson somehow takes away the intimidation. Now it can be equal. The world can be black and white."

A young white woman, Stephanie Williams, described how Jackson's visit had helped her friend: "The night before, she was talking about suicide. We had a long talk on the telephone, and when I was talking, she was listening, but it was just 'Yeah, right, okay.' I could tell I wasn't getting through to her, but I didn't know what else to say. But she came to the assembly, and she was up there saying, 'I am somebody!' I think she heard what he was saying. I think he made a difference."

Later, on April 27, after Jackson had left Withrow High School, as he moved around Ohio talking to the voters themselves, he began to sound despondent. After his terrible thrashing by Dukakis in Pennsylvania, Jackson's mood noticeably shifted between hope and despair. And for the first time he slipped into describing his campaign in the past tense. He seemed almost elegiac.

But then, later that night anger snapped Jackson out of his depression. He was taken aback when both Gerald Austin and Willie Brown also began to speak of the Jackson campaign as lost. He was furious that they would have dared presume to announce that the Jackson run for the presidency was over. The two top aides had publicly suggested that Jackson had lost and would now focus on the vice presidency.

Jackson reacted in high gear to override and retaliate against his aides for their insubordination. After a rally in Canton, Ohio, on Thursday, April 28, he angrily addressed reporters and denied his aides' comments. His eyes flashing, he firmly stated: "Those statements [by Austin and Brown] are utterly untrue and do not represent the spirit and the thrust of this campaign nor our work. We can win Ohio. We're in this campaign through June 7. California and

New Jersey we can win, intend to win, are working on winning, and I speak for the campaign without fear of contradiction."

The reporters then pressed the candidate to explain how both his manager and his chairman could have presented such a different interpretation of the state of his campaign only the day before. Jackson responded with vehemence: "I can only ask you to accept the most valid interpretation of where our campaign is from the campaigner. There is no source more credible about the state of our campaign than Jesse Jackson."

Then Jackson's anger boiled to the surface, and in front of two thousand Canton residents who had come to his rally and stayed at his invitation to observe his news conference, the candidate called the reporters "barracudas." When the crowd of onlookers cheered, Jackson then proceeded to dictate to the reporters what to write in their notebooks. He instructed: "Let me make this very clear. We are running right through June 7. Write that down. We intend to set the agenda for the national campaign—the war to stop drugs, which Dukakis is now into. He's a lieutenant in it, but I'm the general. I set the pace. We'll keep setting the moral tone of the campaign. There will be distinctions, not divisions. Write that down."

Incited by the cheers of the crowd, Jackson continued giving his dictation to the obedient stenographic reporters: "We intend to get our share of delegates based on popular votes. Write that down. We intend to come out of California, then New Jersey, in search of a management team and a running mate to go against George Bush. Write that down."

By then, the crowd had begun shouting: "Write that down," and Jesse was thrilled with the effect of his performance. He had successfully converted the group of journalists into a sideshow in his circus. They danced and did what he said, and the crowd loved it.

But somehow, in the next primaries, his popularity on the road did not translate into big votes. In the predominantly black District of Columbia on May 3 he won by a landslide. But in the other primaries, Ohio, Indiana, West Virginia and Nebraska, during the first two weeks in May, he suffered further defeats. On the night of

May 3, he proclaimed, once again: "What do I want? I want to move our nation beyond racism, beyond sexism, beyond anti-Semitism." And after the primaries on May 10, Jackson was eager to move on to California. He believed he had a good chance at an upset there, and he was ready to try. But first he went to another Western state—Oregon, where, though he came in second in the primary on May 17, he won 35 percent of the vote.

13

THE CALIFORNIA PRIMARY

"Common ground. What is leadership, if not present help in a time of crisis? And so I met you at the point of challenge—

"In Jay, Maine, where paper workers were striking for fair wages.

"In Greenfield, Iowa, where family farmers struggled for a fair price.

"In Cleveland, Ohio, where working women seek comparable worth.

"In McFarland, California, where the children of Hispanic farm workers may be dying from poisoned rain, dying . . .

"In an AIDS hospice in Houston, Texas, where the sick support one another, too often rejected by their own family and friends. Common ground."

Jackson listed the places he'd been, the "points of challenge" for America where he'd gone to help in times of crisis. He kept the list going as he traversed America, over the twenty-five years since he'd left college, as he established his vast grass-roots network of people, places, contacts.

California was his last stop on the long schedule of primaries and caucuses that started in Iowa, on February 8, and would end on the West Coast, in America's most populous state, on June 7. On the same day on the East Coast, there was another important last primary in New Jersey. Jesse Jackson had never stopped moving; nor had he stopped collecting names of people and places and points of challenge and poignant incidents that he could then weave adroitly into his dynamic speeches. Those speeches moved his supporters, and even as they inspired fear in his enemies, those enemies could not help but be moved, even if they were also frightened by his tones and rhetoric.

McFarland, California, became one of those special places that Jesse would add to his litany, his list of "points of challenge."

The story of McFarland interested him as soon as he was told about it when he arrived in California that spring of 1988. Some unknown poison, from the air or the water or the land, was sickening and killing the people, mostly the poor Hispanic residents and mainly children, in this farming community in the San Joaquin Valley. Jackson was told that the plague was spreading but no one was doing anything about it. Most of the people affected did not have the power to get anyone's attention, so Jesse Jackson decided to go and help these people at their point of challenge.

In late May, Jackson flew to this once unnoticed, dusty town set in the midst of vast crop fields, blooming orchards and vineyards. He went straight to the poor side of town, to the "cancer area," where there had been fourteen deaths in one small residential area. Sixteen other children had already been diagnosed as having cancer, and many more were being treated for strange, yet undiagnosed ailments. No cause had been pinpointed, but as yet there was little concern for the situation because it was affecting only the poor Hispanics.

McFarland was a town divided by a highway. Like many in America, that road also divided the residents according to their class and race. About a third of the town's population was Hispanic, and they lived on one side of the highway. The mayor, Carl Boston, a white-haired retiree, a conservative Republican, had seldom visited the Hispanic "side of the tracks." He only learned about Jackson's visit when he saw it on the eleven o'clock news that night. The report said that Jesse Jackson was spending the night with a Hispanic farmer's family in McFarland and planned to meet with the mayor the next morning. The mayor heard Jackson say on the news that the cause of the cancer in this community was contamination and corruption. The mayor took this as an affront, but he decided he should meet with the visiting dignitary the next morning.

Mayor Boston met Jesse Jackson just as the presidential candidate was leaving the host farm worker's house. Jackson gave the mayor a friendly welcome and invited him to look at a contaminated well. Then Jackson explained that he was not blaming the mayor, but he considered the cancer cluster to be a "national scandal." Before long, the unlikely pair were holding hands at the well, surrounded by Hispanic women and children, and all together chanting the Jackson slogans: "Keep hope alive!" and "We, the people, can win!"

Later, after leaving the well, Mayor Boston talked with reporters about his unexpected meeting with Jesse Jackson. The old Republican said: "Do I think he was sincere? Yes, I think he was sincere. I didn't think I would say that."

Not only did Jesse go that first time to visit the dying children and sleep overnight among their people; he also returned. Only a few days before the California primary, he came back to stage a nationally televised march. He brought with him celebrities, white California liberals and blacks, the venerable organizer Cesar Chavez of the United Farm Workers and the powerful Texas Agriculture Commissioner, Jim Hightower. They all came to march and turn McFarland, California, into a symbol of economic violence.

Jesse Jackson had been going to such places for years, but now his time had come to tell more Americans who were ready to listen. Jesse would then tell the story time and again, and later at the July convention he would name it in his litany of places where he'd helped "in a time of crisis." For Jesse Jackson, McFarland, California, had become a new symbol of his message. The poor, dying people of this community were powerless to do anything about their plight. They were up against the huge conglomerates of agribusiness and oil companies, all interwoven with the banks, government and water authorities. These Hispanic residents were faced with a cancer they could do nothing about until Jesse Jackson came to town and pointed out the economic violence in McFarland to all of America.

In the last month of the primary campaigning, the Secret Service reported that threats against Jackson's life increased, and one particular death threat in early May interrupted his schedule somewhat, but only slightly. The Reverend Jackson was used to hearing that such threats were being made against him, but this time the Secret Service had taken the May 10 threats more seriously. On May 19 in St. Louis, Missouri, a federal grand jury indicted a thirty-year-old white man, Londell Williams, on a charge of threatening to kill the black presidential candidate. Williams denied the charges. He said, however, that he sympathized with white supremacists but did not actually belong to any extremist group. He acknowledged, "I do have prejudices . . . against anything that isn't white." But he then said of Jackson's quest for the presidency, "If the man makes it to President, more power to him."

Jackson himself was, as always, relatively calm about the threat to his life. Indeed, some people who had known him for years thought he had a martyr complex—that he would be glad ultimately to be martyred and thus immortalized like John F. Kennedy and Martin Luther King, Jr. Sometimes on the road, Jackson would tell his staff that he hoped they would not fall apart and disperse if something did happen to him, as King's disciples had after his assassination.

This time, in May 1988, when reports of threats increased, Jackson commented to reporters, "The pain is how it does affect one's family. It calls one out of campaigning into parenting rather quickly." His youngest child, twelve-year-old Jackie, had telephoned him from her private boarding school where she had been hearing rumors of the threats. She was very upset and worried and wanted to know if her father was all right.

Jesse went on to say of the threats that he himself felt "very spiritual, very philosophical." He said that the "danger factor" simply went with his role, and he explained, "We have this extraordinary burden, because we're not just changing the party or broadening the party. We're changing the culture."

In the glitzy last days of the California campaign, observers reported that the only politician who resembled the Hollywood stars and their film world was Jesse Jackson. He moved easily from one world to another, as if he were the star of whatever movie was playing that time. On the night of June 1, Jesse Jackson had rocked along with country-music singers Kris Kristofferson and Willie Nelson at a fund-raiser at the Hollywood Palace Theater disco. The two stars sang a song they'd composed, "Roll On, Brother Jackson," with the lines "Hold on, brother Jesse Jackson, there's a better world a coming . . . You've been fighting for the future from the start." And the wealthy guests, rich West Coast liberals and other stars, including Martin Sheen, David Crosby, Buffy Sainte-Marie, Mary Wilson, Margot Kidder, Dennis Weaver and Helen Reddy, all joined with Jesse in the chorus.

Then, in almost filmlike split-screen contrast, the next morning Jesse was holding serious talks with the Bounty Hunters, a notorious Watts gang, clad in T-shirts or silk shirts and slacks, earrings and the thick gold rope jewelry that symbolized success in the drug trade. Jesse was wearing a custom-made conservative gray suit and a tie clasp that read DARE. The young men told him their stories. They said they had no economic opportunities other than drugs, and they had to survive. Jesse agreed with them that their problems started outside their community. He said: "Drugs are not growing in Watts." Then he promised them: "I offer the youth today a partnership. I will help fight the flow of drugs. They must cut the supply for drugs."

Jackson spent that night with a family in Watts, in a poor housing project called Nickerson Gardens. What he learned all that day and night would become part of his drug lesson. And later he took their story and told it for all Americans to hear:

We need a real war on drugs. We can't just say no. It's deeper than that. We can't just get a palm reader or an astrologer [referring to Nancy Reagan's reported use of astrology]. It's more profound than that.

We are spending $150 billion on drugs a year. We've gone from ignoring it to focusing on the children. Children cannot buy $150 billion worth of drugs a year. A few high-profile athletes, athletes are not laundering $150 billion a year. Bankers are.

I met the children in Watts . . . Unfortunately . . . their grapes of hope have become raisins of despair and they're turning on each other, and they're self-destructing. I stayed with them all night long. I wanted to hear their case.

They said, "Jesse Jackson, as you challenge us to say no to drugs, you're right; to not sell them, you're right; to not use these guns, you're right. By the way [despite the government's promises], we have neither jobs nor houses nor services, no training, no way out. Some of us take drugs as anesthesia for our pain. Some take drugs as a way of pleasure." Short-term pleasure, long-term pain. "Some sell drugs to make money. It's wrong. We know, but you know we need it. We can go and buy the drugs by the boxes, at the port. If we can buy the drugs at the port, don't you believe the federal government can stop it if they want to?"

They say, "We don't have Saturday-night specials anymore." They say, "We buy AK-47s and Uzis, the latest make of weapons. We buy them across the counter on Long Beach Boulevard."

You cannot fight a war on drugs unless, until you're going to challenge the bankers and the gun sellers and those who grow them. Don't just focus on the children. Let's stop drugs at the level of supply and demand. We must end the scourge on the American culture.

"Down with dope, up with hope" had been a slogan Jesse Jackson had been chanting a long time throughout America, in schools across the country. But that speech, when delivered by Jackson at the Democratic convention, was hailed as the most important statement on drugs ever made by an American politician.

California was a place people had traditionally gone to start a new life. Some called it "the land of second chances." Jesse Jackson was glad that the last major, and the biggest, primary of the season would be held in California. The state, with the largest population in the United States, was full of people who were made to order for his Rainbow Coalition. Many were newly arrived, disaffected from the places they'd left behind, come to California to find the freedom to start anew. Jesse Jackson went there for the last month of campaigning with the same hope. He wanted a second chance to win his party's 1988 presidential nomination.

In the middle of May, Jesse still did not want to talk about the possibility of his "running" for the vice presidency. His campaign manager, Gerry Austin, had made the mistake, just after his defeat in New York, of suggesting publicly that the front-runner, Michael Dukakis, was "going to have to give some consideration" to selecting Jackson as his running mate. Jackson's campaign chairman, Willie Brown, had made the same suggestion.

Jackson was irate. That was why he didn't like anyone, not even his top aides, speaking for him. They always botched things up, he implied. He chastised them in public, treating Austin in particular like an uninformed servant. Jackson was always jealous if anyone around him dared to say something first. If one dared, or even accidentally made that mistake, Jackson would usually rebuke the culprit, but then, within days, or even hours, Jackson himself might be heard saying the same thing, as if he were the first and only one who could state it.

After Austin's error, Jackson had ordered his top policy adviser,

Robert Borosage, to issue another statement. Bob stated, with categorical succinctness, Jackson's position: "Contrary to earlier reports, we are not running for the vice presidency. We're running for the *presidency.*" For nearly a month, most of the time in California, Jackson stuck to that position. But the discussion had been set off, and Jackson could then leave it to his more distant supporters to discuss the possibility of his being the vice president. Only in the last days of the California race did he himself intimate that he might be interested in the number two position.

However, the Austin incident in late April triggered the beginning of other changes Jackson had been planning to make anyway. After his defeat in New York, he had privately blamed his Bronx-reared campaign manager for the debacle. Austin was a Jew from New York, and he hadn't delivered his state. The tension between Jews and blacks within the campaign had been mounting since New York, and Jesse intended to do something about it. His black supporters wanted their people to be given more visibility again as the campaign rolled along. They were tired of seeing all the white faces in the ever-changing inner circle.

Thus, Gerry Austin's mistake in daring to raise the subject of the vice presidency was about his last as campaign manager. Jackson was never comfortable with Austin's independence and his insistence on speaking to the press whenever he thought it appropriate. He'd let Austin get away with getting his own publicity and giving interviews and talking bluntly with Jackson for long enough. There was a limit to people's ordering Jesse Jackson around, even if they thought it was for his own good, as Austin had believed over the months while he tried to bring some semblance of organization to the Jackson campaign chaos he'd found.

Now Austin's usefulness was almost over. He'd managed the campaign to the point where Jackson believed he needed another type of person as his front man. And Austin had failed to win over his own people for Jesse, even though that had never been stated to be his role. Jackson, however, knew he would have to wait until after the Ohio primary on May 3 before making visible changes in his campaign management hierarchy. The reason was that Austin's adopted state was Ohio, where he'd lived most of his adult life and he was well connected politically, having successfully managed Democrat Richard Celeste's two gubernatorial campaigns.

In the meantime, Jackson, who always picked out sensitive points in his aides, decided to signal his displeasure with a weapon that he thought could hurt Austin the most. He wouldn't use a black to issue the rebuke to Austin's rash statement about the vice presidency. No, that could be construed as his returning too quickly to his own people, and Austin could slough off the insult. Instead, Jackson would use Austin's longtime rival, another Jew, Bob Borosage, to deliver his statement. Austin could not then help but realize the extent of Jackson's displeasure. From then on, it was downhill for Austin, and Jackson took every opportunity publicly to try to humiliate him all the way to the convention.

Jackson knew that Austin was smart enough to get the point. Jackson, who never missed a beat on what was happening around him, knew that Austin had been annoyed for months with the way Borosage tried to usurp power and act like the campaign manager as well as chief policy adviser. Jackson sensed it was Austin's Achilles' heel, and since March, he had created many opportunities for Borosage to appear stronger, more influential than Austin. Then when Borosage seemed too independent for Jackson's liking, Jackson would rebuff him in public, and Borosage would go into a shell for a few days, saying: "It's not my place to speak for Reverend Jackson." Jackson privately enjoyed playing aides off against each other, even though publicly he always professed his great concern to maintain staff unity.

Austin could sense he was in real trouble when he heard Borosage formally delivering such an important statement as Jackson's clarification about his position on the vice presidency. He also sensed that he, a Jew from New York, was being blamed by Jackson for his defeat there. (Borosage, although also Jewish, came from Michigan, where Jackson had had his glory.) Austin knew there was nothing he could do about this unjustified blame.

Once the Ohio primary was over, on Tuesday, May 3, Jesse could proceed with his new plan to replace Austin. He had lost Ohio, and he could privately blame Austin for that, too. He would never thank him for all he'd done to give shape to his organization and successfully implement his strategy. No, instead, he would probably remember how this Jew had lost his home state of New York and his adopted state of Ohio.

Austin recognized his power was on the wane, as did some of the press, who even began to refer to his position as titular only. But, always an energetic and hard worker, Austin carried on, using all his organizational skills to make things work. But the scheduling chaos was worse than ever, and Austin had little influence now to force Jackson to make decisions in time. Jackson's visit to Martinsburg, West Virginia, on Monday, May 9, was so poorly planned and decided on at such a last minute that many people eager to see Jesse Jackson never even learned he was coming until after the event. No one except Jackson had any control over the Jackson campaign anymore.

Jesse, as usual, never explicitly told Austin that he was dissatisfied with him. Essentially, as in my own case earlier, Jesse Jackson could never admit what really irritated him about an aide. Thus, he said nothing directly, but steadily pulled the rug out from under him, until all Austin could do was try to maintain a façade of still being the real campaign manager.

After May 3, Jesse made final preparations for bringing blacks to the fore again. He hadn't forgotten them. It was just that in the first five months of the campaign year, he had needed whites more to appear with him on the TV screen. Now he needed to let his base and his largest constituency know that he was loyal to their original support. They had tried to be patient while Jackson had demonstrated he had a real Rainbow Coalition, but their patience was running out. Jackson also needed blacks whom he could trust absolutely to fight for their real interests at the convention. He began making new telephone calls and putting his ducks in a row.

In Washington, on Friday, May 13, less than a month before the last primaries and only two months away from the Democratic convention, Jesse Jackson let the word out that he was planning to make important changes in the structure of his organization.

Ronald H. Brown was named as Jackson's convention manager. The title ostensibly implied that he would have a completely separate position from Austin's, but in essence, the plan and how it worked out was that Ron Brown would be the new campaign chief through the convention. Back in 1987, Brown was one of many to whom Jackson had originally offered the post of campaign manager. Brown demonstrated his intuitive understanding of how Jackson would eventually play out his 1988 campaign and wisely declined that position. Then, once Jackson had chewed up his campaign manager, Brown could accept the new title of convention manager and enjoy the real power and glory during the historic denouement of Jackson's campaign.

Brown was exactly Jackson's age, forty-six that year. In contrast to Jackson's more revolutionary career, Brown followed a more establishment path. He had put in his years in the civil rights movement. But he was also a veteran of the U.S. Army and had gone to law school. A savvy Washington lawyer who had formerly served as Senator Edward Kennedy's deputy campaign manager in 1980, Brown later became deputy chairman of the Democratic National Committee. He was the perfect person to take Jackson through the 1988 convention. Brown was a black with "insider access," known to be a smooth coordinator and to have a rare ability to maneuver within the world of Jackson's traditional constituency as well as within the Democratic establishment. Brown liked to say that he and Jackson were similar kinds of people. "[Jackson], much like me, is a pretty intuitive person who operates on instinct a lot." But Brown also knew how to operate within the establishment rules.

On the same day, May 13, Jackson named another Democratic Party insider, Eleanor Holmes Norton, also a black, to handle the Jackson campaign's platform discussions. She had served as President Carter's chairman of the Equal Employment Opportunity Commission, and she was recognized as a skillful negotiator and spokesperson.

Jackson, always careful to keep the appearance of the Rainbow Coalition, cleverly named two whites to serve with his two new aides. Ann Lewis, former political director of the Democratic National Committee and currently a principal adviser to Jackson, would become deputy to Brown and oversee the convention's standing committees (platform, rules and credentials). Harold Ickes, a New York lawyer experienced in Democratic Party rules, would become deputy to Norton.

As for Gerry Austin, his top management days had essentially ended, but both Jackson and Brown were careful to say he was still the campaign manager. But for the next couple of months, all he was left with was basically to close up shop, pay off the staff, settle the bills and try to oversee getting the books in order. Gerry was proud of his professional skills, and he would see the job to the end. But it wasn't the way he had planned it. By the time the California primary day rolled around on June 7, in Los Angeles, Austin was staying in a different hotel across town from Jackson and the rest of his staff and was seldom seen. Ron Brown was already well entrenched at the forefront, where he would strategically remain through the July convention.

Gerry Austin remained loyal and was determined to the end to put a professional veneer on the organization. Among his last tasks, he took time the day after the last primaries, on June 8, to write a form letter to be sent to all staff members who would soon begin departing. The letter read:

Dear Jackson Staffer:

The Jesse Jackson for President '88 Campaign Committee has made a significant impact on America. Raising the need for a new direction in foreign and domestic policies, welding together a broad-based, multi-cultural coalition, and challenging America's historic racial barriers are major accomplishments which lay the foundation for progressive politics in the 1990's and beyond.

You have played an important role in this process by providing organizational skills, lending aid to the state and local organizations, and serving as part of the national team. We can never thank you enough for the many hours of hard work and sacrifice.

In appreciation of your work, the campaign will pay you through [whatever the particular individual's agreed date was].

Once again, thank you for your work. We made a difference this year and will continue to do so in the future.

The thanks came from Austin, always thoughtful and always professional. Jesse Jackson, the candidate, never said thanks to many of the hardworking professionals and volunteers who contributed to his remarkable 1988 campaign.

On June 7, Jesse Jackson lost all four primaries—in California, New Jersey, Montana and New Mexico. Michael Dukakis had by all counts won his party's nomination for the presidency. But his chief opponent, the runner-up Jesse Jackson, had won thirteen primary and caucus races and had placed either first or second in forty-six. He had won a total of 1,200 delegates with nearly seven million people voting for him across the country against Dukakis's nearly ten million.

Jackson was not throwing in the towel. He said he would now begin preparing for the "second phase" of his campaign—"the struggle for the direction of the party." He intended to continue traveling and campaigning all the way up to the convention. He had to be sure his constituency exerted influence over the party's platform. He never conceded that Michael Dukakis was the winner of the fifty-state marathon. Jesse Jackson's "victory party" that night in Los Angeles was another grand celebration of his continuing candidacy. It far outshone the Dukakis celebration across town. Jackson's California party was a preview of the Jackson show to take place later in Atlanta.

14

PRECONVENTION NEGOTIATIONS: THE VICE PRESIDENCY

"Jackson fights for the homeless—hope.

"Jackson fights for day care—hope.

"Jackson fights to raise minimum wage—hope.

"Jackson fights for comparable worth for women—hope.

"Jackson fights to save our farms—hope.

"He fights to end the flow of drugs—hope.

"He fights to end the nuclear race—hope.

"He fights to revive the people—hope.

"We, the people, will win.

"Thank you very much. We, the people, will win."

The themes were "Jesse Jackson fights for the people" and brings "hope" to America. The video showed Jesse Jackson delivering one of his standard speeches. It could have been anywhere in America. He had said it over and over again. Now his '88 presidential campaign was preparing the film that would be shown on the huge screens at the Democratic convention to introduce the candidate. The film showed Jackson, the hope of the party, promising to save the people and lead them to victory. And he *had succeeded* in persuading many Americans over the course of the 1988 primary season that he could and would do just that. It was a miracle of history. It was a great step forward in fulfilling the American dream.

Jesse Jackson would fight until the end in more ways than one, not only to "save the people" but to carry on his campaign until the end. Many observers had thought the end had come on June 7, when the primary season ended. Michael Dukakis had won enough popular votes and delegates to take the party's nomination. Jesse Jackson had run a valiant race, against all odds, and had placed a powerful second. The race was over in the view of most. It was time for Jesse Jackson to congratulate the winner and step back to give him the limelight. But that was not how Jesse wanted it. On June 8, Jackson announced: "The season of the convention begins." He was continuing the race.

Jesse, who had once confided that "it was all just drama," had to create real drama now. His campaign was the only one that had given the 1988 season any excitement, yet he had been restrained with his dramatic effects throughout the primaries. But now he wanted to turn the story into a cliff-hanger. The audience couldn't know until nearly the end what would happen. Even then, the kind of drama Jesse really preferred was that which never had an end, was like a never-ending serial in which there would always be a new cliff-hanging episode. His drama seduced the audience so that they kept coming back for more.

Jackson knew that if he conceded after the last primary the convention would be boring, the cameras would leave him, and the virtual nominee would begin the U.S. presidential election campaign; but he was not willing to let that happen, not yet anyway. He wanted to get more attention and to gain influence over the Democratic Party's national platform. He wanted to win places for his top supporters on the Democratic National Committee, and he wanted the nominee to realize that he, Jesse Jackson, was vital to the success of the party and to Dukakis's winning the election. Jackson confided to several people, including Mondale's old campaign manager, Bob Beckel: "Sometimes you have to stir up the pot."

Jackson's hard-core supporters were thrilled that their leader was going to fight to the end, that he would carry their demands all the way to the convention and beyond. Many of his more recent, perhaps less vocal and less excitable supporters were a bit uneasy about his not giving up gracefully, not playing by the rules and being polite. And his critics and detractors within the party watched his old behavior return to the fore, and they said: "We told you so. It's the same old Jesse, always wanting his own way, always eager to spoil things." Outside the party, the Republicans gloated that he seemed to be resorting to spoiling tactics, which, they hopefully believed, would hurt the Democrats and their nominee. How could Michael Dukakis ever act as if he were in control with Jackson's sideshow always going on and threatening to become center stage?

Jackson wouldn't just threaten to be the center of attention, he would make sure he remained the central figure, for his ego could not tolerate otherwise now. The way to do that, he knew, was to keep the media guessing. Then his story—"What will Jesse do?"—would be the ongoing drama. Every day, he told his close aides, we must do something to keep the focus on our campaign, our message, our direction. A few advisers dared suggest that perhaps Jesse should be somewhat tempered in the next month and not antagonize the party establishment now that he'd come so close to being accepted. But Jesse didn't buy that. He planned to push to keep their attention, to remind them that he could no longer be ignored.

In Los Angeles on June 8, the day after the California primary, the defeated candidate refused to concede to the winner. Jackson vowed he would try to win more party rules changes and platform positions for his constituents. He said: "The notion that we'll just fold up now is as crazy as [the old question] 'Can a black run?' We have brought progressive political ideas back as a permanent force in American politics."

Also on that day, he fueled the speculation that, after all, he would like the vice presidency. He was passionate as he said: "I've gone all the way from 'Should he run?' to 'The vice presidency is beneath him.' There's only one job on earth above that job."

Then he added: "Now, for some people who have come by way of the stars and who have had silver spoons in their mouths and many job options: Shall they run their father's ranch? Shall they run his plantation? Shall they run the family corporation? Shall they be a university president? Shall they be a Supreme Court judge? With those job options, maybe Vice President is a step down for them. But do you understand my background? The vice presidency is not quite the top. But it's a long way from where I started."

For the next two days, Jesse Jackson and his inner circle and his traveling press corps relaxed, or were supposed to relax, at the luxurious La Costa resort and spa in Carlsbad, California. But Jesse's idea of relaxing is hardly anyone else's. The media christened the place "Camp Jackson." He couldn't go a day without planning activities and keeping his campers busy.

Even his top aide, clearly now Ron Brown, was quoted as complaining: "Even when I was getting a massage, I was being talked to." They were at each other's side all the time. Absent were Jackson's campaign chairman, Willie Brown, and manager, Gerry Austin, who went back to Chicago to begin closing up some books at headquarters.

Jesse himself relaxed enough to wear jeans, sandals and a polo shirt instead of his usual dapper suits, shirts and ties. But he spent most of the time strategizing about how he could persuade Dukakis to name him as his running mate, not infrequently breaking into the reporters' attempts at relaxation to give them more quotes alluding to his latest ambition. He had now set himself on the path toward becoming Vice President. His supporters wanted it, too, if he couldn't be President. He believed he deserved to be appointed by the nominee. It became an obsession, and he knew the media would follow him daily as speculation mounted over whether Michael Dukakis would choose him. And if not, then what would Jackson do?

For the next month, Jackson focused on almost nothing else except the vice presidential nomination. To be the heartbeat away from the presidency would be better than nothing. It would still be a historic achievement. He genuinely believed that Dukakis would ultimately have to give in and offer it to him.

For days, Jackson kept up the pressure on Dukakis. Everywhere he went, the media followed. And every day he would add another line, another quote to his long list of qualifications for the job.

Polls were produced showing that Jackson would hurt the ticket more than help it if he was the vice presidential nominee. Jackson and his supporters did not buy that line. They argued, with some validity, that the millions of his constituents who would turn out to vote because he was on the ticket would offset any losses.

The pundits went wild with speculation. Jackson loved it and fed into their gristmill every day. Few observers outside the Jackson camp could believe that Jackson would be a containable Vice President. His celebrated ego would soon overwhelm his superior.

Some speculated that perhaps Jackson really didn't want the vice presidential slot and that he would turn it down if Dukakis had the courage to offer it. Then others raised the question whether Dukakis would be able to trust Jackson to say no. They pointed to the historical example of 1960, when John F. Kennedy didn't really want Lyndon B. Johnson on his ticket but dutifully offered the position, trusting that Johnson would not accept.

Such speculation about Jackson was similar to the original naïve question: "What does Jesse want?" There was really no doubt about what he wanted, first in his running for the presidential nomination and now in his quest for the vice presidency.

Jesse insisted publicly, frequently and loudly that he deserved "special consideration." Yet this was not the way candidates traditionally went about being chosen. No defeated candidate necessarily "deserved" to be Vice President. It was the choice of the presidential nominee, and often it would be someone with whom he could feel comfortable. Dukakis and Jackson had never had much of a rapport. Each thought himself far superior to the other, for divergent reasons, and their very personalities were antithetical. The cool manager Dukakis had come up with his own self-ascribed "competence" back in the days after the Michigan caucus to distinguish his qualifications from Jackson's "charisma." Now Jackson's behavior and incessant pressure were making Dukakis even more uncomfortable about the man.

Few ever expected Dukakis to give Jackson the nod. But Dukakis had his friend and confidant Paul Brountas, who was in charge of the vice presidential search, include Jackson's name in the list of potential nominees. Sources in the Dukakis camp maintained that he had a consistently difficult time with Jackson. They complained that, in contrast to the others under consideration, Jackson at first refused to supply all the financial information requested. Also, he constantly harassed the search committee with calls and his insistence that he deserved special treatment. This only antagonized the Dukakis people even more.

For a little while, it seemed that Jackson realized his unabashed insistence might be hurting him. He backed off. On Sunday, June 12, he told NBC's Sunday-morning news show *Meet the Press* he didn't want to "push" Dukakis. Then, once again, he fanned the fires of the national guessing game by refusing to say whether he would even accept the number two spot on the ticket if he was actually offered it.

By midweek, Jackson had decided that his best tactic would be to get influential politicians to say that he should be the vice presidential nominee on the Democratic ticket. On Wednesday, June 15, he met in Washington with black Democrats in Congress, and they urged him to go for it. He refused again to say whether he would. But he believed that pressure from blacks, the traditional solid core of the party, might be useful leverage on Dukakis.

Jesse then proceeded to continue on his campaign whirl as if the primary season hadn't ended. His campaign plane was almost empty, but there were always enough reporters and cameras covering him so that he could make news every day. He flew all over the country, zigzagging from city to city. Sometimes there were public meetings at which he gave rousing speeches; other stops were for private meetings with political backers.

It irritated Jesse when reporters suggested that his continuing, apparently frenzied travel after the primary season had ended was

the result of his own personal craving for attention and the limelight. He insisted the purpose was to continue stirring up enthusiasm for his constituents' concerns. He would often mock news stories: "All this stuff about how 'they don't know how to wind down
the campaign, emotional distress and stuff.' You don't wind down
for a convention."

Jackson began adding some new lines to his speech repertoire.
Now he would ask the rhetorical question "What has Jesse built?"
He would say to the crowds that still overwhelmed his every stop:
"What does Jesse want? That's not the right question. The real
question is: What has Jesse built? I've built a family. I've rebuilt the
progressive wing of the Democratic Party. I've expanded our party.
We can only talk of winning in '88 because of what we built in '84
and did in '85, '86 and '87. What have I built? I've built a movement to shift to humane priorities at home and human rights
abroad."

Yet foremost on his mind was the vice presidential slot. Jackson
continued, however, to be cryptic when asked whether he would
accept it if offered. He admitted that "privately" he had made up
his mind. His goal was to keep tantalizing the public, and thus the
media, or vice versa, and to keep attention on himself. He kept
cautioning his aides that he had to keep people guessing. "It's all a
matter of timing and respect." It was all part of his sense of the
dramatic.

Then, the last weekend in June, Jackson began sending strong
signals. First, campaigning in the American Virgin Islands, he told
the throngs who had come to hear him speak: "How we look at the
vice presidency is a new tradition . . . My grandfather wasn't considered. Unless there is a new tradition, I will not be considered. We
must have a new tradition."

Later that same weekend, at a PUSH convention on Sunday
night, June 26, in Chicago, Jackson gave another strong hint to his
supporters: "They say, 'Jesse, you keep raising the issue of the vice
presidency.' I'm just trying to educate the people on what belongs
to the party . . . The vice presidency is not a retirement gift for

party leaders. It's not a wimp job, even though there have been some wimps in it."

Then the weekend of July Fourth rolled around. Much to everyone's surprise, Governor Michael Dukakis and his wife, Kitty, invited the Reverend Jesse Jackson and Jacqueline to come to a private dinner at their house in suburban Brookline, Massachusetts. As Jesse arrived in Boston, two hours behind schedule, he was asked again whether he would tell Dukakis his decision on whether he wanted the number two slot. He replied: "It's a private meeting, and we should not discuss it. It's really a night for a family and national celebration." But already at the airport, Jackson was offended because the Dukakis campaign organizers hadn't thought to send anyone to meet the Jacksons.

The media mistakenly played the event as if it represented a budding new relationship. Rather, the entire evening was most unpleasant and uncomfortable for both the Jacksons and their hosts. It was described by both camps as a fiasco. From the beginning, the Jacksons felt insulted that Dukakis greeted them in his shirtsleeves. Even the meal served offended Jackson—it began with New England clam chowder, which of course has a milk base, and Jackson is allergic to milk.

Jackson later confided to aides and friends and a few select journalists that he was stunned that Dukakis barely touched on the subject of the vice presidency. At one point, when the two candidates were finally alone in the living room and Jackson hoped they would discuss the matter, in strolled one of Dukakis's daughters asking if they wanted dessert. Jackson later reported that the maximum time they gave to it was about eight minutes when the governor asked Jackson about his "academic views" of the Vice President's role. At the same time, he countered Dukakis's slight by continuing to refuse to offer him his endorsement. Jackson let Dukakis know that he considered himself still to be a presidential candidate and would have his name put in nomination at the convention.

After dinner, the two couples attended the traditional Independence Day concert by the Boston Pops orchestra and fireworks display on the bank of the Charles River. By then, the air between Jackson and Dukakis was so foul that they were both relieved to be at a performance where they needn't talk much. A photograph printed in *Time* the following week showed it all—Jesse and Jackie Jackson looking haughtily in one direction and Mike and Kitty Dukakis staring in the opposite direction.

Both Jesse and Jackie came away from the evening feeling they'd been "violated," used only as part of a charade by Dukakis. Seasoned political observers tended to think the same. They believed that Dukakis was merely making a publicly friendly gesture of dinner at home with the Jacksons before announcing that he was in fact choosing someone else to be his running mate. Jesse sensed this, too.

Afterward, however, at a news conference, Jackson was careful to cover up his annoyance and put the best face on his disappointment. All he would say was that "my name is part of the process" of selecting a running mate. He added vaguely: "We keep working on our partnership because in the final analysis that is what is required for us to win in November. Of course, the governor is very rational, very methodical and very studious, and therefore he has this amazing capacity to expand, to grow."

Throughout the following week, Jackson played his game to the limit. He flitted across the country. In the week following his July 4 soiree with the Dukakises, Jackson visited nine cities in seven days —Chicago, Boston, New York, Atlanta, Memphis, Dallas, Los Angeles, San Francisco and Fort Worth, in that order. He gave more than four times that number of speeches, and he sent out ambiguous signals. He sometimes seemed to be trying to allay the fears of the party leadership that he would become a spoiler if he wasn't handed the number two spot. At other times he would make threatening statements to drive them crazy. His primary motivation seemed to be to continue to heighten the expectations of his supporters. He was behaving now in his natural style, saying one thing, then another, going here, going there. He was striving in every way possible to keep the limelight on himself, and that often revealed an apparent loss of self-control.

In the middle of the week, he suddenly announced that he would be arriving in Atlanta for the convention in typical Jackson publicity-grabbing style—aboard a Rainbow Express bus caravan. It would take two days to travel from Chicago down through the middle of the United States to Atlanta. It was designed to seize the media's attention, and it succeeded.

Next came the threat that as many as ten thousand Jackson supporters would demonstrate outside the convention hall if Jackson wasn't treated right. And rumors were circulated that Jackson himself might make his speech outside the convention hall if he wasn't given the time he requested inside. Later Jackson denied this, but not before the threat had sent shivers through the mainstream Democratic Party. Memories of Chicago in 1968 were still strong with some old party regulars, and the young Jackson himself had participated in those demonstrations.

The Dukakis camp was furious. When would Jesse stop? Would he never let the rightful presidential candidate step forward and perform without threats from Jackson? One article discussing Jackson's recent actions, plans and threats implied that Jackson was taking the bus to Atlanta because he was psychologically unbalanced. Jesse took umbrage and called the report "crazy."

Then he decided to try to explain why he behaved his way. He pointed out the difference between an intelligent mind and a creative mind. He said the intelligent person reads a book and does what it says, actually follows the establishment direction. But he said, referring to himself: "The creative person doesn't have the book, so he creates something out of nothing. We're always creating things, thinking things up." It was an accurate description of his brilliance.

But Jackson's "creativity" didn't impress Michael Dukakis. He was reaching the limit of his patience. On Sunday, July 10, the usually controlled Massachusetts governor broke his silence and said: "Jesse Jackson can do anything he wants to do. I'm going to the convention, and I'm going to win it." On the same day, Jackson continued to talk about the upcoming convention as the occasion for celebrating his successful campaign, still never mentioning the fact that its purpose was really to nominate Michael Dukakis. Jackson thought he could strong-arm Dukakis into naming him as his running mate. He seemed blinded to the reality that he was actually alienating Dukakis and entirely eliminating the vice presidential possibility.

The next day, Monday, July 11, just one week before the opening of the convention, Dukakis's aide Paul Brountas called Jackson in for another meeting about the vice presidential hunt. Brountas bluntly told him that the Dukakis campaign was afraid of appearing to be "pandering" to Jackson. Brountas explained that they had to be able to say "We don't make deals." At the same time, he added, they did want "to give all the ex-candidates equal treatment."

Jackson became incensed at being included among the "ex-candidates." He had not conceded. His name would be going in for nomination. He had twelve to fifteen million votes to deliver to the Democratic ticket when he was ready. Didn't the Dukakis people realize that? No other ex-candidate was so powerful, he said.

Then he saw finally that Dukakis had never seriously considered offering him the number two slot. He complained to Brountas that no woman, no Hispanic, no black, no Jew, no labor leader, no minority member was under consideration. Jackson threatened the Dukakis aide that he would fight till the end at the convention.

After that exchange, it was all over for Jackson's wishful thinking about the vice presidency in 1988. Brountas immediately advised Dukakis that he should make his decision as soon as possible in order to "give Jackson a couple of days to pout" before the convention opened in a week. That night, July 11, the Dukakis inner circle met in the Dukakis house and made the decision about his running mate.

The next morning, Tuesday, July 13, the bomb dropped. Michael Dukakis had chosen Texas senator Lloyd Bentsen as his running mate.

But worse, Jackson learned about the choice only from a reporter when he landed at Washington's National Airport minutes before Bentsen was leaving to fly to Boston for the official announcement. Jackson was thrown completely off guard. His face unmistakably reflected anger. Only within the past hour, on his flight from Cincinnati to Washington, Jackson had said he did not expect Dukakis to announce his running mate during the next twenty-four hours.

Dukakis had notified all the other candidates for the number two slot that morning to tell them of his decision, but he had not got word to Jackson. The Dukakis people publicly maintained that they had tried to place a call to Jackson before he left Cincinnati but had missed him. Privately, it was said by some that the rebuff was intentional, "a calculated snub." It was intended as an affront to Jackson in retaliation for his behavior over the past five weeks since the California primary. It also served as a way of preventing Jackson from doing anything to upset the announcement. One Dukakis staff member said it was simply Bostonian insensitivity. Dukakis himself was angry that his aides had not reached Jackson, for whatever reason. But by then it was too late to make amends.

Later, after Jackson had regained his composure, he spoke at a news conference and denied that he was angry. He said: "No, I'm too controlled. I'm too clear. I'm too mature to be angry. I am focused on what we must do to keep hope alive." But his tight voice, his stiff demeanor, instead of the usual easy broad smile, belied his words.

Everyone close to him that day knew how furious, and hurt, he really was. Not only had Dukakis not chosen him as his running mate, but, to make things worse, he had allowed, perhaps directed, his aides to insult him by not informing him beforehand. He described their actions as "arrogance and insensitivity." Jesse Jackson was seething with inner rage.

After the news conference, he holed up most of the day in his suite at the Grand Hotel in Washington, where he talked with aides and supporters. A long line of commiserators, like mourners at a wake, filed through to offer him their condolences, support and advice. His old friends Washington's mayor Marion Barry and Congressman Charles Rangel of Manhattan were among the visitors.

He asked different help from different people. For example, to certain friendly syndicated columnists and advisers who could write Op-Ed pieces, he suggested that they issue strong hints that perhaps his supporters would stay angry through election day. He wanted it leaked that he would probably contest the vice presidential position at the convention the next week, as Estes Kefauver did in 1956.

Many Jackson supporters had come to Washington that day to attend the annual NAACP convention. They were shocked by the Dukakis team's action. The NAACP's executive director, Benjamin L. Hooks, said at a news conference: "I don't think there's any question that there will be a dampening of enthusiasm."

In Washington that day, most black politicians, Jackson's new and old allies, openly threatened that the Dukakis-Bentsen ticket would not get the overwhelming support blacks usually gave the Democratic Party. Jackson's friend and supporter Representative Ronald V. Dellums of California said that blacks would still vote "ninety percent" Democratic, "but the question is ninety percent of what turnout."

Some black politicians, however, such as Pennsylvania congressman William H. Gray III, though a Jackson supporter, praised Dukakis's selection of Senator Bentsen as a "good choice." Gray himself had been suggested as a possible running mate for Dukakis. Some analysts believed that Dukakis could have defused the whole issue by having the courage to name a black with whom he would be more comfortable, like Gray or Mayor Andrew Young of Atlanta, to demonstrate to blacks and all America that blacks were acceptable running mates, even though Jesse Jackson was not the right one. It would have opened up the political arena to blacks in a way that Jackson's seizing power couldn't. It was unknown, however, whether Gray or Young would have had the courage to accept the offer with an angry and resentful Jackson in the background.

One black syndicated columnist, Carl T. Rowan, wrote later that week that "Dukakis will get the votes of a majority of Jackson's constituency, black and white, but he cannot count on ninety percent of it when Bush is regarded as a reasonable advocate of racial justice and is reaching out to blacks. Dukakis must worry more about how many of Jackson's people will still be pouting and stay home on Election Day." Rowan predicted that, as a result, the convention would not be a coronation of Dukakis but a celebration of Jackson.

But the very morning after Dukakis's rejection of Jackson and selection of Bentsen, another black columnist at *The Washington Post,* William Raspberry, wrote differently. He pointed out that Jackson's campaign had represented for black Americans "a measure of our own acceptance in the American mainstream." But then, Raspberry said, Jackson's post-primary behavior first embarrassed Dukakis and now Jackson himself and the blacks who were relying on him to give them acceptability.

Raspberry wrote: "Jackson's bold and intelligent campaign for the presidential nomination came close to achieving the miracle that would have advanced most dramatically the status of black America. But his rash and egomaniacal campaign for the vice presidential nomination not only resulted in embarrassment to both him and us but may also have diminished his influence on our behalf. It may even have created a situation in which his supporters at the convention will be preoccupied not with a Democratic victory but with black revenge."

Other pundits, such as Pulitzer Prize winner Haynes Johnson at the *Post,* were even more critical of Jackson. Johnson wrote, also that same week, that through his behavior after fairly and cleanly losing the presidential nomination and then demanding special treatment for the vice presidency, "Jackson demonstrates that he is a poor loser. He can't, or won't, let go. He seems driven compulsively to greater and greater celebration of self through his unending campaign. His self-portrait, sketched in countless appearances, has been one of egoism run amok. He acts as if he believes himself to be the great I-Am of American politics."

Sadly, too, for Jackson and his campaign, his behavior over the past weeks had alienated many whites within his own Rainbow Coalition. They were disappointed that he felt compelled to behave in this way after they had supported him and believed he was a new man who sincerely wanted to bring hope to them and their causes.

Jesse Jackson dismissed such criticism as representative of the continuing racism in the country. He spent the rest of the week repeating his displeasure over Dukakis's decision. Everything he said and did threatened to disrupt the convention, which was to open in a matter of days. As always, his actions and words kept the media's spotlight squarely on him. Every day was a new story, another dramatic sequel: Jackson at last had the media eating out of his hand.

At the same time, he allowed his cooler convention manager, Ron Brown, to issue calmer, conciliatory words in order not to tip the balance to chaos. Already in Atlanta, Brown began as early as Thursday, July 14, to maintain that "good, open lines of communication" had been restored between the Jackson and Dukakis campaigns, and he predicted that the relationship damaged by Dukakis's handling of the vice presidential announcement had a chance to "get back on track" within days, and thus, by implication, in time for the convention to run smoothly.

On the same day, however, Jackson added more drama, more fuel to the fire. First he made headline news by suggesting that former President Jimmy Carter should be called in to mediate the dangerously disruptive dispute between himself and Michael Dukakis. A Carter spokesman said the former President would be glad to help. Dukakis, however, implied that next week's convention would not be a time for bending to Jackson's demands. On Thursday he said in response to Jackson's threats and fuming: "In a contest like this, somebody wins and somebody loses."

Then Jackson lowered himself to the level of comparing Dukakis's treatment of him to the relationship between a plantation owner and a cotton-picking slave. It was often the way Jackson talked privately, but this was the first time he'd allowed himself to stoop to such rhetoric in public. He said: "It is too much to expect that I will go out in the field and be the champion vote-picker and bale them up and bring them back to the big house and get a reward of thanks, while people who do not pick nearly as much voters, who don't carry the same amount of weight among the people, sit in the big house and make the decisions."

This was the last straw for Dukakis. Jackson's ongoing insults had been pushing him to the limit. Now Jackson's implying he was acting like a slave master was the trigger. Dukakis would keep his cool, but he would clearly show Jackson in Atlanta that he was the party's nominee and he would not give in to threats. Later Jackson backed down and tried to say that he hadn't really meant that he was comparing the current situation in the Democratic Party to slavery.

On the same day that Jackson grabbed more headlines with his call upon President Carter and his allusion to slavery, he seized other news slots with his departure from Chicago, bound for Atlanta aboard his Rainbow Express.

Thursday afternoon, the colorful caravan set forth from the Windy City on its nearly eight-hundred-mile trek south. Despite his caustic attack on Dukakis just before he boarded the bus, Jackson looked the picture of joviality and relaxation in his short-sleeved white safari shirt with epaulets. He was holding court as he loved to do. There he was sitting at the front of the first of seven brightly decorated buses. His bus had its own kitchen in the center and two sitting areas. Secret Service men were with him in force. Jesse's five children accompanied him, but Mrs. Jackson, after being with him to see the show on the road, got off and said she would fly to Atlanta. A few of Jackson's aides were also along—including longtime adviser Frank Watkins, top policy adviser Bob Borosage, lawyer and platform negotiator Harold Ickes and the former mayor of Gary, Indiana, Richard Hatcher.

This was Jesse's kind of show. Lots of razzmatazz, cameras everywhere and more than a hundred reporters on the other buses. Only a couple of dozen supporters and delegates had managed to get seats on the press buses. Secret Service limousines flanked Jackson's bus. Police escorted the caravan. Television helicopters flew overhead. Many reporters maintained that they had been hoodwinked by Jackson into thinking the Rainbow Express would be full of hundreds of his supporters. Instead, it turned out that he had taken the press "hostage" to be with him as he traveled overland to the convention. Along the way, Jackson would stop for rallies in Indianapolis, Louisville, Nashville, Chattanooga and finally Atlanta on Saturday morning. The Rainbow Express was on its way to Jesse Jackson's convention. His drama rolled on. Jesse Jackson would not give up.

15

THE 1988 DEMOCRATIC CONVENTION IN ATLANTA

"America must never surrender to a high moral challenge. Do not surrender to drugs. Never surrender, young America. Go forward. America must never surrender to malnutrition. We can feed the hungry and clothe the naked. We must never surrender. We must go forward. We must never surrender to illiteracy. Invest in our children. Never surrender and go forward. We must never surrender to inequality. Women cannot compromise ERA or comparable worth. Women deserve to get paid for the work that you do. Never surrender, my friends. Those with AIDS deserve our compassion. You with AIDS, do not surrender. You in your wheelchairs, don't you give up. (We cannot forget that fifty years ago, when our backs were against the wall, Roosevelt was in a wheelchair. I would rather have Roosevelt in a wheelchair anytime than Reagan or Bush on a horse.) Don't you surrender, and don't you give up."

On the last stretch of the road, after Jackson's Rainbow Express had stopped in Calhoun, Georgia, to pick up his chum Bert Lance, Jackson talked candidly to reporters on his bus about his tactics. He was sitting between Percy Sutton, a longtime black adviser from New York, and Lance, who had his arm around Jackson. The candidate stated: "I'm methodical." He was resting one hand on Lance's knee as he talked.

"Very methodical," Jackson emphasized, and then elaborated: "I follow a process: the Five A's—first get their attention; then get their attendance; then create the atmosphere; then affect their attitude; and then you achieve."

He explained that he learned these tactics and got many of his ideas from the civil rights movement. He said, as if from memory: "Make it tense, but not ugly. From creative tension, new life comes."

The idea of arriving in Atlanta in a bus caravan, he pointed out, was a way to get the attention of Dukakis and other Democratic leaders at the convention. He got the idea "straight from Dr. Martin Luther King, Jr.," twenty years ago as he led the SCLC and the civil rights movement. Jackson said: "I didn't need no book, no ad agency. Where did the idea for the bus caravan come from? From 334 Auburn Avenue [SCLC headquarters], where they always come from."

All along the caravan route, Jackson had been holding news conferences to send out signals that he wanted "partnership, equity and shared responsibility" in the campaign and in the party. And if he wasn't assured of that, he had told the press, he would put his name in nomination for Vice President. But now that Lance was on board, Jackson was talking in a more conciliatory manner. Lance had already told him on the telephone that morning that he should stop talking about challenging Bentsen. Lance had warned Jackson that if he continued he would look like a spoiler.

Over the last miles before the bus pulled into Atlanta, Jesse Jackson said he would follow Lance's advice. Jackson said: "If we come out of the convention without common ground, it's a lose-lose situation."

Lance congratulated Jackson in front of the reporters. "You've done well," he said, slapping him on the back and grinning, "You're using mature political judgment."

Atlanta, Georgia, "the cradle of the old South, the crucible of the new South," as Jesse Jackson would call it, was the site for the Democratic convention in July 1988. It was the first time a national convention had been held in the South in this century, and this was the first convention that would see the name of a black who was runner-up go into nomination for the presidency of the United States of America. It was a historic event for Democrats, for blacks, for whites, for all Americans. Jesse Jackson had indeed performed a miracle.

Jackson's arrival in Atlanta, just two days before the opening of the convention, contrasted sharply with the style of arrival of the many other dignitaries who flocked into Atlanta later that weekend. Michael Dukakis and Lloyd Bentsen would fly in and receive official, humdrum welcomes at the Atlanta airport and then would be whisked off in long black limousines to their respective hotels. And others would take the train.

But Jesse Jackson came straight through the middle of Atlanta in the lead bus of his caravan, the Rainbow Express. On Saturday night, July 16, Jackson's "moving media event" rolled into Piedmont Park in Atlanta's "Midtown" section, where thousands of supporters were waiting to greet him. Hundreds more journalists were encamped to begin their minute-by-minute coverage of Jesse Jackson at "his" convention.

The setting was historic because there, on the same site in the 1890s, Booker T. Washington had urged blacks to try to accommodate themselves to whites. As a result of his speech, a short time later in Atlanta another black, Yusef Dubois (for whom Jesse Jackson had named his youngest son), countered Washington and called on blacks to rebel to obtain equal rights with white Americans. That conflict led to the birth of the civil rights movement, a movement Martin Luther King, Jr., was to carry forward from Atlanta more than half a century later. Now tonight the new, undisputed leader of African-Americans, Jesse Jackson, had come back to Atlanta to inherit King's mantle and to lead the blacks forward in a Rainbow Coalition with other Americans.

Jackson delivered yet another emotional speech that Saturday night before the convention and many in the crowd of twelve thousand wept. They had been waiting so long for this moment. He proclaimed: "I got off [the bus] here as a black American and as a political leader who's turned the mainstream into a wide river. The threat [we posed] was not that we would leave, but that we'll stay and expand and grow. The issue is common ground."

All along the caravan route, he'd promised crowds in different cities that "I won't let you down." But over the past day, he'd begun toning down his rhetoric some in comparison with that of earlier in the week. There he had been speaking again of "healing" and "unity." Tonight he promised: "We're going to have a good convention," but what he meant by that was not clarified when he added: "We're not talking about concessions or conquests." He could not then refrain from alluding once again to his being like a slave hand to the Dukakis team and gibed: "I don't mind working. I'll go out and pick some votes."

He then issued his latest demand—that he wanted to be granted a special position in the coming Democratic presidential campaign that would signify "shared victory and shared responsibility," never spelling out exactly what that meant. Jackson proclaimed that he sought a vague and unprecedented "partnership" with the party's presidential and vice presidential nominees. The party's establishment was horrified by his brashness. Sunday morning, on CBS News's *Face the Nation,* Jackson reiterated his demands and said everything had to be worked out in face-to-face meetings with Michael Dukakis.

Both the media and the Dukakis-Bentsen team went wild with speculation about his meaning. What was he demanding now? The Republicans watching from outside gloated that Jackson intended to rearrange the structure of American leadership and turn it into a "troika" with three at the top, not just the President and Vice President.

Jackson had spent much of Sunday in Atlanta talking with his core constituency in the black community. At Salem Baptist Church, he exhorted the congregation: "It's just Sunday. It's not over until it's over, and even then it's not over." Jackson preached, as he always did, about persisting against all odds. After his sermon, the choir sang a version of the hymn "Be Ye Steadfast and Unmovable."

Later in the day, Jackson addressed labor delegates. With them he was more cautious, as he explained the aim of his tactics. He said people wondered why he kept campaigning, but, he said, "they don't realize that wearing down the opposition is a great strategy."

Again, he exercised caution when he talked at a private meeting with a hundred and fifty of his delegate whips, those who would be in charge of all his delegates on the convention floor. "Some of you are saying to me, 'Jesse, you don't seem quite your normal self,' " Jackson said to them. "Well, I've got more weight on my shoulders. I can't just flip out. I can't lead you if I have unresolved conflict. If you get down, remember, we are right where our parents prayed we would be someday. And right here in the heart of Dixie."

The nominee, Michael Dukakis, flew into town that evening, Sunday, July 17, and he was given a formal reception at the airport by Mayor Andrew Young and Senator Bentsen. Jackson was miffed that the Massachusetts governor had not bothered to come earlier when he knew that there was "serious sorting-out" to be done between the two of them. Jesse had already phoned him early that morning to tell him they needed to talk face to face to work things out. Jesse had also phoned New York governor Mario Cuomo and asked his help in talking with Dukakis.

Speaking at the Lockheed Air Terminal of Atlanta's Hartsfield International Airport, Dukakis sent an immediate signal to Jackson when he firmly stated: "Every team has to have a quarterback— that's the nominee. You can't have two quarterbacks. On the other hand, every team has to have terrific players in the backfield and up in the line. That's the way you win."

Jackson's blood boiled when he heard this remark. Dukakis had hit him where it hurt. Jesse was still in a denial state of not yet accepting the fact that he wouldn't be the Democratic Party's quarterback this year. Ever since freshman year in college in Illinois, Jesse had been decrying the fact that black football players weren't allowed to play quarterback, instead always only backfield and line positions. Finally, the previous winter, a professional football team, the Washington Redskins, had won the Super Bowl with a black quarterback. Jackson had often cited that event as a major achievement for blacks in general.

Both Jackson and Dukakis continued to rub each other completely the wrong way. Neither had ever been comfortable with the other, and now the signals they were sending each other seemed designed specifically to irritate. Jackson had at least twice accused Dukakis of treating him like a slave, and now he interpreted the quarterback remark as intentionally racist. Jackson still could not admit that he'd lost to Dukakis, who physically appeared to be a dwarf next to the giant Jackson. Jackson was never unaware of that: he looked down on him and thus it galled him all the more that such a person could have beat him.

Dukakis's patience had run out, and the day before the convention opened, he was determined to take control. Sunday night Dukakis placed a telephone call to Jackson at the Fox Theater, where Jackson was attending a gospel concert. Jackson took the call in a holding room at the old theater. In cool, formal tones, Dukakis invited Jackson to meet him for breakfast talks the next morning at eight-thirty. The meeting would take place in Dukakis's suite at the Hyatt Regency Hotel. The Jacksons were staying in another hotel, the Marriott Marquis, across the street. Jesse accepted.

After he got off the phone, however, he told listeners at the mostly black gala that negotiations between the two teams had not progressed enough to permit a successful meeting. He recalled the last time he'd met with Dukakis, that disappointing Fourth of July occasion in Brookline. Jackson sent word that his aides were to continue thrashing things out through the night with the Dukakis people. What Jesse didn't seem to grasp was that Dukakis had made up his mind about what he wanted and further lower-level talks were irrelevant.

And so Jesse himself turned to the medicine that always made him feel best—oratory. Speaking, whether on the telephone or preferably to crowds, always had both a calming and an energizing effect on Jesse Jackson. That night, after his brief and stilted conversation with Dukakis, Jackson marched out to address the crowd that had come to this Jackson tribute at this old Atlanta theater. The Fox was decorated like an emporium in the Moorish style, with the balcony resembling the walls of an old city and stars twinkling from the vaulted ceiling. Nearly 1,500 people had turned out to hear him and Al Green, among other musicians. The audience was mostly middle-class blacks, dressed in tuxedos and evening gowns, and though their Cadillacs and Mercedes-Benzes were parked outside, they responded as enthusiastically as any poorer group would to Jackson's rousing "I am somebody" chant. They were on their feet, yelling along with him as he ended his Sunday-night sermon by shouting repeatedly into the microphone: "Hold on! Hold on! Hold on!" It was midnight on the eve of the 1988 Democratic convention. The crowd's response to him and his speech once again gave Jesse Jackson his strength, and he was ready for tomorrow.

Monday morning, July 18, at eight-thirty, Jesse Jackson left his hotel to meet with Dukakis. Flanked by Secret Service agents, Jackson strode up to the door of the Dukakis suite. He left his guards at the door with those of Dukakis and entered, accompanied only by his top aide, Ronald Brown. The only Dukakis aide to attend the meeting was his campaign chairman, Paul Brountas.

Jackson said later that at that point he suddenly remembered that it was twenty-one years ago that he had first gone into this Hyatt to attend the annual meeting of SCLC that turned out to be the last one Dr. King attended before his death. That morning in 1988 Jackson recalled how impressed he had been in 1967 by this hotel's grand atrium, but now he was so used to staying in hotels that it no longer was a situation that could ruffle him. It was, he confided later, the personal atmosphere of a situation that could unsettle him. He was relieved now that there would be a couple of witnesses to this meeting.

The meeting lasted nearly three hours, while people in Atlanta and across America waited for the result. Many Americans stayed tune to their radios and televisions to learn what the two fighters would have to say when they emerged. It was a cliff-hanger, but this time Jackson was not completely in control of the script.

At the beginning, it was unusually stormy. Both men spoke candidly. Each told the other about things he had said and done over the past months that were irritating. Jackson said that he resented not being told in advance about Bentsen's appointment and instead having to learn of it from journalists. Jackson had also been irritated the day before by Dukakis's use of the "quarterback metaphor." Dukakis resented Jackson's several remarks that implied that their relationship was that of a slave owner to a field slave. For the first time, the two men were being honest with each other. Jackson later said that the whole conversation highlighted great culture clashes over language.

Then they came to Jackson's demands for "partnership, equity and shared responsibility," and Dukakis voiced his great discomfort with all those terms. Jackson later recalled their semantic dispute. He said that Dukakis said: "You know, when you say partnership, it sends a political signal to my supporters. I'm a lawyer, and to me partnership implies a contract. That implies a deal." Then Jackson recalled that he explained to Dukakis that in the South the term "partnership" had a different meaning, "It means friend, it means participating in, it means understanding, it doesn't mean contract."

They then argued over other terms Jackson had used. Dukakis said that he would never accept the notion of shared power, but Jackson corrected him by saying he'd used the term "shared responsibility." And Jackson explained: "Power sends one kind of signal— responsibility means I'm willing to work, willing to make a difference."

Finally, they were able to work out an arrangement whereby Jackson would play a significant part in the fall campaign and his supporters would be given roles in the campaign and on the Democratic National Committee. But the irony, as many noticed, was that the very person who had symbolized the rift in the first place, the vice presidential running mate, Lloyd Bentsen, was the one who helped patch over the rift that Monday morning in Atlanta. After Jackson and Dukakis had got their resentment and anger out in the open and discussed their respective points, they placed a call to Senator Bentsen to invite him to join them. He was in another hotel at the time, addressing the New Jersey delegation, but when he finally arrived, his presence lifted the air in the room. He and Jackson had something in common: they were Southerners. The Southern heritage was unique in the United States, and it was shared by blacks and whites alike. That always provided a bond between blacks and whites that Northerners like Massachusetts governor Dukakis could never understand.

Jesse himself later commented on this common bond: "There is a certain sensitivity that grows out of the Southern environment. A politician of any prominence has had to learn to grapple with the language, style and nuance of black people. It's Elvis Presley and B. B. King—separated by race but bound by grits, bound by biscuits, bound by circumstance, bound even by the Civil War division in the sense that in the North whites are innocent until proven guilty, in the South they are guilty until proven innocent."

At last they emerged from the suite—Dukakis and his top aide, Jackson and his chief aide, and Bentsen. They descended to the lobby of the Hyatt Regency with its vast atrium reaching to the sky, and they spoke to the sea of microphones and cameras. The bottom line, they said, was that there would be peace among the Democrats. The feud was over, they claimed.

For the next twenty-four hours, Jesse Jackson had to fight hard within himself to keep his morale up. Immediately after his meeting with Dukakis and their conciliatory news conference, he had met with his 1,200 delegates at his hotel headquarters. He encouraged them and praised them for their work, but he knew they had lost by then. That night, Monday, July 18, Jackson was visibly thrown off by a question from ABC News's Peter Jennings, who had asked bluntly if he was depressed, as someone close to Jackson had reportedly disclosed that day. Jackson flatly denied it during the live television interview, and he went on to maintain that there never was any acrimony between him and Dukakis. But he had also that night watched Jennings interview Dukakis and ask him directly why he hadn't chosen Jackson as his running mate. Dukakis's stumbling and vague answer was no more satisfactory than anything Jackson had heard before. His closest aides knew he was depressed.

The next day, Tuesday, July 19, Jackson attended a civil rights breakfast with Speaker of the House Jim Wright, but after that he returned to his suite on the forty-sixth floor of the Marriott to spend most of the day ensconced and working on his convention speech, which he knew would be the highest point in his political career to date. He would spend most of the time in his bedroom, surrounded by his closest advisers and his family. He was down, but for Jackson, this kind of "down" mood was useful because he was also preparing himself by letting his mind have time to go over that night's performance.

His aides knew this Jackson mood, and they were careful not to push him but at the same time to stay with him, to encourage him and be a sounding board for whatever ideas he might toss out. They provided him with ample, but not too many, background papers, some of which he kept on his lap and others nearby on the floor. He would glance over them briefly, then store them in the computer of his brain, but he kept them around like security blankets.

Not that Jesse Jackson sat quietly in his grand bedroom at such a time. The scene, as often around Jackson, was not unlike that of some Eastern potentate in his royal suite surrounded by courtiers and with minions coming and going. There were constant phone calls and visitors with questions about that night's show at the Convention Center. Jesse himself was also thinking ahead to the next night and had to consult with numerous friends and advisers about his decision to ask the Machinists' Union leader, William Winpisinger, to place his name in nomination.

The main order of business for the day, however, was the preparation of Jackson's speech, and ostensibly he was working on it as he kept leafing through his sheafs of papers in between talking on the phone and receiving visitors. Jackson ordered his aides Frank Watkins and Bob Borosage to write it, and they spent much of the day with him writing out a draft using major points from his hundreds of 1988 stump speeches. They knew this was something of a wheel-spinning task because Jackson himself would deliver most of the speech from his head. But they also knew that their writing something out for him was important for his own creative process in that it gave him necessary security. Frank Watkins had been doing this for Jackson for years. As they sat with him that day, they told him about the lines, the old anecdotes from his many previous speeches that they were including in this speech, and Jackson digested their suggestions as they wrote and spoke.

But they couldn't decide what he should say about Dukakis. They talked about it intermittently throughout the day: Borosage and Watkins and the others bounced suggestions at Jackson, and he listened. Then, finally, Jackson told them to take notes as he dictated his own thoughts: "Tonight I salute Governor Michael Dukakis. He has run a well-managed and a dignified campaign. No matter how tired or how tied, he always resisted the temptation to stoop to demagoguery. I have watched a good mind fast at work, with steel nerves, guiding his campaign out of the crowded field without appeal to the worst in us. I have watched his perspective grow as his environment has expanded. I've seen his toughness and tenacity close up, knew his commitment to public service. His foreparents came to America on immigrant ships. My foreparents came to America on slave ships. But whatever the original ships, we are in the same boat tonight."

Jesse Jackson was thinking not only about his own speech and his political career but also, perhaps more nervously, about the introductory speeches his five children would be making that night. Their appearance at the convention would be the highlight, he said, for him. It had been mostly his idea that all five of his children would introduce him, their father—starting with Jacqueline, age twelve, and then the brothers, Yusef, seventeen, Jonathan, twenty-two, Jesse Jr., twenty-three, through the eldest, sister Santita, who had just turned twenty-five the week before.

Other politicians had their family perform for them, and some like the Kennedys established dynasties. Jackson's wife and children had been campaigning for him all year all over the country, but they'd never been given the national spotlight. Tonight was the chance, and Jesse Jackson could show off to the world his nearly perfect children who personified all the values that he espoused in his speeches and, moreover, demonstrated that there were some black families, as well as white ones, in which children were raised with sound values. As one close aide put it, Jackson wanted to show that "there are many black families like that. Articulate, good kids not taking drugs, not babies making babies." And there was no question that his five children were true models of those good values. It wasn't just their father, Jesse Jackson, who thought that of his children. All the rest of us who had ever met them and spent time with them were impressed and felt the same about each one of them.

The family understandably felt nervous anticipation before the big event that night, but they all proved they were more than up to the mark. Someone had tried to draft a speech for little Jackie, but she rejected it as "stupid" and wrote her own. Her brother Yusef, who was getting ready to go off in the fall to the University of Virginia on a football scholarship, seemed calmer than the others. He said: "This is nothing compared with a football game." His older brothers, Jonathan and Jesse Jr., prepared only "talking points" for their speeches, the way their father would do, and they used a lot of their father's rhetoric from the campaign. They were both used to making speeches across the country as their father's foremost "surrogates." Always quiet and poised, the eldest, Santita, worked quietly on her own. She remembered how her family had just celebrated her twenty-fifth birthday: "We had prayer. Every day that the Lord gives me, I am happy for."

That night, Tuesday, July 19, the family sat together backstage at the huge Convention Center, waiting through all the political speeches, including that of twenty-seven-year-old John F. Kennedy, Jr., who introduced his uncle, Senator Edward Kennedy. In the Jackson holding room, little Jackie began to panic with fear about going before all those thousands of people. Her mother, Jacqueline, big Jackie, went over to comfort her youngest child. She placed her hands on her daughter's cheeks and said gently: "God bless you. You look right at them. You look them right in the eye."

Then the young girl walked onto the platform with her siblings and was the first to speak. She said that though she wasn't old enough to vote now, if she could, she would vote for her father. Her father later remarked: "The highlight of the week for me was watching little Jackie. She really had the toughest job, because she was first. She had to come into a hall where governors and senators have had some difficulty getting attention . . . and she had the poise to pause and get their attention."

The last of the children to give his introductory speech was Jesse Jr., the budding politician who had shown over the months that he had taken to the political game like a fish to water. He told the crowd of more than twelve thousand in the Omni and the hundreds of millions around the world watching on television that his father had taught them that life's great tragedy was "not failure but a low aim."

Jesse Jr. said: "To many he is a hero; to us he is also our father." And as a campaign film about his father came up on the huge convention screens, young Jackson concluded his introduction: "My father is an odds-buster, a man who fights against the odds, who lives against the odds, the next President of the United States, our dad, Jesse Jackson."

The Jackson campaign film told the story: "In 1988, America began a search for an honest vision for who we are as a people, and we found a vision of hope"—Jesse Jackson delivering one of his many speeches:

"We're bigger than one language, bigger than one culture, bigger than one race, bigger than one religion. This is America. Let's expand. Let's grow. Let's build. Let's keep hope alive," he shouted, and the filmed crowds cheered.

The Jackson '88 presidential campaign had come to Atlanta to celebrate him and his success. As far as Jackson and his supporters were concerned, the fact that another man would be nominated for the presidency was beside the point. The Atlanta convention would be Jesse Jackson's. He had created the scene to make it so, and the

American media followed his lead. Dukakis's "competence" paled in the television lights before Jesse Jackson's "charisma."

Finally, at 10:57 P.M., as the film ended and the convention hall lights were brightened again, the children's father, the black presidential candidate, Jesse Jackson, appeared. Accompanied by his wife, Jacqueline, he walked to center stage. There were only three minutes to go before the networks would end their prime-time coverage of the convention. The Omni convention hall was full of red placards for Jesse, and the crowd went wild with enthusiasm. Inside, the hall was packed to capacity at 12,500, and outside, an estimated 10,000 had been locked out by the fire wardens. Before he even began, Jackson was overwhelmed by a standing ovation. The band played as the crowd clapped and cheered. And suddenly nationwide television viewership increased by quantum leaps. Jesse Jackson was "prime time" whether the networks planned it or not.

On ABC News, anchorman Peter Jennings narrated over the nearly four-minute-long ovation: "And, of course, the Dukakis campaign has made a point of giving this man the respect he sought, the respect he has wanted, it has been argued, for much of his life as a child, as a teenager, as an adult."

Jesse Jackson waved exultantly to the throng. He was dressed impeccably—in a dark gray pin-striped suit, light blue pin-striped shirt, a red tie with white polka dots and a red silk handkerchief in his breast pocket. As he stood surveying the sea of faces and posters, Jackson remembered the words he'd uttered in his speech at the 1984 convention: "God hasn't finished with me yet," and he felt the same this time but didn't say it.

At last he began, slowly and mildly, quietly, as he often did to get the crowd's attention. He began as a preacher, a man of God, about to launch into a sermon: "Tonight we pause and give praise and honor to God for being good enough to allow us to be at this place at this time. When I look out at this convention, I see the face of America, red, yellow, brown, black and white. We are all precious in God's sight—the real rainbow coalition.

"All of us . . ." And he had to pause a moment for the first of the fifty-five times applause interrupted his speech. Then he continued: "All of us who are here think that we are seated. But we're really standing on someone's shoulders. Ladies and gentlemen— Mrs. Rosa Parks."

The audience stood and burst into rousing cheers as Jesse brought up to the podium "the mother of the civil rights movement." Now seventy-five years old, this black woman in 1955 had refused to go to the back of a bus in Montgomery, Alabama. None of us watching Jackson's introduction of her at the Democratic convention thirty-three years later could help but have goose bumps on our arms and lumps in our throats. Standing there together, the two of them symbolized such incredibly wonderful changes in our nation's history.

Jackson then went on to express his "deep love and appreciation for the support my family has given me over the past months." He also thanked Mayor Andrew Young of Atlanta, and gave "a special salute" to former President Jimmy Carter, who was present that night, and thanks to all the Carter family.

And then he hailed the civil rights champions of the past and said: "My right and my privilege to stand here before you has been won—won in my lifetime—by the blood and the sweat of the innocent."

He named many and then brought the past to the present as he said: "Dr. Martin Luther King, Jr., lies only a few miles from us tonight. Tonight he must feel good as he looks down upon us. We sit here together, a rainbow coalition—the sons and daughters of slave masters and the sons and daughters of slaves sitting together around a common table, to decide the direction of our party and our country. His heart would be full tonight."

The great convention hall was quiet as Jackson continued in his elegiac tone: "As a testament to the struggles of those who have gone before; as a legacy for those who will come after; as a tribute to the endurance, the patience, the courage of our forefathers and mothers; as an assurance that their prayers are being answered, their work was not in vain, and hope is eternal, tomorrow night my name will go into nomination for the presidency of the United States of America."

Jesse shuffled his papers as he paused briefly for the applause and then went on: "We meet tonight at the crossroads, a point of decision. Shall we expand, be inclusive, find unity and power; or suffer division and impotence? We've come to Atlanta, the cradle of the old South, the crucible of the new South. Tonight there is a sense of celebration because we are moved, fundamentally moved from racial battlegrounds by law, to economic common ground, with the moral challenge to move to higher ground. Common ground!"

He listed many examples of finding common ground, as he had so often over the months of campaigning. He said: "The Bible teaches that when lions and lambs lie down together, none will be afraid, and there will be peace in the valley. It sounds impossible. Lions eat lambs. Lambs sensibly flee from lions. Yet even lions and lambs find common ground. Why? Because neither lions nor lambs want the forest to catch on fire. Neither lions nor lambs want acid rain to fall. Neither lions nor lambs can survive nuclear war. If lions and lambs can find common ground, surely we can as well, as civilized people."

The applause brought him to a halt again before he could continue: "The only time that we win is when we come together." Jackson then recounted the recent history of the American presidency and the Democratic Party in particular, beginning with John F. Kennedy in 1960, and he continued up to the present with his "salute" to Governor Michael Dukakis, using the words he'd already spoken earlier that day.

But instead of outright endorsing Dukakis, Jesse Jackson called for unity. He suggested a partnership in the party, repeating what he had been urging throughout the past week: "Our choice? Full participation in a democratic government or more abandonment and neglect. And so this night, we choose not a false sense of independence, not our capacity to survive and endure. Tonight we choose interdependency and our capacity to act and unite for the greater good. Common good is finding commitment to new priorities, to expansion and inclusion. A commitment to a shared national campaign strategy and involvement at every level. A commitment to new priorities that insure that hope will be kept alive."

And then he returned to his favorite themes: "Common ground, easier said than done. Where do you find common ground? At the point of challenge. This campaign has shown that politics need not be marketed by politicians, packaged by pollsters and pundits. Politics can be [a] moral arena where people come together to find common ground.

"We find common ground at the plant gate that closes on workers without notice. We find common ground at the farm auction where a good farmer loses his or her land to bad loans or diminishing markets. Common ground at the school yard where teachers cannot get adequate pay, and students cannot get a scholarship, and can't make a loan. Common ground"—Jackson was now shouting the phrase over the applauding crowd—"at the hospital admitting room, where somebody tonight is dying because they cannot afford to go upstairs to a bed that's empty waiting for someone with insurance to get sick. We are a better nation than that. We must do better."

Jackson paused for the cheering, then continued: "Common ground. What is leadership, if not present help in a time of crisis? And so I met you at the point of challenge—in Jay, Maine, where paper workers were striking for fair wages." And the applause rose from the Maine delegation on the floor. He went on through the list of the various places he'd visited at their point of challenge, and in each case halted a moment for the applause from the relevant state delegation: ". . . in Greenfield, Iowa, where family farmers struggled for a fair price; in Cleveland, Ohio, where working women seek comparable worth; in McFarland, California, where the children of Hispanic farm workers may be dying from poisoned rain; in an AIDS hospice in Houston, Texas, where the sick support one another, too often rejected by their own family and friends."

Jesse Jackson then told the story of his grandmother's quilt for all the world to hear. "America is not a blanket woven from one thread, one color, one cloth. When I was a child growing up in Greenville, South Carolina, and Grandmama could not afford a blanket, she didn't complain and we did not freeze. Instead, she took pieces of old cloth—patches—wool, silk, gabardine, croker sack—only patches, barely good enough to wipe off your shoes with, but they didn't stay that way very long. With sturdy hands and a strong cord, she sewed them together into a quilt, a thing of beauty and power and culture. Now, Democrats, we must build such a quilt."

He then listed the groups, the patches, that make up the Democratic Party and America: "Farmers, you seek fair prices, and you are right—but you cannot stand alone, your patch is not big enough. Workers, you fight for fair wages, you are right—but your patch, labor, is not big enough. Women, you seek comparable worth and pay equity, you are right—but your patch is not big enough. Women, mothers, who seek Headstart and day care and prenatal care on the front side of life, rather than jail care and welfare on the back side of life, you are right—but your patch is not big enough. Students, you seek scholarships, you are right—but your patch is not big enough.

"Blacks and Hispanics," he went on, halting briefly for the applause from each of the groups he named, "when we fight for civil rights, we are right—but our patch is not big enough. Gays and lesbians, when you fight against discrimination and a cure for AIDS, you are right—but your patch is not big enough. Conservatives and progressives, when you fight for what you believe, right wing, left wing, hawk, dove, you are right from your point of view, but your point of view is not enough.

"But don't despair," he concluded, returning to the metaphor of his grandmother's quilt. "Be as wise as my grandmama. Pull the patches and the pieces together, bound by a common thread. When we form a great quilt of unity and common ground, we'll have the power to bring about health care and housing and jobs and education and hope to our nation." He was screaming over the applause: "We, the people, can win."

He had to stop for another of the eighteen standing ovations that punctuated his speech, before he continued: "We stand at the end of a long dark night of reaction. We stand tonight united in a commitment to a new direction. For almost eight years, we've been led by those who view social good coming from private interests, who view public life as a means to increase private wealth." And he told this audience his theory of Reaganomics as "reverse Robin Hood." Over the thunderous applause, after he'd described how the Reagan administration had spent the nation's wealth, Jackson shouted: "Use some of that money to build decent housing, use some of that money to educate our children, use some of that money for long-term health care, use some of that money to wipe out these slums, and put America back to work."

He said he just wanted to "make common sense." He explained: "It does not make sense to close down 650,000 family farms in this country while importing food from abroad subsidized by the U.S. government. Let's make sense. It does not make sense to be escorting all our tankers up and down the Persian Gulf, paying $2.50 for every $1 worth of oil we bring out, while oil wells are capped in Texas, Oklahoma and Louisiana. I just want to make sense."

Jesse Jackson moved then to his theme of "economic violence." And as so many times over the past months when he'd delivered his "Ode to the Poor," tonight's audience of millions could not help but be moved. He started his "Ode," as he had countless times before: "Most poor people are not lazy. They're not black. They're not brown. They're mostly white and female and young. But whether white, black or brown, a hungry baby's belly turned inside out is the same color. Color it pain, color it hurt, color it agony.

"Most poor people are not on welfare," he continued, his voice tearful and plaintive. "Some of them are illiterate and can't read the Want Ad section, and when they can, they can't find a job that matches the address. They work hard every day. I know. I live amongst them. I'm one of them. I know they work. I'm a witness. They catch the early bus. They work every day. They raise other people's children. They work every day. They clean the streets. They work every day. They drive the cabs. They work every day. They changed the beds you slept in in these hotels last night. They can't get a union contract. They work every day."

Jackson stopped for the applause and for his words to sink in. Then he shouted: "No, no, they're not lazy. Someone must defend them because it's right and they cannot speak for themselves. They work in hospitals. I know they do. They wipe the bodies of those who are sick with fever and pain. They empty their bedpans. They clean out their commodes. No job is beneath them. And yet when they get sick, they cannot lie in the bed they made up every day."

Over the wild applause, he shouted: "America, that is not right. We are a better nation than that. We are a better nation than that."

Then, in the hall of the 1988 Democratic convention, Jesse Jackson delivered what many later described as the most comprehensive call for a national war on drugs that the world had ever heard. He began by criticizing the Reagan administration's, in particular First Lady Mrs. Reagan's, soft attack on the drug problem. "We need a real war on drugs. We can't just say no. It's deeper than that. We can't just get a palm reader or an astrologer. It's more profound than that." Then he recounted his experience meeting with the youth of Watts, and he concluded, "You cannot fight a war on drugs unless, until you're going to challenge the bankers and the gun sellers and those who grow them. Don't just focus on the children. Let's stop drugs at the level of supply and demand. We must end the scourge on the American culture."

After the enthusiastic applause, Jackson turned to foreign policy. He called for a "no use" nuclear policy, and he urged that the United States pay more attention to the Third World, the "real world," the seven-eighths of the world outside the United States and the U.S.S.R. He issued the key principles of his foreign policy: "Support international law. We stand the most to gain from it. Support human rights. We believe in that. Support self-determination. We're built on that. Support economic development. You know it's right. Be consistent, and gain our moral authority in the world. I challenge you tonight, my friends, let's be bigger and better, as a nation and as a party."

Then as Jesse Jackson began to conclude his masterful speech, he returned to himself: "I am often asked, 'Jesse, why do you take on these tough issues? They're not very political. We can't win that way.' If an issue is morally right, it will eventually be political. It may be political and never be right . . . If we're principled first, our politics will fall in place. 'Jesse, why do you take these big, bold initiatives?' "

He recited: "A poem by an unknown author was something like this: 'We've mastered the air. We've conquered the sea, annihilated disease and prolonged life. But we're not large enough to live on this earth without war and without hate. As for Jesse Jackson, I'm tired of sailing my little boat far inside the harbor bar. I want to go out where the big ships float, out on the deep where the great ones are. And should my frail craft prove too slight, a wave sweep those billows o'er, I'd rather go down in the stirring fight than drown to death in the sheltered shore.' We've got to go out, my friends, where the big boats are."

Then Jackson exhorted: "Young America, hold your head high now. We can win. We must not lose to the drugs, and violence, premature pregnancy, suicide, cynicism, pessimism and despair. We can win. Wherever you are tonight, now I challenge you to hope and to dream. Don't submerge your dreams. Exercise above all else —even on drugs, dream of the day you are drug-free. Even in the gutter, dream of the day that you will be up on your feet again. You must never stop dreaming. Face reality, yes, but don't stop with the way things are. Dream of things as they ought to be. Dream."

He delivered his "Never surrender" exhortation, and then he told the story of his illegitimate birth and poverty-stricken childhood in Greenville, South Carolina. He gave all the details, as he had to so many audiences before, but never to one as large as he had that night. He said: "When you see Jesse Jackson, when my name goes in nomination, your name goes in nomination. I was born in the slum, but the slum was not born in me. And it wasn't born in you, and you can make it."

The applause never stopped for the rest of his speech: "Wherever you are tonight, you can make it. Hold your head high. Stick your chest out. You can make it. It gets dark sometimes, but the morning comes. Don't you surrender. Suffering breeds character, character breeds faith, in the end faith will not disappoint."

Jackson's voice was hoarse, and his forehead was sweating, as he shouted his conclusion to the audience: "You must not surrender.

You may or may not get there but just know that you're qualified and you hold on and hold out. We must never surrender. America will get better and better. Keep hope alive. Keep hope alive. Keep hope alive for tomorrow night and beyond. Keep hope alive. I love you very much. I love you very much."

As the Omni convention hall erupted into joyful pandemonium at the conclusion of Jackson's speech, the television cameras turned back to the commentators for their analysis of the oration. It was after midnight in the East, fifty-two minutes past the scheduled end of that evening's coverage. Dan Rather of CBS News described the past hour's performance as "thunder and lightning from Jesse Jackson. He shook the hall in his own way, just as he has shaken up the Democratic Party." CBS veteran Walter Cronkite speculated aloud that there was probably "gnashing of teeth and cracking of knuckles" at the Dukakis headquarters after viewing Jackson's masterful performance.

On NBC, anchorman Tom Brokaw remarked: "There he is—one generation moved from a slum to prominent American politician. [But] I must say, as a political speech, I was a little surprised that there wasn't something new. These are the same themes that we've heard before, the exact phrases."

That should have been no surprise. Jesse Jackson had been pounding the same message, the same themes and phrases for months, even years, and few had listened. He wanted the world to hear what he was saying, and so it did that night.

EPILOGUE

"**I** may not get there," Jesse Jackson said on the morning after his memorable speech to the 1988 Democratic convention, "but it is possible for our children to get there now." He was addressing a group of black leaders in Atlanta at a meeting of SCLC, the organization in which he had begun his political career.

Jesse Jackson had not given up. He was engaged, as he often explained, in an "endless campaign." And now he was planning how he would carry on that campaign in the months and years ahead. That morning, when Governor Dukakis phoned him to congratulate him on his speech, Jackson took the opportunity to invite himself and his aides for another meeting to work out the details of the "partnership" between himself and the Democratic ticket. Later, he spent much of the day in his suite meeting with New York governor Mario Cuomo, Massachusetts senator Edward Kennedy and his own advisers.

Then, for a brief while, the campaigner was exhausted. And that night, Wednesday, July 20, when Jackson's name was placed in nomination for the presidency, he stayed in bed in his hotel suite and watched most of the balloting on television. In advance, Jackson had directed his campaign chairman, Willie Brown, to proclaim the Dukakis vote unanimous after the tally had been taken.

After that, it was all over for Jesse Jackson's candidacy in 1988. The next day, Thursday, July 21, was the beginning of his new life. Early that morning, before getting out of bed, Jesse began his usual routine of telephoning. The first person he dialed was his old buddy Bert Lance, and he asked for his advice about how he should proceed from here.

Lance had always told Jackson that he had more moves than most, more even, he'd once said, than the professional basketball star Michael Jordan. That morning in Atlanta, Lance advised Jackson, as he later recalled: "I told him he's just had one of the identifiable moments in American politics. I told him the time had come for him to be invisible—wherever that is."

Jesse Jackson listened to Lance's advice, but he wasn't quite ready to heed it. That night the Democratic ticket for 1988 would be put into final and formal shape, and he was not going to let the people forget him.

So on Thursday night, after the Democratic presidential nominee Michael Dukakis had finished delivering his acceptance speech on the last night of the convention, the mood was one of unity and celebration. The stage was soon flooded with supporters, family and former candidates, and as the picture-taking began, photographers found the black runner-up for the Democratic Party's 1988 presidential nomination standing, inches above the party's nominee and his running mate, dominant, at center stage.

The contrast between the tall ex-candidate and the party's nominees was striking. It was the picture the Democratic establishment did not want taken that night. It was the photograph that Jesse Jackson and his supporters wanted most of all. And the Republicans couldn't have asked for a better shot if they'd been able to stage-manage it. They called it the "Democratic troika." It was obvious which man was at center stage. But who was in charge?

After the formal pictures at the podium, Jackson finally moved offstage. He and his family went to a yellow tent to await the Secret Service's arrangements for their departure from the convention hall. As Jesse and his youngest child, little Jackie, stood at the tent's entrance accepting handshakes from passersby, Michael Dukakis came toward them and then stopped to speak. In his speech that night he had mentioned little Jackie and how impressed he had been with her brave performance Tuesday night, when she had courageously stood before all those people as the first of the Jackson children to introduce her father.

Dukakis held out both his hands to her. He said, as he smiled warmly: "You know, I didn't want to embarrass you out there tonight, so I called your father and asked him if I could mention you in the speech. He said it would be all right." The Democratic presidential nominee then hugged Jackie as her father smiled approvingly. It had meant a lot to him that Dukakis had finally done something to show his acceptance of him—first the phone call to ask Jackson's permission, then the mention of his daughter in Dukakis's speech and now the warm greeting after it was all over. At that point the two men seemed reconciled and accepting of each other.

For a short time after the convention, Jesse Jackson followed Bert Lance's advice, although it was difficult. For about a week, Jesse stayed out of sight. Then he began popping up here and there, as if in search of a new script. By the end of July, he was warning that the unity achieved at the convention could be dissipated if he and his supporters weren't brought into the Democratic equation. On July 30, in Chicago, Jackson delivered a campaign speech, ostensibly for the party's ticket, but of its fourteen pages, the first eleven were about Jackson and his campaign. He didn't mention the nominee's name until thirty-six minutes into the forty-two-minute address, and he never mentioned Bentsen's name at all. Listeners reported that Jackson seemed to be grumbling still about the vice presidential choice and about what his own role would be in the campaign.

A few days later, Jackson said he would be operating as a "free agent" in the campaign, but by the end of August, the campaign had decided to limit Jackson's role. Dukakis aides went so far as to tell Jackson they did not want him campaigning in certain states where their polling indicated his presence would hurt the ticket. Jackson became infuriated and began publicly expressing his irritation with the Democratic nominee.

By September, Jackson was openly threatening to disrupt the party if some of his platforms were not incorporated into the campaign, and if changes weren't made in the party's direction. Many believed that Jackson did not want the Democratic ticket to win in 1988, because a Republican victory would pave the way for Jackson to run with even more strength in 1992. Dukakis would not be an incumbent, and Jackson could suggest that the Democrats had in fact lost because they had not had Jackson on the ticket, even as the vice presidential nominee. And by 1992 even more young people he'd long been influencing would be old enough to vote.

By Labor Day the Dukakis campaign itself was apparently foundering. Their treatment of Jackson was alienating black voters and at the same time their indecision about how to deal with him was turning away other voters. In late September, Dukakis's former top aide, John Sasso, who had rejoined the campaign, met with Jackson to try to smooth over the differences. At that point Jesse agreed to do a number of radio spots for the campaign, and he began holding rallies to encourage eligible voters to cast their ballots for the Democratic ticket in November. Observers remarked that such rallies would ultimately help only Jackson, as he continued to build his own support base for 1992. The Dukakis campaign was in so much disarray by then that Jackson's presence or absence was irrelevant.

On November 8 Vice President George Bush was elected President of the United States. The Republican Party had been voted in for a third term. On November 30, President-elect Bush had a luncheon meeting with the Reverend Jesse Jackson to discuss the future course of America.

Whether the establishment, and particularly the Democrats, liked it or not, they had to acknowledge that as 1989 began there was no other Democrat as powerful as Jesse Jackson. Not only had he become the undisputed leader of black America; his popularity had also grown across the country.* Regardless of the widespread belief that he could never win the White House, more because of his personality than his race, that he couldn't govern and that he might rip the party apart, Jesse Jackson was the one force that the Democrats, and America, had to reckon with in charting the future of the party.

February 14, 1989
New York City

---

* On February 10, 1989, Jackson's convention manager Ronald H. Brown was elected Chairman of the Democratic National Committee. Brown was the first African-American to head a major political party. Also in early 1989 Jackson began promoting the change of the common usage of the term "black" to "African-American."

Jesse Jackson's main campaign, however, remained his quest for the presidency of the United States of America.

INDEX

INDEX